... Semantics

Cognition Special Issues

The titles in this series are paperbacked, readily accessible, in some cases expanded and updated editions of the special issues of *COGNITION: An International Journal of Cognitive Science,* edited by Jacques Mehler and produced by special agreement with Elsevier Science Publishers B.V. The first six are available from M.I.T. Press.

VISUAL COGNITION, Steven Pinker, guest editor

THE ONSET OF LITERACY: Cognitive Processes in Reading Acquisition, Paul Bertelson, guest editor

SPOKEN WORD RECOGNITION, Uli H. Frauenfelder and Lorraine Komisarjevsky Tyler, guest editors

CONNECTIONS AND SYMBOLS, Steven Pinker and Jacques Mehler, guest editors

NEUROBIOLOGY OF COGNITION, Peter D. Eimas and Albert M. Galaburda, guest editors

ANIMAL COGNITION, C. R. Gallistel, guest editor

LEXICAL AND CONCEPTUAL SEMANTICS, Beth Levin and Steven Pinker, guest editors

Lexical & Conceptual Semantics

Edited by

Beth Levin and Steven Pinker

BLACKWELL

Cambridge MA & Oxford UK

This edition published by Blackwell Publishers, 1992

238 Main Street
Cambridge, MA 02142

108 Cowley Road
Oxford, OX4 1JF, UK

Reprinted from *Cognition: International Journal of Cognitive Science*, Volume 41, Numbers 1-3, 1991. Blackwell Publishers have exclusive licence to sell this English-language book edition throughout the world.

Library of Congress Cataloging-in-Publication Data

A CIP catalog record for this book is available from the Library of Congress.

isbn: 1-55786-354-7

British Library Cataloging in Publication Data

A CIP catalog record for this book is available from the British Library.

Printed and bound in the United States of America.

This book is printed on acid-free paper.

Contents

1

Introduction*

Beth Levin
Department of Linguistics, Northwestern University.

Steven Pinker
Department of Brain and Cognitive Sciences, Massachusetts Institute of Technology.

It is the fate of those who dwell at the lower employments of life, to be rather driven by the fear of evil, than attracted by the prospect of good; to be exposed to censure, without hope of praise; to be disgraced by miscarriage, or punished for neglect, where success would have been without applause, and diligence without reward.

Among these unhappy mortals is the writer of dictionaries . . . (*Preface*, Samuel Johnson's Dictionary, 1755).

Samuel Johnson's characterization of the lexicographer might apply equally well to the writer of mental dictionaries, those cognitive scientists who attempt to specify the mental representations underlying people's knowledge of word meanings. Research in lexical semantics, though enjoying waves of enthusiasm during the past 30 years, is often regarded as having met with limited success. Although a sense of excitement and progress accompanied the research efforts of the 1960s and early 1970s, including Katz and Fodor's (1963) semantic feature theory, Fillmore's (1968) case grammar, and the theory of generative semantics proposed by Lakoff (1971), McCawley (1973, 1979) and Ross (1972), shortly thereafter the research area fell on hard times, meeting a series of rebuffs both from linguists and psycholinguists. Efforts to constrain syntactic theories led some theoretical linguists to condemn the efforts of generative semanticists to construct a syntactic

*Supported by NSF Grant BNS-8919884 to the first author, and NIH Grant HD 18381 to the second author.

theory in which decompositional representations of word meaning served as the underlying syntactic representation. Meanwhile, Jerry Fodor and his collaborators (Fodor, 1981; Fodor, Fodor, & Garrett, 1975; Fodor, Garrett, Walker, & Parks, 1980) argued that evidence from the psychological laboratory showed that the mental representations of word meaning *had* no internal structure.

Theories of how word meanings are represented in general must be built on research on how particular word meanings are represented. But it is not easy to define a given word, so any attempt to do so becomes an easy target for by now familiar criticisms. If *bachelor* means "unmarried man", why is the Pope not a bachelor? If we amend the definition to "unmarried man legally eligible for marriage", what about a man who has been happily living for 7 years with a woman he has never officially married, or an illegal immigrant who expediently marries a native platonic friend, or a 17-year-old successful entrepreneur living in a penthouse apartment (examples from Winograd, 1976)? If *to paint* means "cause to be covered with paint", why isn't it *painting* when a paint factory explodes or when Michelangelo dips his brush into the can (Fodor, 1981)? These particular definitions can be patched up, but skeptics foresee a never-ending need for such patching with no real increase in watertightness. The whole enterprise then might seem to be at best tedious and at worst post hoc. Is it really scientifically fruitful to write a 50-page paper on the verb *bake*? And could there even be an answer to such seemingly academic questions as whether the verb means "to create a cake by cooking in dry heat in an oven" or "to cook by dry heat in an oven, resulting in the creation of a cake?" Inevitably one thinks of Johnson's entry for *lexicographer*, which defines the term as "... a harmless drudge, that busies himself in ... detailing the signification of words", perhaps with doubts about the "harmless" part. As Johnson put it,

> It appeared that the province allotted me was of all the regions of learning generally confessed to be the least delightful, that it was believed to produce neither fruits nor flowers, and that after a long and laborious cultivation, not even the barren laurel had been found upon it. (Johnson, 1747: 2).

Despite the early pessimism, there has been a resurgence of interest in lexical semantics over the last few years in both linguistics and psychology. The new blossoming was caused by several developments, both theoretical and practical.

Within theoretical linguistics, it is a response to the increased importance of the lexicon in many current linguistic frameworks (e.g., government-binding, lexical-functional grammar, head-driven phrase structure grammar; see Wasow, 1985). As part of the effort to constrain the power of syntactic rules, more and more facets of syntactic constructions were considered to reflect the properties of the lexical items in these constructions. This shift meant that many linguistic phenomena had to be explained in terms of argument structure – the representation of argument-taking properties of lexical items. And once argument structure began to be used to explain facts of sentence syntax, it became necessary in turn to explain properties of argument structure, leading inexorably to the detailed examination of the meanings of predicates. The study of lexical semantics no longer divides the field, as it did during the interpretive semantics versus generative semantics debates of the 1970s, but is becoming a unifying focus. Insights regarding word meaning are being compiled eclectically from a variety of linguistic frameworks, current and past, and are incorporated in not too dissimilar ways in most modern linguistic theories.

The assumption underlying much of this current linguistic research – that syntactic properties of phrases reflect, in large part, the meanings of the words that head them – also provides a powerful new methodology for studying word meaning. Rather than relying exclusively on intuitions and judgments about aspects of verb meaning, researchers can exploit the fact that subtle differences in word meaning correlate with otherwise puzzling differences in the syntactic structures that the word can appear in. Why can you say *Chris cut at the bread* but not *Chris broke at the bread*? The answer, it turns out, depends on the fact that *cut* is a verb of motion, contact, and causation, while *break* is a verb of pure causation (Guerssel, Hale, Laughren, Levin, & White Eagle, 1985; Levin, 1985). This implies that motion, contact, and causation must be represented in the meanings of verbs in a format that the syntax can be sensitive to. When the technique of searching for syntax-relevant distinctions is applied to many words and many constructions, a small set of semantic elements tends to recur. Thus evidence from syntactic judgments provides us with a characterization of the scaffolding of semantic structures that verb meanings are built on. Interestingly, the set of elements picked out by this technique is in many instances similar to the set of elements that can be marked overtly by the morphology of some languages, that define the common thread between literal and quasi-metaphorical uses of a given verb, and that are needed to specify the meanings of hundreds or thousands of verbs in English and other languages (Jackendoff, 1990; Miller & Johnson-Laird, 1976; Pinker, 1989; Talmy, 1985). Such convergences increase confidence that the core content of semantic representations is beginning to be identified, and that researchers are not just indulging their intuitions about the best way to define a word.

The development within computer science of computational and statistical techniques that can be applied to on-line text corpora and machine-readable dictionaries adds powerful new tools to the toolkit available for the study of lexical representation (e.g., Boguraev, 1991; Boguraev & Briscoe, 1989; Byrd, Calzolari, Chodorow, Klavans, & Neff, 1987; Church, Gale, Hanks, Hindle, & Moon, to appear; Church & Hanks, 1989; Zernik, 1991; among many others). These technologies, by providing access to large amounts of data and allowing for the semi-automatic verification of hypotheses, are already showing great promise, and may soon lead to even more striking results. The study of lexical semantics might also repay the favor to computer science. The development of natural language-understanding systems depends on the availability of large-scale comprehensive lexicons. Current systems face what has sometimes been called a "lexical bottleneck" (Byrd, 1989) – limitations in system performance attributable to the inadequacy of their lexicons. In the past, the lexicons of natural language-processing systems were created with the technological requirements of a system in mind (especially in terms of the ability to support inference), regardless of their fidelity to the human mental lexicon. But it is hard to believe that such systems would not profit from insights about how the human mind represents word meaning and maps it onto grammar (Levin, 1991; Pustejovsky & Boguraev, to appear). After all, that's where the words and grammar come from.

Psychology, too, cannot afford to do without a theory of lexical semantics. Fodor (1975, 1981; Fodor et al., 1980) points out the harsh but inexorable logic. According to the computational theory of mind, the primitive (nondecomposed) mental symbols are the innate ones. If people know 50,000 word meanings, and if most of these cannot be decomposed into finer-grained elements, then people must have close to 50,000 primitive concepts, and they must be innate. And Fodor, after assessing the contemporary relevant evidence, concluded that most word meanings are *not* decomposable – therefore, he suggested, we must start living with the implications of this fact for the richness of the innate human conceptual repertoire, including such counterintuitive corollaries as that the concept *car* is innate. Whether or not one agrees with Fodor's assessment of the evidence, the importance of understanding the extent to which word meanings decompose cannot be denied, for such investigation provides crucial evidence about the innate stuff out of which concepts are made. Current evidence that there is some linguistically relevant internal structure to verb meaning has provided an intriguing set of candidates for basic conceptual elements, reviewed in Jackendoff (1990) and Pinker (1989). How much of a speaker's vocabulary can be *exhaustively* captured in terms of these elements is, of course, an open question.

Lexical semantics has also come to play an increasingly central role in the study of language acquisition. Infants do not know the grammar of the particular language community they are born into, but they do have some understanding of the conceptual world that the surrounding language users are expressing. Since concepts are in turn intimately tied to the meanings of words, the child's semantic machinery might play an important role in allowing him or her to break into the rest of the language system, a hypothesis sometimes called "semantic bootstrapping" (see Pinker, 1984). At the same time the semantic representations of particular words, especially verbs, vary from language to language and must themselves by acquired, and the acquisition of verb meaning has become a lively topic in developmental psycholinguistic research (Bowerman, 1989; Clark, 1982; Gentner, 1982; Gleitman, 1990).

The impetus for this special issue of *Cognition* is the revival of interest and research on lexical and conceptual semantics. The issue presents a range of representative recent studies that approach lexical and conceptual semantics from the perspectives of both theoretical linguistics and psycholinguistics. The authors of the papers in this volume come from a variety of backgrounds and bring different perspectives to bear on the common goal of developing a theory of word meaning and explaining our ability to use and understand words. Like other areas in cognitive science the study of word meaning has only benefited from being approached by researchers from various fields. The fruits of the resulting cross-fertilization are evident in the papers in this volume, which together cover a wide range of current research issues in lexical and conceptual semantics. Three of the papers in this volume are primarily from a psycholinguistic perspective and three primarily from a linguistic perspective. Two of the psycholinguistic studies focus on child language acquisition, while the third explores a model of lexical organization that is supported by experimental and theoretical work.

Jackendoff's paper introduces the notion of "conceptual semantics" – a characterization of the conceptual elements by which a person understands words and sentences, to be distinguished from much of formal linguistic semantics which characterize the abstract relation between words and sentences and the external world. This approach is illustrated by means of an investigation of the meanings of words for objects, events, and their parts. The study uncovers unexpected and uncanny grammatical parallels between nouns and verbs, related, presumably, to some underlying conceptual parallel between things and events. Pustejovsky's paper, although focusing on verbs, looks at how verbs come together with nouns, adverbs, and prepositional phrases in determining certain facets of the compositional meaning of a sentence in a model that he calls "the generative lexicon". Lexical aspect – the inherent temporal structure of an event, a facet of word meaning that has recently been shown to be extremely important in explaining properties of words – figures in Pustejovsky's and Jackendoff's papers and to a lesser extent in some of the other papers. Choi and Bowerman's paper studies the development of the meanings of verbs signifying motion with respect to particular directions, objects, and parts, and the relation between these language-specific lexical semantic structures and nonlinguistic conceptual structure. The study, which compares English and Korean-speaking children, documents children's striking ability to acquire the language-particular nuances of word meaning quickly, while demonstrating the importance of cross-linguistic research to our understanding of development of word meaning.

The next two papers also investigate verbs of motion, focusing on a subclass of motion verbs that has figured prominently in recent research within linguistics on lexical semantics and its relation to syntax. Levin and Rappaport Hovav present a linguistic investigation of *clear/wipe* verbs, and Gropen, Pinker, Hollander, and Goldberg study the acquisition of their semantic inverses, the *spray/load* verbs. Both studies show how an appropriate representation of word meaning can be used to predict syntactic behavior, and, in the case of children, misbehavior.

Finally, Miller and Fellbaum discuss a large-scale computational investigation of lexical organization that centers around the semantic relations between words, rather than the semantic components within words. Their paper presents a sample of the discoveries that their group have made while working on this project, with intriguing implications for how words in different grammatical categories are mentally organized and how they develop in the course of language history.

We hope that this collection of papers will bring the new work on lexical semantics to the attention of a broad range of cognitive scientists, and will serve as a framework from which future integrations can proceed.

References

Boguraev, B. (1991). Building a lexicon: The contribution of computers. *International Journal of Lexicography*, *4*(4). To be co-published in M. Bates & R. Weischedel (Eds.), *Challenges in natural language processing*. Cambridge, UK: Cambridge University Press.

Boguraev, B., & Briscoe, E. (Eds.). (1989). *Computational lexicography for natural language processing*. Harlow, Essex: Longman.

Bowerman, M. (1989). Learning a semantic system: What role do cognitive dispositions play? In M. Rice & R. Schiefelbusch (Eds.), *The teachability of language*. Baltimore: Brookes.

Byrd, R.J. (1989). Large scale cooperation on large scale lexical acquisition. Paper presented at the Workshop on Lexical Acquisition, IJCAI, Detroit.

Byrd, R.J., Calzolari, N., Chodorow, M.S., Klavans, J.L., & Neff, M.S. (1987). Tools and methods for computational lexicology. *Computational Linguistics*, *13*, 219–240.

Church, K., Gale, W., Hanks, P., Hindle, D., & Moon, R. (to appear). Substitutability. In B.T. Atkins & A. Zampolli (Eds.), *Computational approaches to the lexicon: Automating the lexicon II*. Oxford: Oxford University Press.

Church, K.C., & Hanks, P. (1989). Word association norms, mutual information and lexicography. *Proceedings of the 27th annual meeting of the Association for Computational Linguistics*, 76–83.

Clark, E.V. (1982). The young word maker: A case study of innovation in the child's lexicon. In E. Wanner & L.R. Gleitman (Eds.), *Language acquisition: The state of the art*. New York: Cambridge University Press.

Fillmore, C.J. (1968). The case for case. In E. Bach & R.T. Harms (Eds.), *Universals in linguistic theory*. New York: Holt, Rinehart and Winston.

Fodor, J.A. (1975). *The language of thought*. New York: T. Crowell.

Fodor, J.A. (1981). The present status of the innateness controversy. In J.A. Fodor (Ed.), *Representations*. Cambridge, MA: MIT Press.

Fodor, J.A., Fodor, J.D., & Garrett, M.F. (1975). The psychological unreality of semantic representations. *Linguistic Inquiry*, *6*, 515–531.

Fodor, J.A., Garrett, M., Walker, E., & Parkes, C. (1980). Against definitions. *Cognition*, *8*, 263–367.

Gentner, D. (1982). Why nouns are learned before verbs: Linguistic relativity vs. natural partitioning. In S.A. Kuczaj II (Ed.), *Language development. Vol. 2: Language, thought, and culture*. Hillsdale, NJ: Erlbaum.

Gleitman, L.R. (1990). The structural sources of verb meaning. *Language Acquisition*, *1*, 3–55.

Guerssel, M., Hale, K., Laughren, M., Levin, B., & White Eagle, J. (1985). A cross-linguistic study of transitivity alternations. *Papers from the parasession on causatives and agentivity*. Chicago, IL: Chicago Linguistic Society.

Jackendoff, R.S. (1990). *Semantic structures*. Cambridge, MA: MIT Press.

Johnson, S. (1747). The plan of a dictionary of the English language; Addressed to the Right Honourable Philip Dormer, Earl of Chesterfield; One of His Majesty's Principal Secretaries of State. [Reproduction edition (1970). London: Scolar Press.]

Johnson, S. (1755). Preface to the dictionary. Reprinted in E.L. McAdam Jr. & G. Milne (Eds.) (1964). *Samuel Johnson's dictionary: A modern selection.* New York: Pantheon.
Katz, J.J., & Fodor, J.A. (1963). The structure of a semantic theory. *Language*, *39*, 170–210.
Lakoff, G. (1971). On generative semantics. In D. Steinberg & L. Jakobovits (Eds.), *Semantics.* Cambridge, UK: Cambridge University Press.
Levin, B. (1985). Lexical semantics in review: An introduction. In B. Levin (Ed.), *Lexical semantics in review.* Lexicon Project Working Papers 1, Center for Cognitive Science, MIT.
Levin, B. (1991). Building a lexicon: The contribution of linguistic theory. *International Journal of Lexicography*, *4*(4). To be co-published in M. Bates & R. Weischedel (Eds.), *Challenges in natural language processing.* Cambridge, UK: Cambridge University Press.
McCawley, J.D. (1973). *Grammar and meaning.* Tokyo: Taishukan.
McCawley, J.D. (1979). *Adverbs, vowels, and other objects of wonder.* Chicago, IL: University of Chicago Press.
Miller, G.A., & Johnson-Laird, P.N. (1976). *Language and perception.* Cambridge, MA: Harvard University Press.
Pinker, S. (1984). *Language learnability and language development.* Cambridge, MA: Harvard University Press.
Pinker, S. (1989). *Learnability and cognition: The acquisition of argument structure.* Cambridge, MA: MIT Press.
Pustejovsky, J., & Boguraev, B. (to appear). A richer characterization of dictionary entries: The role of knowledge representation. In B.T. Atkins & A. Zampolli (Eds.), *Computational approaches to the lexicon: Automating the lexicon II.* Oxford: Oxford University Press.
Ross, J.R. (1972). Act. In D. Davidson & G. Harman (Eds.), *Semantics of natural language.* Dordrecht: Reidel.
Talmy, L. (1985). Lexicalization patterns: Semantic structure in lexical forms. In T. Shopen (Ed.), *Language typology and syntactic description 3. Grammatical categories and the lexicon.* Cambridge, UK: Cambridge University Press.
Wasow, T. (1985). Postscript. In P. Sells, *Lectures on contemporary syntactic theories.* Center for the Study of Language and Information, Stanford University, Stanford, CA.
Winograd, T. (1976). Towards a procedural understanding of semantics. *Revue Internationale de Philosophie*, *117–118*, 262–282.
Zernik, U. (Ed.). (1991). *Lexical acquisition: Using on-line resources to build a lexicon.* Hillsdale, NJ: Erlbaum.

2

Parts and boundaries*

Ray Jackendoff
Brandeis University.

Within the framework of Conceptual Semantics, a family of conceptual features and functions is developed that accounts for phenomena in the semantics of noun phrases such as the mass-count distinction, plurality, the partitive construction (a leg of the table), *the constitutive construction* (a house of wood), *the "Universal Packager"* (three coffees), *and boundary words such as* end, edge, *and* crust. *Using the strong formal parallelism between noun phrase semantics and event structure that is a hallmark of the Conceptual Semantics approach, the features and functions of the NP system are applied to a wide range of problems in event structure, for example the analysis of the Vendler classes, the meaning of the progressive, the "imperfective paradox", and "aktionsarten" such as the syntactically unexpressed sense of repetition in* The light flashed until dawn.

Crucial to the analysis is that these features and functions can be expressed in syntactic structure either by being part of lexical conceptual structure, or by use of a morphological affix, or by being associated with the meaning of a construction such as N of NP *or nominal compounding. Alternatively, they may remain unexpressed altogether, being introduced into the conceptual structure of a phrase by "rules of construal". This shows that lexical semantics and phrasal semantics interpenetrate deeply, and that there is no strict one-to-one correspondence between syntactic and semantic structures. In addition, the analysis provides further evidence that natural language semantics must be based on a psychological view of meaning – it must be concerned with how language users are constructed to understand and schematize the world.*

*This research was supported in part by NSF Grants IST 84-20073 and IRI 88-08286 to Brandeis University. I am grateful to Steven Pinker, Paul Bloom, and three anonymous referees for useful comments on earlier versions of this paper.

1. The framework

Given the many different opinions on what semantics is supposed to be about, I had better begin by situating this study in the overall enterprise of which it forms a part. A convenient starting point is Chomsky's (1986) distinction between two broad views of language. One, *E-language* or "externalized language", sees language as an external artifact, existing independently of speakers. The other, *I-language* or "internalized language", sees language as a set of mental principles that account for linguistic understanding and use. From the standpoint of psychology, the latter view is of greater interest.

One can approach semantics, the theory of linguistic meaning, from either of these views. For the most part, standard versions of truth-conditional semantics are concerned with the relation of language to the world independent of speakers, that is, *E-semantics*. By contrast, this study (along with Jackendoff 1983, 1990) is an inquiry into the principles of mental representation that support thought – that is, it belongs to a theory of *I-semantics*, which in principle should be more compatible than an E-semantic theory with the concerns of both psychology and generative grammar.

The basic hypothesis underlying Conceptual Semantics, the particular version of I-semantics pursued here, is that there is a form of mental representation called *conceptual structure* that is common to all natural languages and that serves as the "syntax of thought".[1] Conceptual structure is envisioned as a computational form that encodes human understanding of the world.[2] Rules of inference, pragmatics, and heuristics can all be thought of as principles that license the formation of new conceptual structures on the basis of existing ones. Since conceptual structure serves as the form of linguistic meaning, there must also be a set of *correspondence rules* that relate it to syntactic representations, which permit the expression of meaning. In addition, since the conceptualization of the world must be related to perception and action, conceptual structure must be linked by further sets of correspondence rules to the mental representations proprietary to the perceptual systems and to the production of action. The overall layout of the theory is shown in Figure 1.

Accordingly, the goal of Conceptual Semantics is to articulate each of the

[1]I use this term to distinguish my notion of conceptual structure from Fodor's (1975) "Language of Thought"; the latter carries with it the property of intentionality, from which I wish to distance myself. See Jackendoff (1990, 1991) for discussion.

[2]However, conceptual structure is not the only form of representation available to encode one's understanding of the world. Aspects of the world that are understood spatially are encoded in another central representation whose properties resemble Marr's (1982) 3D model structure (see Jackendoff, 1987b; Jackendoff & Landau, 1991 for discussion, as well as section 5); there may well be other central representations as well, for instance a "body representation" that encodes the position and state of the body. What distinguishes conceptual structure from these others is its *algebraic* character – its being formalized in terms of features and functions – and its capacity to encode abstractions.

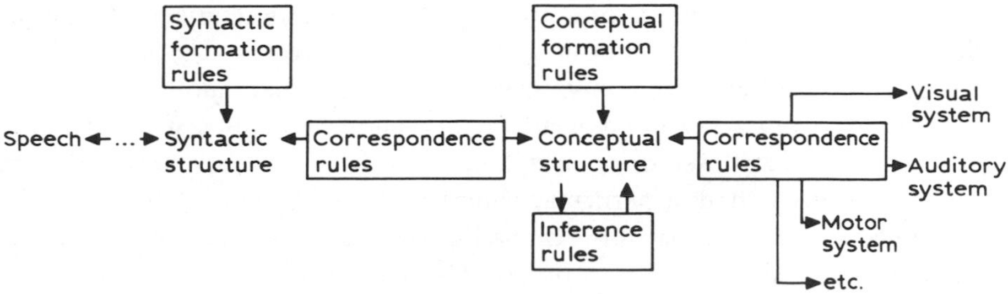

Fig. 1.

systems of principles in Figure 1: (a) the formation rules for conceptual structure, that is, the primitives and principles of combination that collectively generate the infinite class of possible concepts – both lexical concepts (word meanings) and phrasal concepts (including sentential concepts or *propositions*); (b) the rules of inference, pragmatics, and heuristics; (c) the correspondence rules between conceptual structure and the other representations with which it interacts. None of these goals, of course, can be pursued in isolation; they are intimately interdependent. The present study will touch on all of them to varying degrees.

The main issue, however, will be the primitives and principles of combination for a particular conceptual domain, that dealing with parts and boundaries. These are to be universal: they define what there is for language to express, and they do not depend on the vehicle of expression. We will also be concerned with the correspondence rules that determine the translation from conceptual structure into syntactic and morphological structure of English. Such rules are of the form "Such-and-such a configuration in conceptual structure corresponds to such-and-such a syntactic configuration." They thus must contain two structural descriptions, one for each of the levels being placed in correspondence. Since the syntactic side of the correspondence is in part language-particular, it is to be expected that the correspondence rules will also be language-particular, though undoubtedly constrained by principles of Universal Grammar that pertain to the correspondence rule component.

Within this framework, a lexical item can be seen as a correspondence between well-formed fragments of phonological, syntactic, and conceptual structure. Hence the lexicon is conceived of as part of the correspondence rule component. The leading questions of lexical semantics then come to be framed as: (a) What fragments of conceptual structure can be encoded in lexical items (of, say, English)? (b) When lexical items are combined syntactically, how are they correspondingly combined in conceptual structure, and what principles license these correspondences?

When one claims that conceptual structure can be described in terms of primitives and principles of combination, and in particular that lexical items can be conceptually decomposed into primitives,[3] the question arises of how one justifies primitives. This question in turn falls into two parts. The first is how to tell in general whether one putative primitive is better than another. In fact, an isolated primitive can never be justified; a primitive makes sense only in the context of the overall system of primitives in which it is embedded. With this proviso, however, I think a particular choice of primitives should be justified on the grounds of its capacity for expressing generalizations and explaining the distribution of the data. That is, a proposed system of primitives is subject to the usual scientific standards of evaluation.

The other part of the question concerning the justification of primitives is how to tell whether the primitives one has proposed are *really* primitive – with the insinuation that if one can't tell whether one is all the way at the bottom, the enterprise is hopeless. My answer is that one probably can't tell whether one is all the way at the bottom, but that this is not a matter for worry. Consider that the decomposition of all substances into 92 primitive elements was a major breakthrough 100 years ago, but that these primitives in turn have been further decomposed, first into electrons plus nucleus, then into electrons plus protons and neutrons, then all of these into quarks, which in turn are combinations of more primitive features such as spin, color, up/down, etc. Each level of decomposition explained more about the nature of matter and raised new questions of its own; and each step was cause for excitement, not discouragement. We will see parts of a similar progression here, when later in the paper some of the categories treated as primitive in Jackendoff (1983) undergo further decomposition in terms of a more explanatory set of primitives.[4]

A final general issue I must mention is that of the *reference* of linguistic expressions. Standard formal semantics seeks to explicate the relation of reference between language and the external world, usually modeling the world set-theoretically and often using the notion of possible worlds. In the present framework of I-semantics, the relation between language and the external world is taken to be mediated by the way the mind understands the world, as encoded in mental representations. Thus this theory contains no notion of reference in the standard sense. Rather, the corresponding construct is the mind's *construal* of the world, or how the speaker is at the moment inviting the hearer to *view* the world. This difference will play an important role in what is to follow, since the semantics

[3] Jerry Fodor, in an influential series of publications (Fodor, 1970, 1981; Fodor, Fodor, & Garrett, 1975; Fodor et al., 1980), has denied that lexical items have semantic decompositions. For replies, see Jackendoff (1983, Ch. 7; 1990, Ch. 1).

[4] Among other things, it will develop that there are probably no *words* that directly express conceptual primitives; all words are composite. This should not be cause for alarm. In chemistry/physics, after all, none of the quarks (not to mention quark-features) appear in isolation. Closer to home, no phonological primitives appear in isolation either; one of the major points of Prague School phonology, preserved in the generative tradition, is that the phoneme is always divisible into features which themselves never occur in isolation.

of parts and boundaries proves in many respects to depend crucially on what construals of objects and events are possible and salient.

2. The technology of conceptual semantics

Much of the theory of conceptual semantics (Jackendoff, 1976, 1983, 1987a, 1990) has been concerned with the encoding of verb-argument structure. To give the reader a feel for the notation and the claims it makes, consider a simple syntactic structure like (1):

(1) $[_S[_{NP}\text{ Bill}][_{VP}[_V\text{ went}][_{PP}[_P\text{ into}][_{NP}\text{ the house}]]]]$

This corresponds to the conceptual structure (2):

(2) $[_{\text{Event}}\ \text{GO}([_{\text{Thing}}\ \text{BILL}],[_{\text{Path}}\ \text{TO}([_{\text{Place}}\ \text{IN}([_{\text{Thing}}\ \text{HOUSE}])])])]$

Let me unpack this expression. Paralleling the notation for syntactic structure, the square brackets in (2) identify *conceptual constituents*. Each constituent is labeled as belonging to a *major conceptual category* or "semantic part of speech" – one of the kinds of entities the world is conceptualized as containing, for example Thing (or physical object), Event, State, Path (or trajectory), Place (or location), Property, Time, and Amount.

Within the brackets, the expressions in capital letters denote conceptual content. The expressions BILL and HOUSE are for present purposes undecomposed. The three other pieces of material are the functions IN, TO, and GO. IN is a one-place function that maps an object (its *reference object*) into a region or Place that encompasses the interior of the object. TO is a one-place function that maps a Thing or Place into a Path that terminates at that Thing or Place. Thus the Path constituent in (2) can be read roughly as "a trajectory that terminates at the interior of the house". GO is a two-place function that maps a Thing and a Path into an Event consisting of the Thing traversing the Path. Thus the entire Event in (2) can be read roughly as "Bill traverses a path that terminates at the interior of the house" ((2) does not encode tense or determiners, a gap in the theory at present).

Notice that the standard thematic roles of Theme and Goal are encoded structurally in (2): Theme, the thing in motion, is the conceptual constituent that serves as the first argument of GO; Goal, the point at which motion terminates, is the conceptual constituent that serves as the argument of TO. Thus [BILL] is Theme of (2) and [IN([HOUSE])] is Goal of (2). This is an essential feature of Conceptual Semantics: thematic roles are treated as structural positions in conceptual structure, not as an independent system of diacritics (or case-markers).

Statement (2) is placed in correspondence with the syntactic structure (1) by virtue of the lexical entries in (3):

(3) a. $\begin{bmatrix} \text{into} \\ \text{P} \\ [_{\text{Path}}\ \text{TO}([_{\text{Place}}\ \text{IN}([_{\text{Thing}}\ ]_A)])] \end{bmatrix}$ (phonological structure) (syntactic structure) (conceptual structure)

b. $\begin{bmatrix} \text{go} \\ \text{V} \\ [_{\text{Event}}\ \text{GO}([_{\text{Thing}}\ ]_A, [_{\text{Path}}\ ]_A)] \end{bmatrix}$ (phonological structure) (syntactic structure) (conceptual structure)

(3a) specifies that the phonological material *into* corresponds to a preposition in syntactic structure and to a certain expression in conceptual structure – the item's "lexical conceptual structure" or LCS. The LCS in (3a) is a function of one argument, a Thing; the argument is marked with the "linking subscript" *A*. An argument so marked must be expressed by a syntactic argument; by virtue of a general principle of linking, this syntactic argument will appear as the object of the preposition.[5] Thus the PP *into the house* in (1) is mapped into the full Path-constituent in (2).

Similarly, (3b) specifies that the phonological material *go* (ignoring the morphological alteration to *went*) corresponds to a verb in syntactic structure and to a two-place function in conceptual structure. The two arguments of the function are subscripted *A*, and therefore must be expressed in the syntax; by the linking principles, they are expressed as the subject and postverbal PP.

An alternative way of expressing conceptual structure (2) is as the English sentence (4a), whose verb has the lexical entry (4b):

(4) a. Bill entered the house.

b. $\begin{bmatrix} \text{enter} \\ \text{V} \\ [_{\text{Event}}\ \text{GO}([_{\text{Thing}}\ ]_A, [_{\text{Path}}\ \text{TO}([_{\text{Place}}\ \text{IN}([_{\text{Thing}}\ ]_A)])])] \end{bmatrix}$

The LCS of *enter* can be thought of as "incorporating" the LCS of *into* with that of *go*. By virtue of this incorporation, both arguments of *enter* are Things. The result is that the verb occurs with two NPs (subject and object) rather than with an NP and a PP. Thus it is possible for the same conceptual structure to correspond to more than one syntactic structure, depending in part on the argument structure of the lexical items involved.

We can see from these examples that Conceptual Semantics treats the "argument structure" or "θ-grid" of a lexical item not as a separate level of lexical

[5]This treatment of linking differs from treatments in Jackendoff (1983, 1987a), where linking was stipulated by coindexing between the LCS and the syntactic subcategorization feature. The present treatment, which is more general, is developed in Jackendoff (1990, Ch. 11).

representation (as in Grimshaw, 1990; Higginbotham, 1985; Rappaport & Levin, 1985, 1988; Stowell, 1981; Williams, 1984; and others), but simply as the collection of A-markings in the item's LCS. The structural positions of the A-marked constituents in turn determine the θ-roles of the syntactic arguments in the sentence; hence the process of "θ-marking" amounts essentially to linking syntax to conceptual structure.

More generally, this approach to conceptual decomposition bears a resemblance to other such theories, for example Schank's (1973) "conceptual dependency theory". It differs from Schank's approach in that (a) it takes seriously the contribution of syntactic structure to the form of a sentence, whereas Schank rejects an independent syntax; (b) it attempts to determine general primitives and principles of combination that explain facts of linguistic distribution, whereas Schank appears to be concerned primarily with covering the semantic facts with minimal concern for linguistic generalization.

All this said, we are finally ready to get to the problem at hand.

3. The puzzle and a preliminary solution

The problem that motivates the present study might be first illustrated with a sentence discussed by Talmy (1978):

(5) The light flashed until dawn.

Statement (5) conveys a sense of the light flashing repetitively. However, the "core" sentence *the light flashed* suggests not repetition but a single flash. Nor does the sense of repetition come from *until dawn*: *Bill slept until dawn*, for instance, does not express repeated acts of sleeping. Hence there is evidently no lexical item in the sentence that can be said to contribute to the sense of repetition; it must arise from combining the words into the sentence. Thus three questions must be answered: (a) How is repetition encoded in conceptual structure? (b) What principles of correspondence license its use in (5), despite the absence of a lexical item that contains it? (c) Why is it required in the interpretation of (5)?

To get a little more feel for the problem, let us explore some related examples:

(6) Until dawn,

a.	Bill slept.	
b.	the light flashed.	[*repetition only*]
c.	lights flashed.	[*each may have flashed only once*]
d.	*Bill ate the hot dog.	
e.	Bill ate hot dogs.	

f. *Bill ate some hot dogs.
g. Bill was eating the hot dog.
h. ?Bill ran into the house. [*repetition only*]
i. people ran into the house [*each may have entered only once*]
j. ?some people ran into the house. [*each person entered repeatedly*]
k. Bill ran toward the house.
l. Bill ran into houses. [*he may have entered each house once*]
m. Bill ran into some houses. [*he entered each house repeatedly*]
n. Bill ran down the road.
o. *Bill ran 5 miles down the road. [*OK only on the reading where 5 miles down the road is where Bill was, not on the reading where 5 miles down the road is how far he got*]

Some of the phrases in (6) combine with *until dawn* without changing sense; some add the sense of repetition; some are ungrammatical. Moreover, the possibilities are influenced by the choice of verb (6a vs. 6b vs. 6d); by the choice of singular versus bare plural versus *some* + plural in subject (6h, i, j), object (6d, e, f), or object of a preposition (6h, l, m); by the choice of aspect (6d vs. 6g); by the choice of preposition (6h vs. 6k vs. 6n); and by the choice of prepositional specifier (6n vs. 6o). We are thus dealing with a semantic system whose effects are felt in practically every part of the syntax. A properly general solution to the sense of repetition in (5) must therefore be an account of this entire system, and it must extend naturally to all the cases in (6).

With this in mind, let's sketch out the overall form of the solution, beginning with the sense of repetition. As has been pointed out many times (e.g., Gruber, 1967; Hinrichs, 1985; Langacker, 1987; Talmy, 1978; among others), the semantic value of repetition is identical to that of the plural, that is, it encodes the multiplicity of a number of entities belonging to the same category. In the case of objects, the plural maps an expression denoting an instance of a category (say *apple*) into an expression denoting a multiplicity of instances of the category (*apples*). In the case of repetition, an expression denoting a single instance of a particular category of events (*the light flashed*) is mapped into an expression denoting multiple instances of the same category. In English, the resulting expression does not differ in form; but there are languages such as Hungarian and Finnish that have an iterative verb aspect used for this purpose. Note also that if the event is expressed in English with a noun, for instance *a flash*, then its plural denotes repeated events, for instance *flashes*. Thus the identification of repetition with plurality is syntactically justified as well.

A consequence of this analysis is that the multiplicity of entities is a feature of conceptualization that is orthogonal to the distinction between objects and events. Such a result is consistent with the evidence from (6) that the system of conceptual encoding we are looking for cuts across this conceptual distinction.

Next consider the rule that permits (5) to be interpreted as repetitive despite the absence of any iterative morpheme. This rule appears to belong to a class of rules that might generally be called "rules of construal". Example (7), adapted from Nunberg (1979), is a standard case that invokes such a rule:

(7) [One waitress says to another:]
The ham sandwich in the corner wants another cup of coffee.

The lexical entry for *ham sandwich* certainly does not specify a potential reading "customer with a ham sandwich"; nor is there any other lexical item in the sentence that licenses such a reading. Rather, there is a general principle of construal that may be stated roughly as: "A constituent identifying an individual X may be used/understood to identify an individual contextually associated with X." This principle licenses the insertion of nonlexical material into the conceptual structure of a sentence, roughly "individual contextually associated with". In the process, the lexical material identifying X comes to be subordinated to the role of modifier of the new material, so that the subject of (7), for example, is understood as "individual contextually associated with a ham sandwich".[6]

Of course, if the rule used in (7) could operate freely, chaos would result. What renders its application appropriate in (7) is the fact that the literal interpretation of (7) is ill-formed: a ham sandwich can't want anything. This seems characteristic of this class of rules: the interpreter avails him/herself of them to understand otherwise ill-formed or pragmatically inappropriate utterances. (Jackendoff, 1990, suggests that rules of this sort fall into the same class as what Levin and Rapoport (1986) have called rules of "lexical subordination" and what Jackendoff (1990) calls "superordinate adjuncts".)

The rule of construal responsible for (5) has the effect of substituting "multiple events of category X" for "event of category X". What motivates its application? The basic insight is that the conceptual structure of *until dawn* places a temporal boundary on an otherwise temporally unbounded process. So, for instance, *Bill slept* expresses a process that is conceptualized as unbounded: the speaker's focus for the moment lies within the process, excluding the boundaries from view. The full sentence *Bill slept until dawn* then expresses the termination of this process. However, *the light flashed* expresses an inherently bounded occurrence: the light goes on, then goes off, and the event is over. Thus it cannot be subject to the extrinsic bounding imposed by *until dawn*. This is the ill-formedness, parallel to that of the literal interpretation of (7), that motivates applying a rule of construal. The effect of applying the rule is to map the "core" event into a sequence of flashes that can go on indefinitely; this sequence can then be bounded in time by the expression *until dawn*. By contrast, *Bill ate the hot dog* is inherently bounded and *cannot* be repeated (barring regurgitation), so applying the rule of construal

[6]This is how the rule looks from the point of view of syntax. From the point of view of semantics, a rule of construal licenses leaving material out of syntax, hence economizing the overt expression of thought.

to (6d) does not result in a well-formed reading; the sentence is therefore unacceptable.[7]

The basic formal shape of this solution appears in (8), a first approximation to the conceptual structure of (5):

(8)

$$\left[\begin{array}{l} \text{UNTIL}\left(\left[\begin{array}{l}\text{PLURAL}\left(\left[\begin{array}{l}\text{LIGHT FLASHED}\\ \text{BOUNDED}\end{array}\right]_{\text{Event}}\right)\\ \text{UNBOUNDED}\end{array}\right]_{\text{Event}}, [\text{DAWN}]_{\text{Time}}\right)\\ \text{BOUNDED}\end{array}\right]_{\text{Event}}$$

Unpacking this, UNTIL is a function that bounds an unbounded event (its first argument) with a time (its second argument), producing a bounded event. PLURAL is a function that maps a bounded entity (its argument) into an unbounded multiplicity of entities of the same type; in the interpretation of (5) this function is contributed by the rule of construal.

The idea behind this solution appears in many sources (e.g., Declerck, 1979; Dowty, 1979; Hinrichs, 1985; Mourelatos, 1978; Platzack, 1979; Pustejovsky, 1991; Talmy, 1978; Vendler, 1957; Verkuyl 1972, 1989). In the course of subsequent sections, this solution will be refined and placed in the context of the larger system that is responsible for the facts in (6) and many other phenomena. In particular, my strategy is to make full use of the cross-categorial properties of this system, using the much richer grammatical resources of the noun system to elucidate the properties of the verbal system standardly called aktionsarten or event structure. (There is no space here to compare my proposals at any length with those in the extensive literature, only a small portion of which is cited above and later in the text. I hope to address the differences in future work.)

4. The features b(ounded) and i(nternal structure)

To begin approaching a more general solution, we introduce a pair of fundamental conceptual features. Consider first the feature of boundedness. It has frequently been noted (Bach, 1986; Fiengo, 1974; Gruber, 1967; Talmy, 1978; among many others) that the distinction between count and mass nouns strongly parallels that between temporally bounded events and temporally unbounded processes. For example, one hallmark of a count noun, say *apple*, is that one cannot divide its referent up and still get something named by the same count noun, i.e. another apple. By contrast, with a mass noun such as *water*, one can divide its referent up

[7] Notice that in a language like Chinese, which lacks a plural morpheme, this rule of construal will be responsible for the interpretation of plurality in noun phrases as well as sentences.

and still get something describable as water (as long as one does not divide it up so small as to break up the molecular structure). The same criterion applies to events versus processes. One cannot divide up the event *The light flashed* and get smaller events describable as *The light flashed*, but one can divide up a process described as *Bill slept* into smaller parts also describable as *Bill slept*.

Accordingly, we will introduce a feature ±*bounded*, or ±b, in both the object and the event system. Individual objects (usually described by count nouns) and completed events will be encoded as +b (replacing the notation BOUNDED in (8); unbounded substances (usually described by bare mass nouns) and unbounded processes will be encoded as −b (replacing UNBOUNDED in (8)).

Let me be slightly more specific about what is intended by −b. As suggested in the previous section, a speaker uses a −b constituent to refer to an entity whose boundaries are not in view or not of concern; one can think of the boundaries as outside the current field of view. This does not entail that the entity is absolutely unbounded in space or time; it is just that we can't see the boundaries from the present vantage point.

A second feature encodes plurality. As is well known, plurals and mass nouns pattern together in various respects, in particular admitting many of the same determiners, including *some*, *all*, *a lot of*, *no*, *any*, and, significantly, the zero determiner. Bare mass nouns and bare plurals, but not singulars, can occur in expressions of distributive location such as (9). When they serve as direct object of a verb such as *eat*, the resulting sentence is a process (10a, b) by contrast with singulars, which create closed events (10c):

(9) a. There was water all over the floor.
 b. There were books all over the floor.
 c. *There was a book all over the floor.[8]

(10) a. Bill ate custard until dawn.
 b. Bill ate hot dogs until dawn.
 c. *Bill ate a hot dog until dawn.

We will therefore group bare mass nouns and bare plurals together as unbounded (−b). Talmy suggests the term *medium* to encompass them both. The difference between the two kinds of media is that plurals entail a medium comprising a multiplicity of distinguishable individuals, whereas mass nouns carry no such entailment. We will encode this difference featurally; the difference in entailment

[8]A reader has observed that *There was a copy of the NY Times all over the floor* is grammatical. It appears that in this sentence the newspaper is being conceptualized as an unbounded aggregate of sheets of paper.

can then be a consequence of inference rules that refer to the feature in question. I will call the feature ±*internal structure*, or ±i. *Aggregates* – the entities normally expressed by plural nouns – will be +i. *Substances* – the entities normally expressed by mass nouns – will be −i. (Note: the value −i does not mean lack of internal structure, but rather lack of necessary entailment about internal structure.)

The +i distinction can be applied in the +b domain as well as the −b: it provides a way of encoding the difference between *individuals* and *groups*. (Here I begin to move away from standard proposals.) A group entity is bounded, but there is a necessary entailment that it is composed of members. An individual may have a decomposition into parts, but that is not a necessary part of its individuality. Thus the feature system, applied to objects and substance, comes out as (11):

(11) +b, −i: individuals (*a pig*)
+b, +i: groups (*a committee*)
−b, −i: substances (*water*)
−b, +i: aggregates (*buses*, *cattle*)

Individuals correspond to the conceptual category of Thing employed in section 2. We therefore need a larger supercategory that contains all of the entities in (11). Let us call it Material Entity (*Mat* for short). The term thing, previously regarded as primitive, now becomes composite: it is an abbreviation for [Mat, +b, −i]. Note, however, its privileged status: of the four subcategories of Mat, only Thing has an inherent shape. Therefore it is the only subcategory that has physical boundaries. (Groups are bounded in quantity but do not have an inherent shape.)

The features *b* and *i* can be applied in the event/process domain as well. A closed event such as *John ran to the store* is [+b, −i]; an unbounded homogeneous process such as *John slept* is [−b, −i]; an unbounded iterative process such as *The light flashed continually* is [−b, +i]; a bounded iterative event such as *The light flashed until dawn* is [+b, +i]. Thus the feature system cuts across major conceptual categories, expressing the generality of the phenomena of boundedness and plurality.

5. Functions that map between values of b and i

5.1 PL

How is the notion of plurality to be represented? There are two possibilities. Suppose (12a) is the conceptual structure of *a dog*, where the features [Mat, +b, −i] set the entity within the major category of individual objects, and DOG is a stand-in for the conceptual information that distinguishes dogs from other categories of individual objects. Then there are two possible ways to encode the term *dogs*, shown in (12b) and (12c)

(12) a. $\begin{bmatrix} +\text{b}, -\text{i} \\ _{\text{Mat}}\ \text{DOG} \end{bmatrix}$ = a dog

b. $\begin{bmatrix} -\text{b}, +\text{i} \\ _{\text{Mat}}\ \text{DOG} \end{bmatrix}$ = dogs

c. $\begin{bmatrix} -\text{b}, +\text{i} \\ _{\text{Mat}}\ \text{PL}\left(\begin{bmatrix} +\text{b}, -\text{i} \\ _{\text{Mat}}\ \text{DOG} \end{bmatrix}\right) \end{bmatrix}$ = dogs

In (12b), the plural has been expressed by changing the b and i features of *a dog* from those for an individual to those for an aggregate. The plural morpheme is thus conceived of as expressing a feature-changing process. In (12c), by contrast, the lexical entry for *dog* has been left unchanged; it appears as the argument of a conceptual function PL that maps its argument into an aggregate. The plural morpheme is then taken to express this function.

I will adopt the latter solution, because it permits correspondence rules along lines known from the principles of verb argument structure illustrated in section 2. In particular, it gives the correspondence rules a property of "morphological transparency": for the most part, addition of syntactic information (including morphology) does not change features of the base element, but rather adds operators around the base. In the present case, the LCS of *dog* is found directly in (12c), embedded in the operator PL; by contrast, in (12b) the LCS of *dog* has disappeared.

One reason for adopting representation (12c) is what happens when we pluralize a group-noun such as *herd* or *committee*. Under the feature-changing treatment, the plural comes out as (13a), which is no longer distinct from the plural of an individual. Under the functional treatment, it comes out as (13b), in which one can still discern that the plurality is of groups rather than individuals:

(13) a. $\begin{bmatrix} -\text{b}, +\text{i} \\ _{\text{Mat}}\ \text{COMMITTEE} \end{bmatrix}$ = committees

b. $\begin{bmatrix} -\text{b}, +\text{i} \\ _{\text{Mat}}\ \text{PL}\left(\begin{bmatrix} +\text{b}, +\text{i} \\ _{\text{Mat}}\ \text{COMMITTEE} \end{bmatrix}\right) \end{bmatrix}$ = committees

The plural morpheme thus has the conceptual structure (14a); the LCS of the noun to which it applies fits into the A-marked argument slot. A lexical plural such as *people* or *cattle* has an LCS like (14b):

(14) a. $\text{N} + \text{plur} = \begin{bmatrix} -\text{b}, +\text{i} \\ \text{PL}([+\text{b}]_{\text{A}}) \end{bmatrix}$

b. $\text{people} = \begin{bmatrix} -\text{b}, +\text{i} \\ _{\text{Mat}}\ \text{PL}\left(\begin{bmatrix} +\text{b}, -\text{i} \\ _{\text{Mat}}\ \text{PERSON} \end{bmatrix}\right) \end{bmatrix}$

Note that the plural morpheme cares only that the noun to which it applies designates a bounded entity. It does not care whether that entity is Material or an Event (such as *earthquakes*), nor whether it is an individual or a group. On the other hand, the entity must be bounded, so that mass nouns, which are −b, cannot be pluralized. (We return to apparent counterexamples like *three coffees* in section 5.3.)

In the verbal system, PL is the function that iterates events. Thus a constituent of *The light flashed until dawn* is (15). This expression is the unbounded process that will eventually be bounded by *until dawn*; it replaces the notation for the first argument of UNTIL given in (8):

(15)
$$\begin{bmatrix} -\text{b}, +\text{i} \\ \text{PL}\left(\begin{bmatrix} +\text{b}, -\text{i} \\ \text{LIGHT FLASHED} \end{bmatrix}_{\text{Event}}\right) \end{bmatrix}_{\text{Event/Process}}$$

In this case, PL is not introduced by a morpheme in the sentence. Rather, as argued in section 3, it is introduced by a rule of construal.

There are verbs that appear to lexically include PL, parallel to the lexically plural nouns. For example, *pound* and *hammer* normally describe not a single blow (as *hit* does), but a sequence of blows iterated into a process.

PL is one of a class of functions that map an entity with one value of b and i into another entity with different values. Having myself considered and rejected numerous hypotheses about the constitution of this class, I am not completely confident that the functions about to be proposed are properly characterized. (A different but related set is proposed by Winston, Chaffin, & Herrmann, 1987.) However, the discussion to follow shows the range of phenomena for which any competing analysis of this class of functions must be responsible.

5.2 ELT

A sort of inverse of PL is evoked in phrases like *a grain of rice*, *a stick of spaghetti*. In these phrases, the second noun is grammatically a mass noun, but it happens that it denotes an aggregate rather than a substance. The first noun picks out an individual of the aggregate. Hence, to express the meaning of the phrase, we need a function that maps an aggregate into a single element of the aggregate. I will call the function ELT (element of). *A grain of rice* then comes out as (16):

(16)
$$\text{a grain of rice} = \begin{bmatrix} +\text{b}, -\text{i} \\ \text{ELT}\left(\begin{bmatrix} -\text{b}, +\text{i} \\ \text{RICE} \end{bmatrix}_{\text{Mat}}\right) \end{bmatrix}_{\text{Mat}}$$

A possible extension of ELT to another feature combination might be *a drop of water*, in which *a drop* is conceptualized as the natural unit into which the substance water divides itself:

(17)
$$\text{a drop of water} = \left[\begin{array}{l} +\text{b}, -\text{i} \\ \text{ELT}\left(\left[\begin{array}{l} -\text{b}, -\text{i} \\ \text{WATER} \end{array}\right]_{\text{Mat}}\right) \end{array}\right]_{\text{Mat}}$$

This extension is not, however, a natural inverse of the plural, since it conceptualizes a multiplicity of individuals (drops) combining into a substance rather than an aggregate. I will leave open whether this extension is correct.

PL and ELT thus form a pair that can be thought of as approximate inverses. I will call PL an *including function*: the function maps its argument into an entity that includes the argument as a subentity. By contrast, ELT is an *extracting function*: the function maps its argument into a subentity of the larger entity denoted by the argument. It is a characteristic of including functions that they transmit existential claims to their arguments. For instance, if there are dogs around, there is a dog around. By contrast, extracting functions do not transmit existential claims to their arguments. For instance, having a grain of rice around does not entail that there is a larger aggregate body of rice around – this single grain may be all we have.

The other functions to be introduced form pairs in the same way as PL and ELT: one member of the pair will be an including function and one an extracting function.

5.3 COMP

Consider an expression like *a house of wood*. The phrase *of wood* describes the substance of which the house is composed. To encode this relation, let us introduce a function COMP. Preserving the syntactic relations of subordination, this function will take a substance as its argument and map it into an individual:

(18)
$$\text{a house of wood} = \left[\begin{array}{l} +\text{b}, -\text{i} \\ \text{HOUSE} \\ \text{COMP}\left(\left[\begin{array}{l} -\text{b}, -\text{i} \\ \text{WOOD} \end{array}\right]_{\text{Mat}}\right) \end{array}\right]_{\text{Mat}} \quad \text{("a house composed of wood")}$$

Substituting an aggregate for the substance in (18), we can create expressions like *a house of bricks*:

(19)
$$\text{a house of bricks} = \left[\begin{array}{l} +\text{b}, -\text{i} \\ \text{HOUSE} \\ \text{COMP}\left(\left[\begin{array}{l} -\text{b}, +\text{i} \\ \text{PL}\left(\left[\begin{array}{l} +\text{b}, -\text{i} \\ \text{BRICK} \end{array}\right]_{\text{Mat}}\right) \end{array}\right]_{\text{Mat}}\right) \end{array}\right]_{\text{Mat}}$$

In (18) and (19), the noun *house* contributes only the content [+b, −i, HOUSE]; it is presumably not part of the LCS of *house* that it *has* to be composed of something. In other words, the COMP function is contributed by the modifying construction *of wood* or *of bricks*. However, there are other nouns whose LCS contains COMP as an essential part. For instance, *a pile* or *a stack* is an inherently bounded collection of smaller elements, combined to create a particular form. Thus the LCS of these items is something like (20):

(20) a.
$$\text{pile} = \begin{bmatrix} +\text{b}, -\text{i} \\ \text{PILE} \\ {}_{\text{Mat}}\ \text{COMP}([-\text{b}]) \end{bmatrix}$$

b.
$$\text{stack} = \begin{bmatrix} +\text{b}, -\text{i} \\ \text{STACK} \\ {}_{\text{Mat}}\ \text{COMP}([-\text{b}, +\text{i}]) \end{bmatrix}$$

The difference between the two expresses the fact that one can have *a pile of bricks* (aggregate) or *a pile of sand* (substance), but only *a stack of bricks*, not **a stack of sand*.[9]

In the examples above, the COMP function maps its argument into an individual. But COMP can also provide an analysis for group-nouns such as *herd*, *flock*, and *group*:

(21)
$$\text{a flock of birds} = \begin{bmatrix} +\text{b}, +\text{i} \\ {}_{\text{Mat}}\ \text{COMP}\left(\begin{bmatrix} -\text{b}, +\text{i} \\ {}_{\text{Mat}}\ \text{PL}\left(\begin{bmatrix} +\text{b}, -\text{i} \\ {}_{\text{Mat}}\ \text{BIRD} \end{bmatrix}\right) \end{bmatrix}\right) \end{bmatrix}$$

Note the difference between *stack* and *flock*: a stack has an inherent shape, which makes it [+b, −i], while a flock has no shape of its own, which makes it [+b, +i].[10]

So far COMP has been introduced by a lexical item or by the *of*-construction. It can also be introduced by a rule of construal, in which case it serves as what has been called the "universal packager", attributed in the literature to David Lewis:[11]

[9]Notice that *a stack of wood* implies that the wood is in discrete largish pieces, that is, an aggregate rather than just a substance. However, one cannot have **a stack of wood chips*, even though *wood chips* is plural. That is, *stack* imposes further selectional restrictions that are not addressed here, probably having to do with orderly geometric arrangement of the elements of the stack.

[10]This extension does not appear to have full generality: an individual can be composed of either a substance or an aggregate, but a group may be composed only of an aggregate – the notion of a group composed of a substance seems anomalous or conceptually ill-formed. I leave open how this asymmetry in the COMP function is to be resolved.

[11]David Lewis has informed me (personal communication) that he has not used this term in print; he in turn attributes the notion to lectures or writings by Victor Yngve in the 1960s which he is now unable to trace. The same goes for the notion of the "Universal Grinder" in section 5.4.

(22) I'll have a coffee/three coffees.

Here *coffee* is construed as "bounded individual composed of coffee". The syntax of the construction is that of count nouns: it uses the indefinite article and the plural, which are conceptually incompatible with the LCS of *coffee*, a substance. Therefore a rule of construal, inserting the operator COMP, must apply to make the representation well formed:

(23) a.

$$\text{a coffee} = \begin{bmatrix} +\text{b}, -\text{i} \\ \text{COMP}\left(\begin{bmatrix} -\text{b}, -\text{i} \\ \text{COFFEE} \end{bmatrix}_{\text{Mat}}\right) \end{bmatrix}_{\text{Mat}} \quad \text{"a portion of coffee"}$$

b.

$$\text{coffees} = \begin{bmatrix} -\text{b}, +\text{i} \\ \text{PL}\left(\begin{bmatrix} +\text{b}, -\text{i} \\ \text{COMP}\left(\begin{bmatrix} -\text{b}, -\text{i} \\ \text{COFFEE} \end{bmatrix}_{\text{Mat}}\right) \end{bmatrix}_{\text{Mat}}\right) \end{bmatrix}_{\text{Mat}} \quad \text{"portions of coffee"}$$

(Note: this reading of *coffees* is distinct from the reading that means "varieties of coffee", as in *The store sells seventeen coffees, each from a different country*; the latter is due to a separate rule of construal.)

A more general situation in which a rule of construal makes use of COMP appears in examples like (24):

(24) a. Will you mop up *that water*, please?

b. They loaded *the sand* into the truck.

c. *The boys* were impressed.

In each of these, the italicized NP expresses a bounded entity composed of a substance or aggregate. One might think that the definite article is the source of COMP. But in fact in other contexts the very same phrases can be unbounded. *That water* in (25a), for instance, denotes a contextually identifiable medium, not a fixed amount:

(25) a. *That water* kept spurting out of the broken hose.

b. *The sand* stretched out as far as we could see.

c. *The boys* arrived for hours on end.

Apparently, then, definiteness contributes only the content "contextually identifiable"; the determination of boundedness depends on other constraints. The unbounded reading (26a) can be derived directly from the LCS of *that* and *water*; the bounded reading (26b) is the result of applying a rule of construal that inserts COMP (DEF is the conceptual structure associated with definiteness):

(26) a.
$$\text{that water (in (25a))} = \begin{bmatrix} -\text{b}, -\text{i} \\ \text{WATER} \\ \text{DEF} \end{bmatrix}$$

b.
$$\text{that water (in (24a))} = \begin{bmatrix} +\text{b}, -\text{i} \\ \text{DEF} \\ \text{COMP}\left(\begin{bmatrix} -\text{b}, -\text{i} \\ \text{WATER} \end{bmatrix}\right) \end{bmatrix}$$

5.4 GR

COMP, like PL, is an including function: it maps its argument into a larger entity that includes the argument. It therefore has the existential entailment characteristic of an including function: if there is a house of wood around, there is wood around. The inverse of COMP therefore ought to be an extracting function whose argument is an individual or group, and which maps its argument into a substance or aggregate of which the individual or group is composed.

Such a function is found in the so-called "universal grinder" (see footnote 11), illustrated in the grisly (27):

(27) There was dog all over the street.

Here the bare singular and the distributive location force the term *dog* to be interpreted as a substance. As usual, the relevant rule of construal does not simply change the lexical features of *dog* to make it into a substance. Rather, it preserves well-formedness by introducing a function GR, whose argument is the LCS of *dog*:

(28)
$$\text{dog (substance)} = \begin{bmatrix} -\text{b}, -\text{i} \\ \text{GR}\left(\begin{bmatrix} +\text{b}, -\text{i} \\ \text{DOG} \end{bmatrix}_{\text{Mat}}\right) \end{bmatrix}_{\text{Mat}}$$

Given this operator, we can also use it in the lexicon to express the relation between animals and their meat (29a), animal body parts and their meat (29b), and similar paired words like *rock*/*a rock* and *stone*/*a stone*:

(29) a.
$$\text{pork} = \begin{bmatrix} -\text{b}, -\text{i} \\ \text{MEAT} \\ \text{GR}\left(\begin{bmatrix} +\text{b}, -\text{i} \\ \text{PIG} \end{bmatrix}\right) \end{bmatrix}$$

b.
$$\text{liver} = \begin{bmatrix} -\text{b}, -\text{i} \\ \text{MEAT} \\ \text{GR}\left(\begin{bmatrix} +\text{b}, -\text{i} \\ \text{LIVER} \end{bmatrix}\right) \end{bmatrix}$$

GR applied to an individual yields a substance. For symmetry, it is useful to stipulate that GR applied to a group yields the aggregate of which the group is composed. This makes it not quite a true inverse of COMP, but it is close.

As required, GR is an extracting function: its output is a subentity of its argument. Like our other extracting function ELT, it does not transmit existential claims to its argument: if there is dog all over the place, it does not follow that there is a dog around.

In the verbal system, GR appears to be (one of) the reading(s) of the progressive aspect in English. For example, *Bill is running to the store* can be construed as "the process out of which the event *Bill runs to the store* is composed". This analysis allows us to incorporate Bach's (1986) solution to the "imperfective paradox" – the fact that even if it is true that *Bill is writing a novel*, there need not yet (or ever) be a novel such that Bill is writing it. Bach, drawing on Link's (1983) treatment of the semantics of the mass/count distinction, points out that the existence of a part of an object does not entail the existence of the whole object. For instance, one may find (or make) a part of a violin without there being (now or ever) a violin of which this is a part. Similarly, Bach argues, the progressive is extracting a part of an event, and hence carries no entailment that the event is ever carried to completion. Since the existence of the (complete) novel depends on the completion of the event, the novel too carries no existential claim. In the present analysis the same conclusion follows from the claim that the progressive involves applying the extracting function GR to the event, which does not transmit existential claims (or in the case of events, truth claims) to its argument.

Before going on to the next function, notice that all the functions discussed so far can be introduced by rules of construal, and that at least two, ELT and COMP, show up in the *N of NP* construction. This is one of the difficulties of separating these functions clearly – their great degree of syntactic overlap, when they are expressed at all.

5.5 PART

Another *N of NP* construction occurs in (30):

(30) a. a leg of the table

b. the roof of the porch

c. a part of the group

This *partitive* construction takes as its argument a bounded entity and addresses its internal articulation, picking out an identifiable bounded part. It is thus an extracting function like ELT and GR; as noted by Bach, it shares the characteristic entailment of extracting functions. Unlike GR, it extracts a bounded part, not an unarticulated substance. Unlike ELT, it presumes that the entity extracted from is nonhomogeneous: a house can have different kinds of parts, but rice has only one kind of internal element, a grain. Thus it appears that the partitive is a distinct function from the other two. I will encode (30a), for example, as (31)

$$(31)\quad \begin{bmatrix} +\mathrm{b}, -\mathrm{i} \\ \mathrm{LEG} \\ \mathrm{PART}\left(\begin{bmatrix} +\mathrm{b}, -\mathrm{i} \\ \mathrm{TABLE} \end{bmatrix}\right) \end{bmatrix}$$

Note that words like *leg* and *roof* are lexically partitive – a leg has to be a leg *of something*. Statement (30c) shows the same operator applied to a group noun, yielding a smaller group:

$$(32)\quad \text{part of the group} = \begin{bmatrix} +\mathrm{b}, +\mathrm{i} \\ \mathrm{PART}\left(\begin{bmatrix} +\mathrm{b}, +\mathrm{i} \\ \mathrm{GROUP} \end{bmatrix}\right) \end{bmatrix}$$

A word like *subcommittee* lexically incorporates the whole complex in (32).

PART also appears to be able to map its argument into a substance. An example is (*the*) *blood of a pig*, which seems altogether parallel to *a/the heart of a pig* in its structure. A possibly more controversial extension would be to cases with an unbounded argument, as in *an ingredient of stew*, whose proper analysis I leave open.

Another frequent syntactic realization of the PART function is as a nominal compound. So, for example, parallel to the examples above we have *table leg*, *porch roof*, *pig blood*, *pig heart*, and *stew ingredients* (though not **group part*).

5.6 CONT

Each of the other functions has an approximate inverse. This suggests that PART should too. What would be its properties? It would have to be an including function that mapped its argument into an entity containing the argument as a part.

One possible instance of such a function is in compounds like *drop-leaf table* ("a table whose identifying part is a drop-leaf") and *beef stew* ("stew whose identifying ingredient is beef"). By extension, it would also be invoked by a rule of construal in synecdoche and exocentric compounds, where a distinguishing part is used to identify the whole (*Hey, Big-Nose!*). Another possible case is NPs containing a *with*-modifier, such as *table with a drop-leaf* and *house with an orange roof*. It is clear that this relation is distinct from the other including functions, PL and COMP; let's call it CONT ("containing"). Then *beef stew*, for instance, would have the structure (33):

(33)
$$\text{beef stew} = \begin{bmatrix} -\text{b}, -\text{i} \\ \text{STEW} \\ \text{CONT}\left(\begin{bmatrix} -\text{b}, -\text{i} \\ \text{BEEF} \end{bmatrix}\right) \end{bmatrix}$$

Thus we have found six functions that map one combination of the features *b* and *i* into another, expressing different relations of parts to wholes. (34) summarizes:

(34) Including functions: PL COMP CONT
Extracting functions: ELT GR PART

6. Dimensionality and directionality

We next have to look briefly at the dimensionality and directionality of entities and how they are encoded in conceptual structure.

The basic observation about dimensionality is that a point is conceptualized as 0-dimensional, a line or curve as 1-dimensional, a surface as 2-dimensional, and a volume as 3-dimensional. (The notion of dimensionality here is essentially the number of orthogonal degrees of freedom within the object.) However, following and extending Marr's (1982) theory of encoding of object shapes, we can decompose an object's dimensionality into a hierarchical arrangement of dimensions.

Consider for example a road, a river, or a ribbon. These can be schematized as a line (the primary dimension) elaborated by a linear cross-section (the secondary dimension), yielding a surface. The primary dimension of these objects may be bounded or unbounded; the secondary dimension is bounded. In order to encode dimensionality in conceptual structure, we will introduce a 4-valued feature *DIM nD*, where *n* varies from 0 to 3. Statement (35) illustrates the use of this feature; the secondary dimension appears in the inner brackets:

(35)
$$\text{road, river, ribbon} = \begin{bmatrix} \pm\text{b}, -\text{i} \\ \text{DIM 1D} \\ \begin{bmatrix} +\text{b}, -\text{i} \\ \text{DIM 1D} \end{bmatrix} \end{bmatrix}$$

Contrast these items to a layer or a slab, which are basically thickened surfaces. Here the primary dimension is a bounded or unbounded surface, and the secondary dimension is an orthogonal dimension that is bounded and linear, giving a volume. Statement (36a) shows this representation. A different case arises with a tube or a beam, whose primary dimension is linear, and whose cross-section is a 2-dimensional shape (36b):

(36) a.

$$\text{layer, slab} = \begin{bmatrix} \pm\text{b}, -\text{i} \\ \text{DIM 2D} \\ \begin{bmatrix} +\text{b}, -\text{i} \\ \text{DIM 1D} \end{bmatrix} \end{bmatrix}$$

b.

$$\text{tube, beam} = \begin{bmatrix} \pm\text{b}, -\text{i} \\ \text{DIM 1D} \\ \begin{bmatrix} +\text{b}, -\text{i} \\ \text{DIM 2D} \end{bmatrix} \end{bmatrix}$$

On the other hand, a sphere has no salient decomposition into axes, so its dimensionality is just [DIM 3D].

The dimensionality feature can easily be extended to time and to states and events. Points in time, states at a point in time, and point-events are [DIM 0D], while periods of time and states and events with duration are [DIM 1D]. This of course does not leave much room for distinctions of primary versus secondary dimensionality, but we will see shortly that such possibilities arise nevertheless.

The dimensionality feature is subject to a principle of reconstrual that I will call the *zero rule*: a bounded object can always be idealized as a point. Under this idealization, the object's intrinsic dimensionality becomes secondary and the primary dimensionality is 0d. (This is the principle that allows cities to be represented by points on maps.)

(37) (Zero rule – idealizing object as point)

$$\begin{bmatrix} \text{X} \\ +\text{b} \\ \text{DIM nd} \end{bmatrix} \Leftrightarrow \begin{bmatrix} \text{X} \\ +\text{b} \\ \text{DIM 0d} \\ [\text{DIM nd}] \end{bmatrix}$$

The use of this principle will become evident in the subsequent sections.

A further wrinkle in the dimensionality feature is that any 1-dimensional axis can have a *direction* or *orientation*. So, for example, a line has no intrinsic direction, but a vector and an arrow do. We can encode this by adding a further distinction to the dimensionality feature, marking vectors and arrows as [DIM 1d DIR] and ordinary lines as just [DIM 1d].[12]

[12]I am treating DIR as a "privative" feature, that is, one that is either present or absent. Alternatively it could be treated as a binary feature ±DIR. However, the only descriptions in the present paper where the feature −DIR is necessary are Place and State (see (38)), which may not prove to need independent definitions – they may be just the residue of Spaces and Situations when Paths and Events are removed.

A surface or volume can acquire directionality only by being decomposed into linear axes. For instance, the human body has a primary directed up–down dimension, a secondary directed front-to-back dimension, and a tertiary side-to-side dimension that is symmetric rather than directed. However, a sphere and a layer have no inherent directionality.

I would like to use the directionality feature to resolve a problem in the set of major conceptual categories in Jackendoff (1983, 1990). This class includes Thing (now expanded to Material), State, Event (now including processes), Place, Path, Time, and others. When these categories were proposed, there was clearly a close relation between States and Events and between Places and Paths, but this relationship found no formal expression.

So let us consider the relation between Places and Paths. Places can be regions of any dimensionality: *at this point* is 0-dimensional, *along the line* is 1-dimensional, *in the circle* is 2-dimensional, and *in the cup* is 3-dimensional. Thus Places share the dimensionality features of objects. But Paths can be only 1-dimensional and must moreover be directed: there is an intrinsic direction in which they are viewed – in the standard case, from Source to Goal. This suggests that Places and Paths can be combined into a supercategory that may be called Space. Paths are the subset of spaces whose dimensionality feature is [DIM 1d DIR] and places are the rest. In other words, the relation of Places and Paths can be formally expressed by a feature distinction.

I would like to extend this, a little speculatively, to the relation between Events and States. States like *X is red* or *X is tall* are conceptualized as "just sitting there" – they have no inherent temporal structure. (The "state" of being in continuous motion, however, is now encoded as a process, or unbounded Event.) Events, by contrast, do have an inherent temporal structure which proceeds in a definite direction. I would like to suggest therefore that the two categories be combined into a supercategory called Situation, with States as the undirected case and Events as the directed case. (Bach, 1986, uses the term *eventuality* in the same sense.)

Statement (38) summarizes this further analysis of the *S&C* primitives:

(38)
$$[\text{PLACE}] = \begin{bmatrix} \text{SPACE} \\ -\text{DIR} \end{bmatrix}$$

$$[\text{PATH}] = \begin{bmatrix} \text{SPACE} \\ \text{DIM 1d DIR} \end{bmatrix}$$

$$[\text{STATE}] = \begin{bmatrix} \text{SITUATION} \\ -\text{DIR} \end{bmatrix}$$

$$[\text{EVENT}] = \begin{bmatrix} \text{SITUATION} \\ \text{DIR} \end{bmatrix}$$

There is a slight asymmetry in this reanalysis, forced by the existence of point-events such as *The light turned on* or *The clock ticked once*. According to our treatment of dimensionality, these should be 0-dimensional; but as Events, they are directional. Thus we have to admit the possibility of 0-dimensional directed Situations, whereas the original intuitions motivating directionality pertained only to 1-dimensional entities. One can think of a number of solutions for this asymmetry, but nothing much hangs on it for now, so I will leave it unresolved.

The main point, however, is that the dimensionality and directionality features, developed to account for conceptual properties of objects, turn out to permit an insightful unification of completely independent conceptual categories.

7. Boundaries

What sort of entity is a boundary? It follows from the definition of the feature system that only a [+b, −i] category – an individual – can have a boundary. If an entity is conceptualized as [−b], this means it is conceptualized without a boundary; in order to discuss its boundary, we have to first reconceptualize it by applying the COMP function. A [+b, +i] entity, a group, is bounded in quantity, but it has no inherent shape – it is just a collection of individuals. Hence it has no discernible entity serving as a boundary.

A basic condition on boundaries is that a boundary has one dimension fewer than what it bounds: a line can be bounded by a point, a region by a line, and a volume by a surface. However, this basic condition is an idealization of the actual situation. Consider a stripe that bounds a circle: it is locally 2-dimensional, not 1-dimensional. What makes the stripe a boundary for the circle is its schematization as a line (its primary dimension) elaborated by a cross-section (its secondary dimension). At the schematic level of primary dimensionality it *is* 1-dimensional, as the basic condition stipulates. From this we can see that the actual condition on dimensionality of boundaries is that the *schematization* of a boundary has one dimension fewer than the *schematization* of what it bounds.

This enables us to make an important generalization in the conceptual structure of words like *end* and *edge*. Consider what kinds of things can have ends, and their dimensionality. A line (1d) has a 0d end; a ribbon (2d) has a 1d end; a beam (3d) has a 2d end. This is not very enlightening. However, the proper analysis emerges if we observe that each of these objects has a 1d primary dimensionality, that is, they are all schematized as lines. By descending to the level of the 1d schematization, we can treat the end in each case as a point bounding the line.

How then does the end acquire its actual dimensionality? Consider again the beam, whose dimensionality is given in (36b). The 2d secondary dimensionality here represents the cross-section of the beam, say an H shape. The end of the beam inherits its shape from this cross-section. More generally, an end can be schematized as having a 0d primary dimension, elaborated by the same secondary dimension as the object it bounds:

(39) a. line $= [\text{DIM 1d}]$ end of line $= [\text{DIM 0d}]$

b. ribbon $= \begin{bmatrix} \text{DIM 1d} \\ [\text{DIM 1d}] \end{bmatrix}$ end of ribbon $= \begin{bmatrix} \text{DIM 0d} \\ [\text{DIM 1d}] \end{bmatrix}$

c. beam $= \begin{bmatrix} \text{DIM 1d} \\ [\text{DIM 2d}] \end{bmatrix}$ end of beam $= \begin{bmatrix} \text{DIM 0d} \\ [\text{DIM 2d}] \end{bmatrix}$

Using the zero rule (37) from right to left, the end of the ribbon and the end of the beam can be reanalyzed as entities in their own right, with one and two dimensions respectively.

An end is therefore fundamentally a point that bounds a line. An *edge*, by contrast, is fundamentally a line that bounds a surface. For instance, the edge of a ribbon (2d) is 1-dimensional. A table-top can be conceptualized as a surface (2d) elaborated by a thickness (1d). The edge of a table-top is the boundary of the surface (1d) elaborated by the same thickness, hence a ribbon-like surface:

(40) a. ribbon $= [\text{DIM 2d}]$ edge of ribbon $= [\text{DIM 1d}]$

b. table-top $= \begin{bmatrix} \text{DIM 2d} \\ [\text{DIM 1d}] \end{bmatrix}$ edge of table-top $= \begin{bmatrix} \text{DIM 1d} \\ [\text{DIM 1d}] \end{bmatrix}$

Notice that a ribbon is conceptualized under different schematizations depending on whether one is identifying its end or its edge.

One further very important wrinkle – what do you do when you *cut off the end of a ribbon*? It would be absurd to think of just cutting off the geometric boundary, as the analysis so far would suggest. Rather, in this context, the end of the ribbon includes the geometric boundary plus some pragmatically determined but relatively small part of the body of the ribbon – similarly for *putting the cup on the end of the table*, in which the end includes some part of the top surface. These examples show that the primary dimension of an end, the one that bounds the linear axis of the object, need not be just 0d, but can be expanded a small amount along the axis. I will encode this expansion by the notation $0 + \varepsilon$d, as in (41). This notation may be thought of as designating a dimensionality that is something more than a point but something less than a line:

(41) object $= \begin{bmatrix} \text{DIM 1d} \\ [\text{DIM nd}] \end{bmatrix}$ end of object $= \begin{bmatrix} \text{DIM 0}(+\varepsilon)\text{d} \\ [\text{DIM nd}] \end{bmatrix}$

The expansion of the boundary is optional in the case of *end*, and one might want to attribute this possibility to a general rule of construal. However, there are other boundary words for which the expansion is obligatory. Consider a *crust*.

This is a surface bounding a volume, plus an expansion of the surface some small pragmatic distance into the volume; it is hard to tell where the crust of a loaf of bread breaks off and the body of the bread begins. We can express the dimensionality of a crust therefore as [DIM 2 + εd]. Similarly, the *border* of a rug is liable to extend further into the rug from the geometric boundary than does the *edge*. Thus, to distinguish *surface* from *crust* and *border* from *edge*, something like the epsilon notation is necessary in lexical conceptual structure. In turn, the optional expansion of *end* may be either lexical or supplied by a rule of construal; in either case, though, the formal effect is encoded by the epsilon notation.

This treatment of the dimensionality of ends gives us an immediate solution for a well-known puzzle in event structure. If the end of a talk is located at its temporal boundary, it must take place at a *point* in time. However, it is perfectly acceptable to say *Fred is ending/finishing his talk*, where the use of progressive implies a process taking place over a *period* of time. What is going on? The solution lies in the optional expansion of the end some small pragmatically determined distance back into the body of the talk, so that the end has dimensionality [DIM 0 + εd]. The expanded end takes up a period of time, and the activity within this period can therefore be described as *ending the talk*. In short, the analysis of *end* developed to account for obvious geometric intuitions generalizes to the less transparent temporal case, providing a natural explanation.

We complete this section by offering a formalism for the functions that relate boundaries to what they bound. As in the case of the functions introduced in section 5, there is a pair of boundary functions that are approximate inverses of each other. Statement (42) gives a first pass:

(42) a. $$\begin{bmatrix} \text{X} \\ +\text{b}, -\text{i} \\ \text{DIM n} - \text{1d} \\ \text{BD}\left(\begin{bmatrix} \text{Y} \\ +\text{b}, -\text{i} \\ \text{DIM nd} \end{bmatrix}\right) \end{bmatrix} = \text{“an X that bounds Y”}$$

b. $$\begin{bmatrix} \text{Y} \\ +\text{b}, -\text{i} \\ \text{DIM nd} \\ \text{BDBY}\left(\begin{bmatrix} \text{X} \\ +\text{b}, -\text{i} \\ \text{DIM n} - \text{1d} \end{bmatrix}\right) \end{bmatrix} = \text{“a Y that is bounded by X”}$$

For our purposes here, one refinement is necessary in these functions.[13] Just in

[13]The definitions in (42) and (43) stipulate that the entity being bounded and its boundary both be [+b, −i]. This pertains, of course, only to the dimension whose boundary is being determined. A river, for instance, has boundaries for its secondary dimension (its edges), while its primary dimension may be regarded as unbounded.

case the entity being bounded (Y in (42)) is directed, the two boundaries must be distinguished as *top* and *bottom*, *front* and *back*, or *beginning* and *end*. Accordingly, we introduce the notation in (43) as a subcase of (42):

(43) a. $$\begin{bmatrix} \text{X} \\ +\text{b}, -\text{i} \\ \text{DIM } 0(+\varepsilon)\text{d} \\ \text{BD}^{\pm}\left(\begin{bmatrix} \text{X} \\ +\text{b}, -\text{i} \\ \text{DIM 1d DIR} \end{bmatrix}\right) \end{bmatrix} = \text{“an X that terminates (+) or originates (−) Y”}$$

b. $$\begin{bmatrix} \text{Y} \\ +\text{b}, -\text{i} \\ \text{DIM 1d DIR} \\ \text{BDBY}^{\pm}\left(\begin{bmatrix} \text{X} \\ \text{DIM } 0(+\varepsilon)\text{d} \\ +\text{b}, -\text{i} \end{bmatrix}\right) \end{bmatrix} = \text{“a Y that has X as a terminus (+) or origin (−)”}$$

Thus, assuming an axis directed from back to front, the front of an object will be its BD^+ and the back its BD^-; the beginning of an event will be its BD^- and the end its BD^+.

Another refinement is necessary to specify that a boundary inherits its secondary dimensionality from the object it bounds, as shown in the cases of *end* and *edge* in the previous section. However, this plays no formal role in what is to follow, so I will leave it for another occasion.

8. Using the formalism

I have introduced a fair amount of new machinery here, but each piece was motivated by its ability to capture aspects of the conceptualization of objects and substances as well as their linguistic reflexes. We now apply the machinery to a variety of analyses in path and event structure.

8.1 Paths

The first case is the Path-function TO, whose argument position defines the thematic role Goal, and which is treated as a conceptual primitive in Jackendoff (1983, 1990) (and most other sources as well). This function is most directly expressed by *to* in English but is also incorporated in a wide range of other prepositions and verbs, as seen in section 2.

We can now decompose TO. It defines a Path that terminates at the Thing or Place that serves as its argument. This is easily encoded in terms of the features and functions introduced here:

(44) $$\text{TO X} = \left[\begin{array}{l} \quad +\text{b}, -\text{i} \\ \quad \text{DIM 1d DIR} \\ {}_{\text{Space}}\ \text{BDBY}^{+}([_{\text{Thing/Space}}\text{X}]) \end{array} \right]$$

That is, TO specifies a 1-dimensional bounded directed Space (i.e., a bounded Path), bounded on its positive end by the Goal. FROM, the function whose argument defines Source, differs from TO only in that BDBY^{+} is replaced by BDBY^{-}. That's all there is to it.

VIA is a path-function that defines routes, again primitive in Jackendoff (1983). It forms part of the LCS of prepositions like *through* ("via the interior of") and *past* ("via near"). In the present notation it can be analyzed as (45):

(45) $$\text{VIA}[_{\text{Place}}\text{X}] = \left[\begin{array}{l} \quad -\text{b}, -\text{i} \\ \quad \text{DIM 1d DIR} \\ {}_{\text{Space}}\ \text{CONT}([_{\text{Space}}\text{X}]) \end{array} \right]$$

This is a directed 1-dimensional Space (a Path) that is unbounded – if you tell me you went *past* my house I have no idea where you started or ended. The only thing I know about your path is that it includes the region near my house as a significant part. That is precisely what CONT was designed to encode in expressions like *beef stew* (section 5.6).

The other two major Path-functions in Jackendoff (1983) are TOWARD and AWAY-FROM, which are like TO and FROM except that they do not include the Goal and Source respectively. In the mass-count test they behave like substances: any part of a Path *toward the house* is also describable as *toward the house*, whereas this is not true of *to the house*. We therefore want to describe TOWARD as unbounded. Statement (46) gives two possible analyses:

(46) a. $$\text{TOWARD X} = \left[\begin{array}{l} \quad -\text{b}, -\text{i} \\ \quad \text{DIM 1d DIR} \\ \quad \text{GR}\left(\left[\begin{array}{l} +\text{b}, -\text{i} \\ \text{DIM 1d DIR} \\ \text{BDBY}^{+}([\text{X}]) \end{array} \right]\right) \\ {}_{\text{Space}} \end{array} \right]$$

b. $$\text{TOWARD X} = \left[\begin{array}{l} \quad -\text{b}, -\text{i} \\ \quad \text{DIM 1d DIR} \\ {}_{\text{Space}}\ \text{BDBY}^{+}([\text{X}]) \end{array} \right]$$

Statement (46a) treats TOWARD X as a "ground-up" version of TO X, that is, roughly as the "Path-substance" of which TO X is made. Statement (46b) treats it by analogy with the notion of an "open interval" in mathematics – a space that is bounded by but does not include the Goal. In this treatment, we have to admit the possibility of [−b] entities that have boundaries. In either case, AWAY-FROM is identical except that $BDBY^-$ replaces $BDBY^+$. At present I do not know how to decide between these alternatives.

The inverse of TO is a function called AT-END-OF in Jackendoff (1990). This appears as part of the reading of a number of prepositions, for instance *across* in *Bill is across the road from here*. In this example, *across the field* expresses a Place that is at the terminus of a Path that begins here and extends across the field. (47) analyzes this function:

$$(47)\quad [_{\text{Place}}\text{AT-END-OF}([_{\text{Path}}\text{X}])] = \left[\begin{array}{l} +\text{b}, -\text{i} \\ \text{DIM 0d} \\ _{\text{Space}}\ \text{BD}^{+}\ ([\text{X}]) \end{array}\right]$$

8.2 Aspectual functions

INCH (inchoative) is a function that maps a state into an event culminating in that state. It is an optional element in the conceptual structure of such verbs as *stand*, *sit*, *point*, *cover*, *extend*, and *surround*. In Jackendoff (1990) (and many other sources) INCH is treated as primitive, but again the present analysis permits a decomposition:

$$(48)\quad \text{INCH}([_{\text{State}}\text{X}])(\text{"State X comes about"}) = \left[\begin{array}{l} +\text{b}, -\text{i} \\ \text{DIM 1d DIR} \\ _{\text{Sit}}\ \text{BDBY}^{+}([_{\text{Sit}}\text{X}]) \end{array}\right]$$

Notice that this is identical to the analysis of TO, except that the major category feature *Situation* replaces *Space*! That is, the present analysis formally captures a deep parallelism between the end of a Path and the state at the end of an Event.

The last section spoke of beginning and finishing as Events that serve as boundaries of other Events. Here is a formal treatment of *finish*; *begin* replaces BD^+ with BD^-:

$$(49)\quad \text{Situation X finishes/ends} = \left[\begin{array}{l} +\text{b}, -\text{i} \\ \text{DIM } 0(+\varepsilon)\text{d DIR} \\ _{\text{Sit}}\ \text{BD}^{+}[_{\text{Sit}}\text{X}] \end{array}\right]$$

Section 5.4 analyzed the progressive aspect as "grinding up" an action into a process, showing how this solves the "imperfective paradox". This analysis can be extended to express the difference between *stop doing X* and *finish doing X*. Both are termini of an action; but you can stop doing something without finishing it. Here is a possible analysis for *stop running to the store*:

(50)
$$\begin{bmatrix} +\mathrm{b}, -\mathrm{i} \\ \mathrm{DIM}\ 0(+\varepsilon)\mathrm{d}\ \mathrm{DIR} \\ \mathrm{BD}^{+}\left(\begin{bmatrix} +\mathrm{b} \\ \mathrm{COMP}\left(\begin{bmatrix} -\mathrm{b} \\ \mathrm{GR}\left(\begin{bmatrix} +\mathrm{b} \\ \text{RUN TO STORE} \end{bmatrix}\right) \end{bmatrix}\right) \end{bmatrix}\right) \end{bmatrix}_{\mathrm{Sit}}$$

This unpacks as follows: the bounded event *run to the store* is ground up by GR into a process; some of this process is gathered up into a unit by COMP; the end of this unit is picked out by BD^{+}. It is this boundary event that is expressed by *stop running to the store*. In turn, since *run to the store* has been ground up, there is no inference of completion.

Statement (50) has a lot of functions in it. Which ones are lexical? My guess is that BD^{+} and COMP are due to the verb *stop*, which can also apply to States and Processes such as *Paul stopped being sick* and *Paul stopped sleeping*. GR in (50) is likely inserted by a rule of construal that converts a closed Event into an unbounded entity so that it can be bounded again internally.

An alternative rule of construal available in this context inserts our old friend PL, which creates a different kind of unbounded entity. This is the most likely reading of *The light stopped flashing*, and a secondary reading of *Bill stopped running to the store* (*all the time*), namely the termination of a sequence of iterations:

(51)
$$\begin{bmatrix} +\mathrm{b}, -\mathrm{i} \\ \mathrm{DIM}\ 0(+\varepsilon)\mathrm{d}\ \mathrm{DIR} \\ \mathrm{BD}^{+}\left(\begin{bmatrix} +\mathrm{b}, +\mathrm{i} \\ \mathrm{COMP}\left(\begin{bmatrix} -\mathrm{b}, +\mathrm{i} \\ \mathrm{PL}\left(\begin{bmatrix} +\mathrm{b} \\ \text{RUN TO STORE} \end{bmatrix}\right) \end{bmatrix}\right) \end{bmatrix}\right) \end{bmatrix}_{\mathrm{Sit}}$$

Notice that in (51) there is no extracting function in the chain, so this time we can infer that Bill did run to the store.

8.3 The "Vendler classes"

Much of the discussion of event structure has taken as a starting point the so-called Vendler classes of states, activities, accomplishments, and achievements. It is by now well known that these classifications pertain to entire sentences rather than to verbs as Vendler (1957) thought. There is not space here to discuss the extensive literature. However, I have become convinced, especially by the work of Declerck (1979), that the distinctions have to do with temporal structure, and have nothing to do with causation or volition, as implied by Dowty's (1979) influential analysis. The present formalism provides a straightforward encoding of the Vendler classes and permits us to set up a couple of other cases that Vendler and many later investigators have missed.

States are simply undirected situations, of 0 or 1 dimension. They may be bounded or unbounded; but I don't think they can be intermittent, hence they are [−i]. The formal specification is (52):

(52) $\text{State} = \begin{bmatrix} -\text{i} \\ {}_{\text{Sit}}\ [-\text{DIR}] \end{bmatrix}$

Activities correspond to what have been called here processes: unbounded directed situations. These can be produced either intrinsically (*swim*), by grinding bounded events (*be running to the store*), or by iterating bounded events (*flash repeatedly*). But these latter two cases are just elaborations of the basic case shown in (53), in which the "core" (*run to the store*, *flash*) is embedded as the argument of a GR or PL function (in other words, the "conversion" of an accomplishment (event) into an activity (process) is produced by a rule of construal that adds an operator):

(53) $\text{Activity} = \begin{bmatrix} -\text{b} \\ {}_{\text{Sit}}\ [\text{DIR}] \end{bmatrix}$

Accomplishments (e.g., *run to the store*, *eat an apple*) are directed situations with a final boundary. They intrinsically take place over a period of time, so they have to be 1-dimensional:

(54) $\text{Accomplishment} = \begin{bmatrix} +\text{b} \\ [\text{DIM 1d DIR}] \\ {}_{\text{Sit}}\ \text{BDBY}^{+}([\ ]) \end{bmatrix}$

However, an accomplishment can be subjected to the zero rule (37), which idealizes it as a point. This is what allows us to attribute an accomplishment to a point in time, as in *Bill ate an apple at 6:00.*

The trickiest case is the *achievements* such as *reach the top*, *arrive*, *die*, and, notably, *finish*. Our analysis of this last verb in the previous section provides the key: they are all events that mark the culmination of some larger event. Although they are fundamentally 0-dimensional, the optional expansion with epsilon provides a little temporal window into which we can sneak a progressive:

(55) $\text{Achievement} = \begin{bmatrix} +\text{b}, -\text{i} \\ [\text{DIM } 0(+\varepsilon)\text{d DIR}] \\ {}_{\text{Sit}}\ \text{BD}^{+}([\ ]) \end{bmatrix}$

Related to the class of achievements but not distinguished by Vendler are the *inceptions* such as *leave*, *commence*, and *start*. These are just like achievement except that BD^+ is changed to BD^-:

$$\text{(56) Inception} = \begin{bmatrix} & +\text{b}, -\text{i} \\ & [\text{DIM } 0(+\varepsilon)\text{d DIR}] \\ _{\text{Sit}} & \text{BD}^-([\ ]) \end{bmatrix}$$

Another class includes *point-events* like *flash* and *click*. These are not regarded as having appreciable duration. Statement (57a) gives their schema. A final class is *duratives* like *stay*, *keep*, and *persist*, which like activities are not inherently bounded, but unlike activities cannot be asserted at a point in time. Statement (57b) gives their schema:

$$\text{(57) a. Point-event} = \begin{bmatrix} & +\text{b} \\ _{\text{Sit}} & [\text{DIM 0d DIR}] \end{bmatrix}$$

$$\text{b. Durative} = \begin{bmatrix} & -\text{b} \\ _{\text{Sit}} & [\text{DIM 1d DIR}] \end{bmatrix}$$

The upshot of this analysis is a general agreement with such writers as Verkuyl (1989) and Pustejovsky (1991), who regard the Vendler classes not as a basic division of the aspectual system, but rather as various realizations of a set of more fundamental parameters. Here the parameters available are those of dimensionality and bounding, motivated independently for the conceptualization of objects; and therein lies their novelty.

8.4 Until and since

We finally return to our initial example, *The light flashed until dawn*, which we can now formalize. Recall the informal analysis of section 3: *until* places a boundary on an otherwise unbounded event. This comes out as (58):

$$\text{(58) X until Y} = \begin{bmatrix} & +\text{b} \\ & [\text{DIM 1d DIR}] \\ & \text{COMP}\left(\begin{bmatrix} & \text{X} \\ _{\text{Sit}} & -\text{b} \end{bmatrix}\right) \\ _{\text{Sit}} & \text{BDBY}^+([_{\text{Sit/Time}}\ \text{Y}]) \end{bmatrix}$$

This is a bounded event, composed of the state or process X (*until* doesn't care which), and ended by the situation or time Y.[14]

The fact that X must be unbounded in order to be the argument of COMP explains why *The light flashed*, which has event structure (57a), cannot appear unmolested before *until*. The day is saved by the rule of construal that inserts iteration, to give (59), a more complete version of our original attempt in (8):

(59) The light flashed until dawn =

$$\left[{}_{\text{Sit}}\begin{array}{l} +\text{b} \\ [\text{DIM 1d DIR}] \\ \text{COMP}\left(\left[\begin{array}{l} -\text{b}, +\text{i} \\ \text{PL}\left(\left[\begin{array}{l} +\text{b} \\ [\text{DIM 0d DIR}] \\ \text{LIGHT FLASH}\end{array}\right]\right)\end{array}\right]\right) \\ \text{BDBY}^{+}([_{\text{Time}}\ \text{DAWN}])\end{array}\right]$$

For some reason, the rule of construal that inserts GR instead of PL cannot apply with *until*, so that *Bill ran into the room until we stopped him* can only mean repeated running into the room, not our stopping him before he had a chance to get all the way in. I don't know why. (Using the progressive, *Bill was running into the room until we stopped him*, is cheating – it grinds the event into a process before submitting it to *until*.) However, another variation is available, seen in *Bill went away until Tuesday*. Here the state that results from or is the culmination of Bill going away persists until Tuesday. I am not sure how to formalize this case.

Since is approximately the reverse of *until*. *Bill has liked Sue since 1948* expresses a state beginning with (BDBY^{-}) 1948, containing (CONT) the discourse reference time (in this sentence, NOW), and composed of (COMP) Bill liking Sue. In *The light has flashed since dawn*, the most prominent reading iterates *the light flashed* into a process so that it can be unbounded, as required for it to be the argument of COMP. Another reading, more prominent in *The light has flashed just once since dawn*, appears to substitute CONT for COMP, so that a single flashing can constitute a significant part of the period since dawn. Note that *ever since* can be used only in the first reading:

(60) a. Ever since dawn, the light has flashed. (iterative)

b. *Ever since dawn, the light has flashed just once.

[14]For simplicity, I have treated *until* as a function of two arguments: the Event to be bounded and the Time. This actually does not accord too well with the syntactic pattern of the sentence, in which *until Y* is a modifier of the sentence expressing the event to be bounded. Improving this analysis would take us deeply into the theory of arguments, adjuncts, and modifiers, a topic beyond the scope of this paper.

Some of these complications seem to be tied up with the strongly preferred use of perfective aspect with *since*, a problem beyond the scope of this paper.

We have not dealt with the conceptual structure of measurement and quantity, so we cannot formalize phrases like *for 3 hours, in 3 hours,* and *3 times*, which have been crucial in the study of event structure at least since Vendler (1957). However, the present approach suggests that *for 3 hours* should be constructed so as to be compatible with expressions in the noun system such as *3 inches of rope*, which measures out a quantity of an unbounded substance; by parallelism, *X took place for 3 hours* measures out a quantity of an unbounded Situation (i.e., State or Process). *X took place in 3 hours* ought to be parallel to *Object X is located within 3 miles of Place Y*; both of them require bounded entities for X. *Three times* ought to just put a count on iterations of bounded events, just as *three cows* puts a count on iterations of *cow*. That is, when counting and measuring can be formalized in the noun and preposition system, the treatment should generalize naturally to the aspectual system along the lines seen here in the formalization of parts, composition, and boundaries.

9. Final remarks

I want to make four points in closing. First is that I have proposed what may seem like a substantial amount of machinery, including the features ±b and ±i, the six extracting and including functions (PL, ELT, COMP, GR, PART, and CONT), the dimensionality feature (including the epsilon dimensionality), the directionality feature, and the two boundary functions BD and BDBY. All of these parts have been necessary to get at the proper analysis of our initial puzzle, *The light flashed until dawn*. This may seem like excessive use of force. However, with this machinery we have been able to address along the way a wide range of phenomena, including the plural, collective nouns like *group* and *pile*, *N-of-NP* constructions and *N-N* compounds, boundary nouns like *end* and *crust* and prepositions like *to* and *from*, the Vendler classes, progressive aspect, and the "imperfective paradox". Thus we see that the true scope of the solution has proven to be an extremely broad one. A cornerstone of the solution has been the "X-Bar" character of the major conceptual categories – the possibility of features and functions that apply equally to Things, Places, and Events. To the extent that the description here has been successful, this vindicates and deepens this aspect of the theory of Conceptual Semantics.

Second, despite the fact that this paper is ostensibly about lexical semantics, the distinction between lexical semantics and phrasal semantics has played only an incidental role. The very same features and functions can appear in conceptual structure by virtue of either lexical entries, morphological affixes, constructional meanings (*N of NP* and *N-N* compounds), or rules of construal. In a sense, this supports an even more fundamental tenet of Conceptual Semantics: that conceptual structure is autonomous from language and that there is no intervening level of "purely linguistic semantics" intervening between it and syntax. The conceptual features and functions proposed here are indifferent to how they are expressed syntactically; it just so happens that four different kinds of correspondence rules – lexical entries, morphological affixes, constructional meanings, and rules of construal – are all capable of licensing relations between syntactic and conceptual structure in this domain.

Third, let us return to the issue of semantic primitives raised in section 1: when we propose a conceptual analysis of a word or phrase, how do we know we have got it all the way down to primitives? The answer is that we don't know, but this shouldn't stop us. For instance, the identification in Jackendoff (1983) of a conceptual category Path spelled out by a repertoire of five Path-functions was, I believe, an advance that permitted an insightful description of many phenomena. The fact that these putative primitives have now been subjected to further decomposition in order to bring them into a still larger orbit does not negate the earlier treatment. Similarly, the functions proposed here – PL, ELT, COMP, GR, PART, CONT, BD, and BDBY – will no doubt themselves submit to further analysis, as well may the ontological supercategories Material, Situation, Space, and Time.

I am not disturbed by this state of affairs. Rather, I am cheered by the analogy to our favorite high-prestige model, physics, where, as pointed out in section 1, the decomposition of matter into ever smaller and more general primitives has been one of the major scientific successes of our century, and where the prospect of not yet having hit bottom is an exciting spur to further research. For those who *are* disturbed by semantic decomposition, the phenomena analyzed here present a major challenge for a nondecompositional theory (be it a theory of monads connected by meaning postulates, as in Fodor, Garrett, Walker and Parkes (1980) or a connectionist theory of meaning).

Finally, I return to the issue of I-semantics versus E-semantics, raised at the outset. There has been considerable philosophical dispute (e.g., Fodor, 1987; Putnam, 1988; Schiffer, 1987) over whether a theory of meaning is even possible. Closer examination reveals that the sort of theory in dispute is always a theory of E-semantics, that is, one that asks for a direct connection between language and the real world; it may or may not in addition contain a psychological component. Schiffer concludes that there is no such theory, and that philosophy of language must find a new set of presuppositions under which to pose questions about meaning. I would like to suggest that the proper questions to ask are those of I-semantics, namely the characteristics in terms of which speakers *construe* the reality they experience. These are the presuppositions under which the present study and the others in this volume have been conducted, and under which some progress has apparently been made.

Let me illustrate with one example. As long as one sticks with unanalyzed sentences like *snow is white* and *tigers have stripes*, one can happily remain under the presumption that sentences are connected to the world pure and simple. But consider the word *end*. What do the end of a table, the end of a trajectory, and the end of a speech have in common, such that we use the word *end* for them all? Nothing, unless we admit the possibility of schematizing objects, trajectories, and events in terms of a common abstract notion of bounded 1-dimensionality. It is hard to regard this schematization as an inherent property of *reality*; but it makes a great deal of sense in terms of the psychological organization with which one construes reality. What we have seen here is that such psychological organization lies a very short distance below the surface of everyday lexical items – and that progress can be made in exploring it. This suggests to mc that thc issue for philosophers of language ought not to be whether it is possible to do E-semantics, but rather how one can make sense of the explanations offered by I-semantics within a broader psychological, social, and biological context.

References

Bach, E. (1986). The algebra of events. *Linguistics and Philosophy*, *9*, 5–16.
Chomsky, N. (1986). *Knowledge of language: Its nature, origin, and use*. New York: Praeger.
Declerck, R. (1979). Aspect and the bounded/unbounded (telic/atelic) distinction. *Linguistics*, *17*, 761–794.
Dowty, D. (1979). *Word meaning and Montague grammar*. Dordrecht: Reidel.
Fiengo, R. (1974). *Semantic conditions on surface structure*. Doctoral dissertation, Department of Linguistics and Philosophy, MIT.
Fodor, J.A. (1970). Three reasons for not deriving 'kill' from 'cause to die'. *Linguistic Inquiry*, *1.4*, 429–438.
Fodor, J.A. (1975). *The language of thought*. Cambridge, MA: Harvard University Press.
Fodor, J.A. (1981). The present status of the innateness controversy. In J.A. Fodor (Ed.), *Representations* (pp. 257–316). Cambridge, MA: Bradford/MIT Press.
Fodor, J.A. (1987). *Psychosemantics*. Cambridge, MA: Bradford/MIT Press.
Fodor, J.A., Garrett, M., Walker, E., & Parkes, C. (1980). Against Definitions. *Cognition*, *8*, 263–367.
Fodor, J.D., Fodor, J.A., & Garrett, M. (1975). The psychological unreality of semantic representations. *Linguistic Inquiry*, *6.4*, 515–532.
Grimshaw, J. (1990). *Argument structure*. Cambridge, MA: MIT Press.
Gruber, J. (1967). *Functions of the lexicon in formal descriptive grammar*. Santa Monica: Systems Development Corporation. Reprinted as part of *Lexical structures in Syntax and Semantics*, 1976. North-Holland, Amsterdam.
Higginbotham, J. (1985). On semantics. *Linguistic Inquiry*, *16.4*, 547–594.
Hinrichs, E. (1985). *A compositional semantics for Aktionsarten and NP reference in English*. Ohio State University doctoral dissertation.
Jackendoff, R. (1976). Toward an explanatory semantic representation. *Linguistic Inquiry*, *7.1*, 89–150.
Jackendoff, R. (1983). *Semantics and cognition*. Cambridge, MA: MIT Press.
Jackendoff, R. (1987a). The status of thematic relations in linguistic theory. *Linguistic Inquiry*, *18*, 369–411.

Jackendoff, R. (1987b). On beyond zebra: The relation of linguistic and visual information. *Cognition*, *26*, 89–114.
Jackendoff, R. (1990). *Semantic structures*. Cambridge, MA: MIT Press.
Jackendoff, R. (1991). The problem of reality. *Noûs*, *25*(4).
Jackendoff, R., & Landau, B. (1991). Spatial language and spatial cognition. In D.J. Napoli & J. Kegl (Eds.), *Bridges between psychology and linguistics: A Swarthmore Festschrift for Lila Gleitman* (pp. 145–169). Hillsdale, NJ: Erlbaum.
Langacker, R. (1987). Nouns and verbs. *Language*, *63*, 53–94.
Levin, B., & Rapoport, T. (1986). Lexical subordination. In *Papers from the Twenty-fourth Regional Meeting of the Chicago Linguistics Society* (pp. 275–289). Chicago: University of Chicago Department of Linguistics.
Link, G. (1983). The logical analysis of plurals and mass terms: A lattice-theoretic approach. In R. Bauerle, C. Schwarze, & A. von Stechow (Eds.), *Meaning, use, and interpretation of language* (pp. 302–323). Berlin: Walter de Gruyter.
Marr, D. (1982). *Vision*. San Francisco: Freeman.
Mourelatos, A. (1978). Events, processes, and states. *Linguistics and Philosophy*, *1*, 199–220.
Nunberg, G. (1979). The nonuniqueness of semantic solutions: Polysemy. *Linguistics and Philosophy*, *3*, 143–184.
Platzack, C. (1979). *The semantic interpretation of aspect and aktionsarten*. Dordrecht: Foris.
Pustejovsky, J. (1991). The syntax of event structure. *Cognition*, *41*, 47–81.
Putnam, H. (1988). *Representation and reality*. Cambridge, MA: MIT Press.
Rappaport, M., & Levin B. (1985). *The locative alternation: A case study in lexical analysis*. Manuscript, Center for Cognitive Science, MIT.
Rappaport, M., & Levin, B. (1988). What to do with theta-roles. In W. Wilkins (Ed.), *Syntax and semantics, Vol. 21: Thematic relations* (pp. 7–36). New York: Academic Press.
Schank, R. (1973). Identification of conceptualizations underlying natural language. In R. Schank & K. Colby (Eds.), *Computer models of thought and language* (pp. 187–248). San Francisco: Freeman.
Schiffer, S. (1987). *Remnants of meaning*. Cambridge, MA: MIT Press.
Stowell, T. (1981). *Origins of phrase structure*. Doctoral dissertation, Department of Linguistics and Philosophy, MIT, Cambridge, MA.
Talmy, L. (1978). The relation of grammar to cognition: A synopsis. In D. Waltz (Ed.), *Theoretical issues in natural language processing 2*. New York: Association for Computing Machinery.
Vendler, Z. (1957). Verbs and times. *Philosophical Review*, *56*, 143–160.
Verkuyl, H. (1972). *On the compositional nature of the aspects*. Dordrecht: Reidel.
Verkuyl, H. (1989). Aspectual classes and aspectual composition. *Linguistics and Philosophy*, *12*, 39–94.
Williams, E. (1984). Grammatical relations. *Linguistic Inquiry*, *15*, 639–674.
Winston, M., Chaffin, R., & Herrmann, D. (1987). A taxonomy of part–whole relations. *Cognitive Science*, *11*, 417–444.

3

The syntax of event structure*

James Pustejovsky
Computer Science Department, Ford Hall, Brandeis University.

In this paper we examine the role of events within a theory of lexical semantics. We propose a configurational theory of event structure and examine how it contributes to a lexical semantic theory for natural language. In particular, we argue that an event structure can provide a distinct and useful level of representation for linguistic analysis involving the aspectual properties of verbs, adverbial scope, the role of argument structure, and the mapping from the lexicon to syntax.

1. Introduction

Recent work in linguistic theory has stressed the important role that structured lexical representations can play in natural language, for example, the emergence of argument structure as a distinct level of representation (Grimshaw, 1990; Williams, 1981) and the importance of semantic representations such as f-structure (Bresnan, 1982) and lexical conceptual structure (LCS) (Jackendoff, 1983; Rappaport & Levin, 1988). Similarly, we will explore what advantages there are in positing a separate level indicating the event structures associated with predicates and their arguments.

The conventional view of argument structure is that a verb is given a set of arguments and associated diacritics indicating how they are realized. Some authors, however, have argued that argument structure is a structured representa-

*This paper developed out of earlier work on the event semantics of verbs (cf. Pustejovsky, 1989b). I would like to thank Jane Grimshaw, Beth Levin, Jim Higginbotham, Robert Ingria, Noam Chomsky, and Sabine Bergler, for comments on earlier drafts of this paper.

tion over which prominence relations are defined (Grimshaw, 1990; Williams, 1981). This structure has profound effects on the behavior of the predicates in the language. Similarly, the conventional view of events (e.g., whether a sentence denotes an activity, a state, etc.) within much of linguistic theory has been that of a single, existentially quantified event variable for sentences in the language (Higginbotham, 1988; Parsons, 1985).[1] Extending this view, we will argue that grammatical phenomena do in fact make reference to the internal structure of events, and that a subeventual analysis for predicates is able to systematically capture these effects. The basic assumptions of the theory are as follows:

(I) A subeventual structure for predicates provides a template for verbal decomposition and lexical semantics. Following Vendler (1967), Dowty (1979), and others, we distinguish three basic event types: states, processes, and transitions, where a predicate in the language by default denotes one particular event type. Unlike previous analyses, however, we assume a more complex subeventual structure of event types, where event types make reference to other embedded types.

(II) By examining the substructure of events, one can describe much of the behavior of adverbial modification in terms of scope assignment within an event structure.

(III) The semantic arguments within an event structure expression can be mapped onto argument structure in systematic and predictable ways. The event structure proposed here should be seen as a further refinement of the semantic responsibilities within an LCS (Jackendoff, 1983; Rappaport & Levin, 1988).

We should point out one caveat about the analysis presented below. This paper is not the proper forum for specifying the formal semantics of the event structure proposed here. Rather, what we attempt to show, in broad outline, is the relevance of event structure to lexical semantics and linguistic theory in general. Where appropriate, we will briefly point out the technical details of the analysis, as well as the limitations and shortcomings of the proposal. Details of the formal interpretation of the event semantics presented here can be found in Pustejovsky (1991) and other work in progress.

2. Event types

Temporal aspect can be viewed as the behavior of sets of periods involving the concepts of *initial*, *internal*, and *final* temporal subperiods, as they relate to the

[1]This is assuming that events are represented at all. There are many who still argue that events are not a necessary addition to the ontology of types (see Cresswell, 1985).

semantic roles associated with the arguments of predicates.[2] To make this clear, let us examine the meanings of the sentences below:

(1) a. Mary walked.
    b. Mary walked to the store.
    c. Mary walked for 30 minutes.

It is normally assumed that there are at least three aspectual types: *state*, *process*, and *events*, sometimes distinguishing between *accomplishment* and *achievement* events. The verb *walk* as used in (1a) denotes an activity of indefinite length. That is, the sentence itself does not convey information regarding the temporal extent of the activity. Such a sentence is said to denote a *process* (Dowty, 1979; Kenny, 1963; Mourelatos, 1978; Ryle, 1949; Vendler, 1967; Verkuyl, 1989). Sentence (1b) conveys at least as much information as (1a), with the additional constraint, however, that Mary terminated her activity of walking at the store. Although not making explicit reference to the temporal duration of the activity, (1b) does assert that the process has a logical culmination or duration, such that the activity is over when Mary is at the store. This type of sentence is said to denote an event, or *accomplishment.*

Sentence (1c) also conveys information about a specific activity of walking and its termination. In this sentence, however, there is no explicit mention of a logical culmination to the activity, but rather a durative adverbial is used to impose a temporal specification on the activity's boundedness. Such a sentence denotes a *bounded process*. These examples illustrate the same verb being used for three different aspectual types: process, accomplishment, and bounded process. When the verb *walk* appears alone structurally, it assumes a process interpretation – it is lexically "process-like". The presence of prepositional and adverbial phrases, however, causes the aspectual class of the sentence to change.

Just as the verb *walk* seems to be lexically process-like, there are lexical accomplishments as well. For example, the verbs *build* and *destroy*, in their typical transitive use in (2), denote accomplishment events, because there is a logical culmination to the activity performed by Mary:

(2) a. Mary built a house.
    b. Mary destroyed the table.

In (2a) the existence of the house is the culmination of Mary's act, while in (2b) the non-existence of something denotable as a table is the direct culmination of her act. One useful test for whether a sentence denotes an accomplishment is the ability to be modified by temporal adverbials such as *in an hour*, that is, the so-

[2]Carlson (1981) presents the issues in these terms, and we adopt this statement of the problem.

called frame adverbials. Notice in (3) that both "derived" and lexical accomplishments license such modification:

(3) a. Mary walked to the store in an hour.
    b. Mary built a house in a year.

Even though *build* seems lexically to be an accomplishment, observe how it can be used in a context where it appears to denote a process:

(4) Mary built houses for four years.

Sentence (4) means that Mary engaged in the activity of house building for a bounded period of time. The durative adverbial indicates that the sentence has been reinterpreted as a process due to the bare plural in object position (see Bach, 1986; Krifka, 1987).

Another aspectual type mentioned earlier is that of achievement. An achievement is an event that results in a change of some sort, just as an accomplishment does, but where the change is thought of as occurring instantaneously. For example, in sentences (5a), (5b), and (5c) the change is not a gradual one, but something that has a "point-like" quality to it. In fact, modification by *point adverbials* such as *at noon* is a diagnostic that a sentence denotes an achievement (Dowty, 1979):

(5) a. John died at 3 p.m.
    b. John found his wallet at 3 p.m.
    c. Mary arrived at noon.

What are apparently lexical properties of the verb can be affected by factors that could not possibly be lexical. For instance, consider the sentences in (6), where one sees a shift in the meaning of *drink* from an accomplishment as in (6a) to a process as in (6b):

(6) a. Mary drank a beer.
    b. Mary drank beer.

The presence of a bare plural object shifts the interpretation of a logically culminating event to an unbounded process (see Pelletier & Schubert (1989) and Krifka (1987) for details).

Finally, let us consider the behavior of *states*, such as those sentences in (7):

(7) a. Mary is sick.
    b. Mary believes that John loves her.

There is no change occurring in either sentence and no reference to initial or final periods. In fact, it is the homogeneity of states that distinguishes them from the other aspectual types. States are identified by several diagnostics. First, they allow modification by durative adverbials (8a), and secondly, they do not appear as imperatives (8b) (Dowty, 1979):

(8) a. Mary was sick for two months.
b. *Be sick!

Because of the sometimes elusive nature of aspectual classification, it is useful to consider a few more diagnostics. One well-known test for distinguishing activities from accomplishments, known as the "imperfective paradox" (Bach, 1986; Dowty, 1979), involves the possible entailments from the progressive aspect. To illustrate the nature of this paradox, consider the sentences in (9):

(9) a. John is running. *Entails* John has run.
b. John is building a house. *Does not entail* John has built a house.

What this difference in entailment indicates is whether an action is homogeneous in nature or has a culmination of some sort. Sentence (9a) is an activity and entails the statement *John has run*. That is, John has already engaged in some running. Sentence (9b), on the other hand, does not allow the entailment *John has built a house* because building is not a homogeneous process, but rather culminates in a changed state, i.e. it is an accomplishment. Thus, if *x is V-ing* entails *x has V-ed*, then either the verb or the predicate is a process. A theory of aspect should be able to account for this behavior, and not just use it to classify propositions into aspectual types.

Finally, there is an important distinction between accomplishments and non-accomplishments based on their interaction with scalar adverbials such as *almost*. Consider the sentences in (10) and the possible interpretations associated with each:

(10) a. John almost swam.
b. John almost painted a picture.
c. John almost arrived.
d. John almost left.

In sentence (10a), what is being expressed is that John almost performed an activity of swimming, but did not even begin it. Sentence (10b), on the other hand, allows for two interpretations. One is similar to (10a), where John almost engaged himself in painting, but then did not. The other interpretation is that John was painting but did not quite complete the picture. The interpretation of

(10c), like (10a) is unambiguous, while (10d) permits two readings along the same lines as (10b). Why should there be such a difference? Dowty (1979) claims that an ambiguity arises with *almost* just in case the predicate is an accomplishment. If this ambiguity does not arise, the predicate is not an accomplishment.

Summarizing, we have considered the following categorization of aspectual types for verbs and verb phrases:

(11) a. *Processes:* walk, run
b. *Accomplishments:* build, destroy
c. *Achievements:* die, find, arrive
d. *States:* sick, know, love, resemble

If membership in one of these aspectual classes is viewed as a projection of the lexical properties of the verb, then how is it that the aspectual properties of a sentence may change as the result of other factors, such as adverbials (both durative and frame), the structure of the noun phrase (NP) in an argument position (e.g. definite vs. bare plural), or the presence of a prepositional phrase? In the sections that follow, we will explain these behaviors, which have come to be known as "type-shifting" phenomena (Bach, 1986), in terms of a configurational theory of event structure. We show how the tests normally used as diagnostics for membership in one class or another fall out as the principled consequence of different event structures. Thus, we are able to abandon the feature-based approach to aspect which is generally assumed (e.g., Verkuyl, 1972) in favor of a highly restricted, topological theory of how events are structured.

3. Towards a model of lexical knowledge

In this section, we will outline generally what the basic requirements for a theory of lexical semantics should be. We present a conservative approach to decomposition, where lexical items are minimally decomposed into structured forms (or templates) rather than sets of features. We will provide a generative framework for the *composition* of lexical meanings, thereby defining the well-formedness conditions for semantic expressions in a language.

One can distinguish between two distinct approaches to the study of word meaning: *primitive-based* theories and *relation-based* theories. Those advocating primitives assume that word meaning can be exhaustively defined in terms of a fixed set of primitive elements (e.g., Jackendoff, 1972; Katz, 1972; Lakoff, 1971; Schank, 1975; Wilks, 1975). Inferences are made through the primitives into which a word is decomposed. In contrast to this view, a relation-based theory of word meaning claims that there is no need for the decomposition of word meaning into primitives if words are associated through a network of explicitly defined links (e.g., Brachman, 1979; Carnap, 1956; Collins & Quillian, 1969; Fodor, 1975; Quillian, 1968). Sometimes referred to as *meaning postulates*, these links establish any inference between words as an explicit part of a network of word concepts.[3] What we would like to do is to propose a new way of viewing primitives, looking more at the generative or *compositional* aspects of lexical semantics, rather than the decomposition of words into a specified number of primitives.

Most approaches to lexical semantics making use of primitives can be characterized as using some form of *feature-based* semantics, since the meaning of a word is essentially decomposable into a set of features (e.g., Katz, 1972; Katz & Fodor, 1963; Schank, 1975; Wilks, 1975). Even those theories that rely on some internal structure for word meaning (e.g., Dowty, 1979; Fillmore, 1985) do not provide a complete characterization for all of the well-formed expressions in the language. Jackendoff (1983) comes closest, but falls short of a comprehensive semantics for *all* categories in language. No existing framework, in my view, provides a *method for the decomposition of all lexical categories*.

What, exactly, would a method for lexical decomposition give us? Instead of a taxonomy of the concepts in a language, categorized by sets of features, such a method would tell us the minimal semantic behavior of a lexical item. Furthermore, it should tell us the compositional properties of a word, just as a grammar informs us of the specific syntactic behavior of a certain category. What one is led to, therefore, is a *generative* theory of word meaning, but one very different from the generative semantics of the 1970s (Pustejovsky, 1991). In order to explain why we are suggesting that lexical decomposition proceed in a *generative* fashion rather than the traditional *exhaustive* approach, let me take as a classic example the word *closed* as used in (12) (see Lakoff, 1970):

(12) a. The door is **closed**.
b. The door **closed**.
c. John **closed** the door.

Lakoff (1970), Jackendoff (1972), and others have suggested that the sense in (12c) must incorporate something like *cause-to-become-not-open* for its meaning. Similarly, a verb such as *give* specifies a transfer from one person to another, e.g. *cause-to-have*. Most decomposition theories of word meaning assume a set of primitives and then operate within this set to capture the meanings of all the words in the language. These approaches can be called *exhaustive* since they assume that with a fixed number of primitives complete definitions of lexical meaning can be given. In the sentences in (12), for example, *closed* is defined in

[3]For further discussion on the advantages and disadvantages to both approaches, see Jackendoff (1983).

terms of the negation of a primitive, *open*. Any method assuming a fixed number of primitives, however, runs into some well-known problems with being able to capture the full expressiveness of natural language.[4]

These problems are not, however, endemic to all decomposition approaches. We would like to suggest that lexical (and conceptual) decomposition is possible if it is performed *generatively*. Rather than assuming a fixed set of *primitives*, let us assume a fixed number of *generative devices* that can be seen as constructing semantic expressions. Just as a formal language is described in terms of the productions in the grammar rather than its accompanying vocabulary, a semantic language should be defined by the rules generating the structures for expressions rather than the vocabulary of primitives itself.[5]

How might this be done? Consider the sentences in (12) again. A minimal decomposition of the word *closed* is that it introduces an *opposition* of terms: *closed* and *not-closed*. For the verbal forms in (12b) and (12c), both terms in this opposition are predicated of different subevents denoted by the sentences. In (12a), this opposition is left implicit, since the sentence refers to a single state. Any minimal analysis of the semantics of a lexical item can be termed a *generative* operation, since it operates on the predicate(s) already literally provided by the word. This type of analysis draws on Aristotle's *species of opposition* (see *Categories*, 11b17; Lloyd, 1968), and it will form the basis of one level of representation for a lexical item. Rather than decomposing such a word into primitive terms, evaluate it relative to an opposition.[6]

The essential opposition denoted by a predicate forms part of what we will call the *qualia structure* of that lexical item (Pustejovsky, 1989a, 1991). Briefly, the qualia structure of a word specifies four aspects of its meaning:

- the relation between it and its constituent parts;
- that which distinguishes it within a larger domain;
- its purpose and function;
- whatever brings it about.

[4]For example, Weinreich (1972) faults Katz and Fodor (1963) for the inability to distinguish between word senses of polysemous elements without requiring an unlimited number of differentiating features.

[5]In my opinion, this approach is also better suited to the way people write systems in computational linguistics. Different people have distinct primitives for their own domains, and rather than committing a designer to a particular vocabulary of primitives, a lexical semantics should provide a method for the decomposition and composition of the meanings of possible lexical items.

[6]Aristotle identifies four species of term opposition:
(a) Correlation: e.g., "double" vs. "half".
(b) Contrariety: e.g., "good" vs. "bad".
(c) Privation: e.g., "blind" vs. "sighted".
(d) Contradiction: e.g., "sit" vs. "not sit".
See Horn (1989) for discussion of the logic of negation. See Modrak (1987) and Graham (1987) for discussion of Aristotle's theory of explanation and its relation to perception.

We call these aspects of a word's meaning its *constitutive role*, its *formal role*, its *telic role*, and its *agentive role*, respectively.[7] For example, the telic role of the noun *book* is the predicate *read*, while the agentive role might be *write*.

The minimal semantic distinctions of the qualia structure are given expressive force when combined with a theory of aspectual (or event) types. For example, the predicate in (12a) denotes the *state* of the door being closed. No opposition is expressed by this predicate. In (12b) and (12c), however, the opposition is explicitly part of the meaning of the predicate. Both these predicates denote what we call *transitions*. The intransitive use of *close* in (12b) makes no mention of the causer, yet the transition from *not-closed* to *closed* is still entailed. In (12c), the event that brings about the *closed* state of the door is made more explicit by specifying the actor involved. These differences constitute the *event structure* of a lexical item. Both the opposition of predicates and the specification of causation are part of a verb's semantics, and are structurally associated with slots in the event template for the word. In this case, for example, the *formal* role for the verb *close* is specified as a transition, denoting an opposition. The *constitutive* role specifies the exact content of the event, in terms of what the predicates engaged in opposition actually are (see below). As will be seen in the next section, there are different inferences associated with each event type, as well as different syntactic behaviors (Grimshaw, 1990; Pustejovsky, 1989b).

4. A level of event structure

As mentioned above, the theory of decomposition being outlined here is based on the central idea that word meaning is highly structured, and not simply a set of semantic features. Let us assume this is the case. We will argue that one level of semantic description involves an event-based interpretation of a word or phrase, that is, the *event structure* mentioned above. Event structure is just one level of the semantic specification for a lexical item, along with subcategorization, argument structure, and qualia structure. Because an event structure is recursively defined in the syntax, "event-type" is also a property of phrases and sentences.[8] There are three primary components to event structure:

- the primitive *event type* of the lexical item;
- the rules of *event composition*;
- the *mapping rules* to lexical structure.

Any verb in natural language can be characterized as belonging to one of three

[7]To a large extent, we follow Moravcsik (1975), who distinguishes the different 'aitia' associated with a proposition. For details, see Pustejovsky (1991).

[8]See Tenny (1987) for a proposal on how aspectual distinctions are mapped to the syntax.

basic event types: *states*, *processes*, or *transitions* (see Bach, 1986; Dowty, 1979; Vendler, 1967).[9] Except where otherwise indicated, the event structure will be interpreted as representing both temporal precedence and exhaustive event inclusion. That is, for an event e, represented as $[e_1\ e_2]$, the intended interpretation is that e is an event containing two subevents, e_1 and e_2, where the first temporally precedes the second, and there are no other events locally contained in event e.[10] We will distinguish these event types as follows (where E is a variable for any event type):[11]

(13) a. State (S): a single event, which is evaluated relative to no other event
Examples: *be sick*, *love*, *know*
Structural representation:

b. Process (P): a sequence of events identifying the same semantic expression
Examples: *run*, *push*, *drag*
Structural representation:

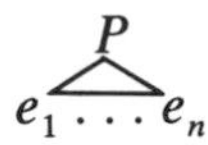

Following Dowty (1979) and others, we will assume that when P is a process verb, then if the semantic expression P' identified with P is true at an interval I, then P' is true for all subintervals of I larger than a moment:

c. Transition (T): an event identifying a semantic expression, which is evaluated relative to its opposition. (Jackendoff, 1972; Lakoff, 1970; Wright, 1963)[12]
Examples: *give*, *open*, *build*, *destroy*
Structural representation (where E is a variable for any event type):

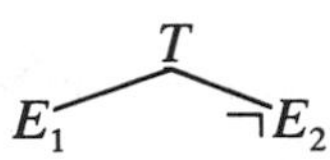

[9] Above we distinguished between four aspectual classes. These classes, we argue, collapse to three distinct structural configurations, where transitions subsume both accomplishments and achievements.

[10] This does not mean that there is no subeventual structure to these events (see below).

[11] The tree structures are given to illustrate the configurational nature of event structures and their combinations. See Pustejovsky (to appear) for discussion of their formal interpretation; cf. Croft (1990) for an alternative suggestion on how lexical items may structure their internal events.

[12] As mentioned in the previous section, Aristotle's *Categories* (194b) makes the same point.

To illustrate the basic distinction in event types, consider the sentences in (12) from the previous section, repeated below:

(12) a. The door is **closed.**
b. The door **closed.**
c. John **closed** the door.

We assume a level of lexical representation similar to that of Dowty (1979), Jackendoff (1983), and Levin and Rappaport (1988), in that verb class distinctions are characterized in terms of an LCS-like structure, which we call LCS′. An LCS is a lexical semantic representation which takes the form of a predicate decomposition. Here we will not assume any fixed set of primitive terms, but rather assume a minimal decomposition of verbs and sentences in terms of the principles of event structure outlined here. This level, using predicates such as *act* (x, y), *at*(x, y), and *on*(x, y), constitutes the LCS′. Thus, the trees represent LCS-like information partitioned according to event structure. Furthermore, we will assume that the LCS representations assumed by Levin and Rappaport (1988) can be constructed by interpreting the event structure together with the LCS′, as we will illustrate below. Let us begin with the sentence in (12a) above. The adjectival form *closed* denotes a state where the event structure is that shown in (14b):

(14) a. The door is closed.
b.

ES: *S* — *e*

LCS′: [closed(the-door)]

LCS: [closed(the-door)]

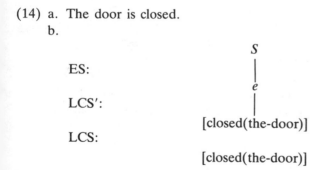

As mentioned in the previous section, a lexical transition, such as *close* in (12b) and (12c), expresses the opposition of a predicate, as illustrated in (15) and (16) below. Here we are assuming that one can interpret the expression of a term opposition as logically equivalent to Dowty's *become* operator (Dowty, 1979, p. 140). Similarly the operator *cause* can be seen as a derivative relation between events, structurally interpreted from an agentive predicate within the initial subevent of an event structure. Furthermore, the conjunction of predicates (&) indicates the simultaneity of the expressions:

(15) a. The door closed.

b.

ES: T → P, S

LCS′:

P: [¬closed(the-door)]

S: [closed(the-door)]

LCS: become([closed(the-door)])

(16) a. John closed the door.

b.

ES: T → P, S

LCS′:

P: [act(*j*, the-door) & ¬closed(the-door)]

S: [closed(door)]

LCS: cause([act(*j*, the-door)], become([closed(the-door)]))

These two structures suggest that *close*, in both the *inchoative* (as in (15)) and *causative* (as in (16)) forms, is a transition from one state to its opposition.[13] Their LCS′ representations differ only in the further specification of an action being performed for the causative cases; that is, the expression & indicates simultaneity of the two expressions within this subevent. But notice that the LCS representations do differ significantly because of the explicit reference to a causal agent. Thus, while the verb *close* is semantically ambiguous at one level (LCS), the logical relatedness of the verb's senses is captured at another (ES and LCS′).

Sentence (17) illustrates how a process verb differs structurally from states and transitions:

(17) a. Mary ran

b.

ES: P → $e_1 \ldots e_n$

LCS′: [run(*m*)]

LCS: [run(*m*)]

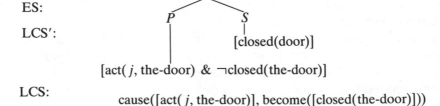

[13]Hale and Keyser (1986) provide independent motivations for treating the inchoative and causative forms of a verb as essentially identical at some level of representation. In our analysis, they differ only in their LCS, but not in their event structures.

The sentence in (18) illustrates how a causative process is represented and subsequently mapped onto an LCS representation:

(18) a. Mary pushed the cart.

b.

ES: P

$e_1 \ldots e_n$

LCS′: [act(m, the-cart) & move(the-cart)]

LCS: cause([act(m, the-cart)], [move(the-cart)])

The aspectual distinctions made by the above trichotomy do not distinguish between achievements and accomplishments in any structural way, as illustrated above with the inchoative *close* and causative *close*, an achievement and accomplishment, respectively. In fact, we will argue that there is no further distinction necessary in terms of event structure for classifying these two aspectual types. Rather, achievements and accomplishments can be distinguished solely in terms of an agentive/non-agentive distinction. We will characterize the difference as follows. When a verb makes reference both to a predicate opposition and the activity bringing about this change, then the resulting aspectual type is an accomplishment (as in (16)). When the verb makes no explicit reference to the activity being performed, the resulting aspectual type is an achievement (as in (15)). This distinction is illustrated in (19) below:

(19) a. Accomplishment:

ES: T

P S

LCS′: [act(x, y) & $\neg Q(y)$] [$Q(y)$]

LCS: cause([act(x, y)], become($Q(y)$))

b. Achievement:

ES: T

P S

LCS′: [$\neg Q(y)$] [$Q(y)$]

LCS: become($Q(y)$)

The role of agentivity for distinguishing event types, explored in Dowty (1979), replaces the notion of "event headedness" introduced in Pustejovsky (1989b). As an example of this difference, notice how the transition verbs *build*, *draw*, and *leave* differ in their event structures from *arrive* and *die*, illustrated with *build* and *die*.

(20) a. Mary built a house.

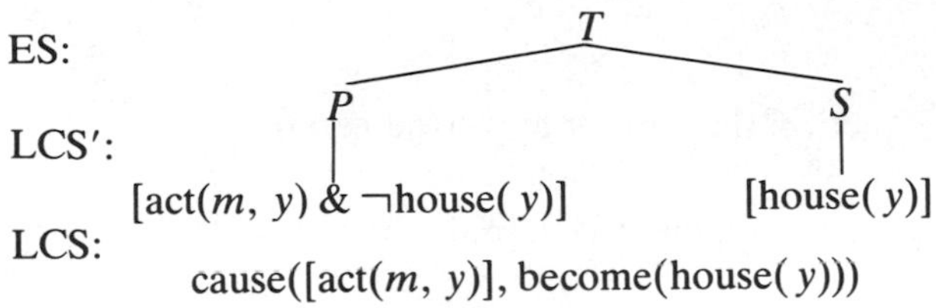

b. Mary died.

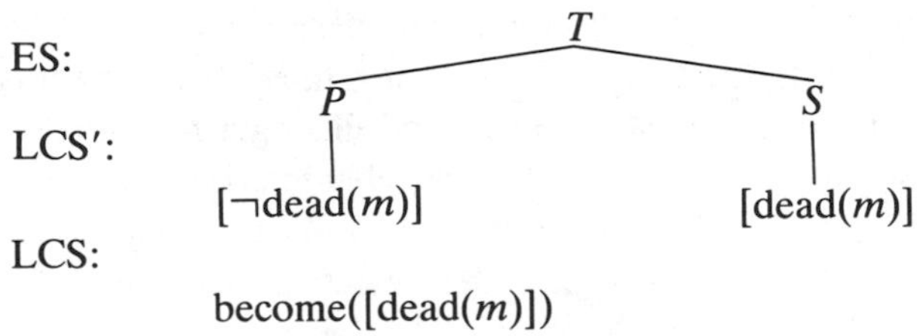

Although this analysis might be intuitive for most cases of achievement verbs, an agentive role does seem implicit in many achievement predicates. For example, the sentences in (21) seem to involve an agent:

(21) a. Mary arrived at the party.
b. John won the race.

The question, however, is whether the agency is part of the verbal semantics of *arrive* and *win* or is contributed by other means, for example, the animacy of the subject, or pragmatic effects. The position that agency is not intrinsically part of the verb's meaning is not as implausible as it might seem. First, notice the absence of agency in the sentences in (22), with the same verbs as in (21):

(22) a. The package arrived at the office.
b. Our anniversary has finally arrived.
c. Mary won the lottery.

The event structure for (22a) is simply the non-agentive transition shown in (22a′).

(22) a.

ES: *T* → *P*, *S*

LCS′: *P*: [¬at(the-package, the-office)] *S*: [at(the-package, the-office)]

LCS:

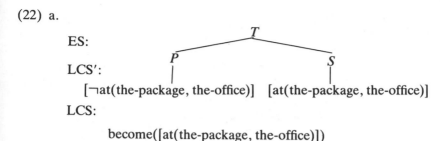

become([at(the-package, the-office)])

Rather than being metaphorical uses of an agentive predicate, we argue that the sentences in (22) are typical instances of non-agentive transitions (i.e., achievements). Secondly, notice how intentional adverbials such as *deliberately* cannot felicitously modify predicates such as *win* and *die*.

(23) a. *Mary won the race deliberately. (But cf. Mary lost the race deliberately.)
b. *Mary deliberately died of cancer.

These data suggest that Dowty's observation concerning agentivity does in fact act to complete the distinctions between the conventional aspectual classes by dividing the class of transitions into two logical subclasses. Configurationally, as event structures, however, the two classes are identical.

5. Event composition

Having studied the basic event structures associated with verbs, we will now turn to how they interact with other syntactic constituents to form derived event representations, that is, the phenomenon of *event composition*. In particular, we look at two classes of event composition, PP attachment and resultative constructions. There are several types of syntactic constructions that directly affect the event type of a phrase: temporal adverbials, adjunct phrases, complement type (e.g., individuated or not), and aspectual coercion (e.g., the progressive). For reasons of space, we consider only the first two types here (for further discussion see Pustejovsky (to appear)). The basic idea is that the event type for a sentence need not be the event type of the main verb. Category changes may occur because of explicit rules setting out the ways events can compose and be modified.

Briefly, as mentioned in the Introduction, temporal adverbials are sensitive to the type of event being modified (Kenny, 1963; Vendler, 1967). For example, the process verb *run* can be modified by a *durative* adverbial, while the transition *build* cannot:

(24) a. Mary ran *for an hour*.
b. *Mary built a chair *for an hour*.

Conversely, *build* can be modified by a *frame* adverbial while *run* cannot:

(25) a. *Mary ran *in an hour*.
b. Mary built a chair *in an hour*.

Within our theory of events, there is one basic principle that accounts for these facts: only when an event contains a logical culmination (e.g., it belongs to the set of transitions) is it modifiable by a frame adverbial. Why should this be? Given our assumptions about the subeventual analysis for verbs, it is possible with our analysis that temporal predicates in the language might make reference to a subevent, or to an assembly of subevents denoted by the verb. Thus, imagine that the frame adverbial *in an hour* requires *two* events to be present for a proper modification, for example, the two subevents of *build*, e_1 and e_2. One can say, then, that this temporal modifier takes as its argument the temporal distance between e_2 and the onset of e_1. The logical form for our sentence (25b) then will be something like (25c):

(25) c. $\exists P, S[build((P, S)) \wedge agent(m, (P, S)) \wedge theme(chair, (P, S)) \wedge in\text{-}an\text{-}hour(P, S)]$

The last conjunct of this expression, *in an hour*, can be interpreted as being:

temporal measure of (time of) S − onset of $P = 1$ hour

Such an analysis would immediately explain why the other event types (states or processes) are ungrammatical with such adverbials, without the "coerce" reading (cf. (25a)).[14]

A second kind of event composition involves the interaction of a prepositional phrase with the event structure of a verb. These include cases of PP attachment that change the event structure of the verb phrase (VP), as shown in (26) and (27):

(26) a. Mary **ran**.
b. Mary **ran** to the store.
(27) a. John **pushed** the wagon.
b. John **pushed** the wagon to Mary.

What the sentence pairs in (26) and (27) have in common is a recognizable shift

[14] I would like to thank an anonymous reviewer for pointing out this analysis to me.

in their event types. In particular, for each case, a sentence denoting a *process* (in the (a) examples) has been transformed into a *transition* by the presence of a prepositional phrase (PP) denoting a bounded path, a *to*-PP. As Chomsky (1957) notes, these are, in fact, examples of a general phenomenon in language, where the grammar allows a syntactic construction to mirror an already existing lexical representation; that is, in this case, a transition (see also Jackendoff (1983) and Talmy (1985) for similar points). When this structure arises from syntactic composition, we have what we will refer to as *event composition*. Informally, the rule can be stated in the following way. In certain constructions, when the verb denotes a *process* (e.g. *run*, *push*), and there is a phrase present which denotes a function from processes to transitions, then the event type of the entire verb phrase (VP) is construed as a *transition*.[15] Notice that this is the same structure carried by lexically specified transitional verbs such as *build*.

Such a process of composition can be made clearer if we consider a specific example. In (26b) above, the event type of the VP containing the lexical process verb *run* shifts to a transition in composition with the PP. In this example, the notation $\langle P, T \rangle$ is taken to represent a function from processes to transitions:

(28)

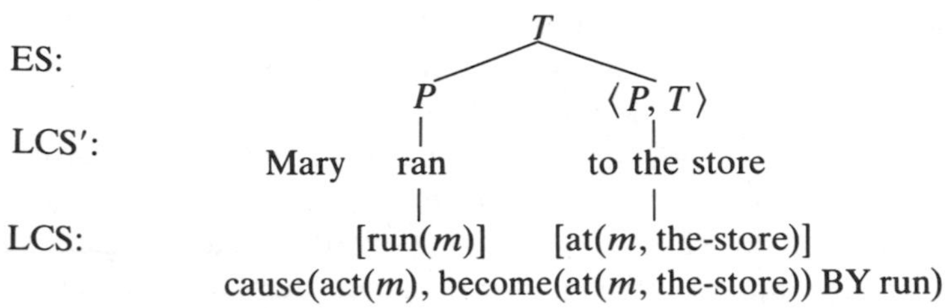

In this example, the prepositional phrase is able to project its own event structure, the *state* of Mary being at the store. It is easy to verify that the above event structure is a transition, since modification by a frame adverbial is well formed, as illustrated in (29):

(29) Mary ran to the store *in an hour*.

To explain the behavior of this type of event composition, we suggest that the preposition *to* is to be analyzed as denoting a relation between states and

[15]This is a slight simplification for illustration purposes. In Pustejovsky (to appear), prepositions such as "to" are treated as relational event functors, applying first to a state, and then to a process, to give a transition: i.e. $\langle S, \langle P, T \rangle\rangle$. The treatment above, however, is useful as a general description of this case of event type-shifting. It should be pointed out that the event type $\langle P, T \rangle$ has consequences for the mapping to LCS as well. Because the event type of the matrix predicate is actually treated as an argument to $\langle P, T \rangle$, it effectively is subordinated in Levin and Rapoport's (1988) sense, hence creating a "BY manner" expression. For discussion, see Pustejovsky (to appear).

processes, such that the resulting event type is a transition. That is, the PP acts like a function from processes to transitions.[16] Importantly, however, as with lexical transitions, this construction sets up a predicate opposition involving the culminating state introduced by the PP. Thus, the LCS derived from this construction looks like that of a lexically specified causative verb.[17]

Similar principles of event composition seem to be operating in the *resultative* construction as well. Resultative constructions are verb phrases, such as those in (30), consisting of a verb with an object, together with an adjunct phrase predicated of the direct object, that specifies the state the object obtains as a result of an action:[18]

(30) a. Mary hammered the metal flat.
b. Mary wiped the table clean.
c. The men drank the pot dry.

Rappaport and Levin (1989) argue that the resultative phrase (e.g. *flat* and *clean*) can only be predicated of the direct object, a restriction they call the *direct object restriction* (*DOR*). We will return to this restriction in section 7, but for now, let us first examine how this construction is relevant to event composition.

The examples are relevant because the resultative construction involves what appears to be a systematic event-type shifting from processes to transitions. This systematic ambiguity, we argue, is the result of principles of semantic composition, rather than an underlying lexical ambiguity in the verb involved. This follows the general methodology outlined in Pustejovsky (1989a, 1991), where, whenever possible, the logical ambiguity of a word should be generated by general principles operating in the grammar rather than by positing multiple lexical entries. Rappaport and Levin's (1989) analysis assumes a similar position with respect to lexical operations. Although we cannot touch on the richness of the problem (see, for example, the discussion in Rapoport (1990, to appear)), consider the resultative interpretations for the verb *hammer* in (30a) and the verb *wipe* in (30b); they arise from a similar event composition rule to that proposed for PP attachment above. That is, both verbs are underlyingly specified as *processes*, while the adjectival phrases *flat* and *clean* have event interpretations as *states*. Notice, then, how the resultative construction requires no additional word sense for the verb, nor any special semantic machinery in order for the resultative

[16]This is similar to the proposals in Hinrichs (1985) and Dowty (1979), where such phrases behave like functions from properties to properties.

[17]For a different approach to such constructions, see Levin and Rapoport (1988), where rules of "lexical subordination" derive such new word senses.

[18]Simpson (1983) and Rappaport and Levin (1989) discuss the connection between resultatives, such as those in (30), and the property of unaccusativity (cf. Perlmutter, 1978). Unaccusatives are intransitive verbs whose subjects behave like direct objects of transitive verbs in many respects (see Levin (1986) and Burzio (1986) for details).

interpretation to be available, beyond the rules of event composition. Briefly, the solution involves analyzing the notion of stage-level predicate (Carlson, 1977) within event semantics as a subset of the states; namely, *those which can be changed by being acted upon*, functions that take processes to transitions, i.e. $\langle P, T \rangle$. Thus, the resultative construction formally reduces to the type of event composition encountered earlier with PP attachment; see (32) below (Ingria & Pustejovsky, 1990) for a discussion of the syntactic consequences of this solution):

(31) a. Mary **hammered** the metal. (*hammer* ∈ process)
b. Mary **hammered** the metal flat. (*hammer* ∈ transition)

(32)

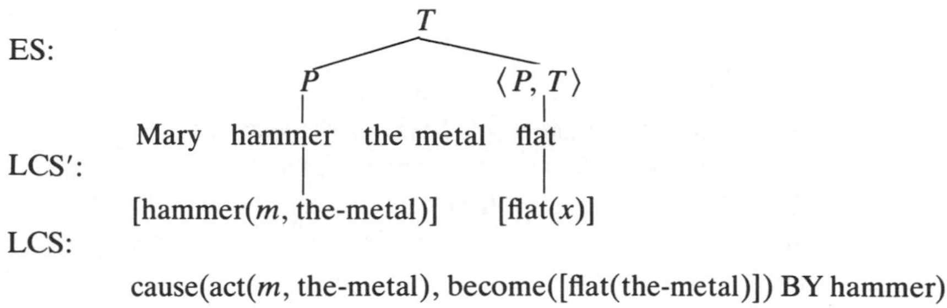

A favorable consequence of this analysis is that it explains why just process verbs participate in this construction, and why the resultative phrase (the adjectival phrase) must be a state. Thus, by proposing that this construction participates in a semantic change at the level of event structure, we can explain the behavior as logically related to that of other subordinating constructions (in Levin and Rapoport's (1988) terms), but where the new sense of the verb arises out of syntactic and semantic composition in the grammar.

To close this section, we will briefly examine the class of psychological predicates such as *fear* and *frighten*, and how event structure contributes to the binding violations associated with the latter set of these verbs. The considerations reviewed briefly here motivate Grimshaw (1990) to analyze such violations in terms of event structure rather than in terms of structural configuration effects.[19]

The normal conditions on anaphoric binding, according to syntactic-based theories of grammar, involve the notions of *precedence*, *c-command*, and a *binding domain*. One class of examples that violates this definition of anaphoric licensing is that involving the *experiencer* verbs (we will not review the literature on this subject here, but will refer the reader to Belletti and Rizzi (1985), Pesetsky (1987), and Grimshaw (1986) for details). The problem can be stated as

[19]For discussion of how this phenomenon extends beyond this verb class, see Pustejovsky (1989b) and (to appear).

follows: there are two types of psych predicates – both with an argument structure of (experiencer, theme) – the first where the argument bearing the experiencer role is expressed as the subject (e.g. *fear*) and the second where the argument bearing the theme is expressed as the subject (e.g. *frighten*).[20]

Although these classes seem to have identical argument structures the syntactic behavior of their members is very different. For example, the *fear* class behaves as expected by the binding theory, while the *frighten* class allows violations of the c-command requirement on anaphoric binding. Normally, an anaphoric pronoun must be structurally c-commanded by its antecedent, as in (34) or (36). Thus, an anaphor in matrix subject position is ill-formed, because there is no possible antecedent to c-command it as in the *fear* sentence (33a). An exception to this rule comes from the *frighten* class of experiencer verbs, however, as illustrated in (33b, c):

(33) a. *Each other's students fear the teachers.
     b. The pictures of each other frighten the teachers.
     c. ??Each other's students frighten the teachers.
(34) a. The women fear each other.
     b. The women frightened each other.
(35) a. *Himself fears John.
     b. *Himself annoys John.
(36) a. John fears pictures of himself.
     b. The women frightened each other's students.

Although both classes disallow backward binding when the anaphor is the subject itself (see (35a) and (35b)), when the anaphor occurs embedded within the subject NP, as in (33b, c), binding is permitted with *frighten* verbs. What is it about *frighten* that allows the violation of the normal binding conditions? Following Grimshaw (1986) and Williams (1987),[21] we claim that the argument structure of the verb contributes information that accounts for the binding ability of its arguments. Grimshaw assumes that the argument structures for the members of the two verbs classes is as given in (37), distinguished only by a case-marking diacritic on one argument, Exp_{acc}, indicating it must appear as a direct object:

(37) a. fear $(Exp(Th))$
     b. frighten $(Exp_{acc}(Th))$

[20]There are of course two readings for "frighten" type verbs: one which is purely causative (*x* occasions fear in *y*), and the other which is being considered here. As Pesetsky (1987) notes, the backwards binding effects introduced below obtains only in the second interpretation.

[21]Williams' (1987) proposal is somewhat different from Grimshaw's, but we will not review the differences here.

Grimshaw argues that the notion of *argument command* is as important for licensing anaphoric binding as is c-command. Briefly, this can be defined as in (38):

(38) *Argument command*: $(\theta_1(\theta_2 \ldots \theta_n))$: members of outermost lists (recursively) a-command all other arguments.

Equipped with two separate dimensions of evaluation (both c-command and argument command), Grimshaw's theory can predict the subtle grammaticality differences that arise. What is left unexplained, however, is this: if such a minimal structural difference between the two verb classes (see (37)) has such a profound effect on binding possibilities, then there should be strong evidence for this distinction.

We will now demonstrate that the theory of event structure outlined above provides a well-motivated semantic explanation for the structural distinctions between the two experiencer verb types, thereby providing evidence for this distinction. Furthermore, the binding violations that the *frighten* class exhibits are part of a much wider phenomenon. We suggest that the event structure for the *frighten* verbs is that of a transition, while the event structure for *fear* verbs is that of a state. The difference between the two classes of experiencer verbs can be given as follows:

(39) a. Type(*fear*) $\in$ state; object is intensional.
b. Type(*frighten*) $\in$ transition; subject is extensional.

Although it has long been noted that verbs such as *fear* are stative and those such as *frighten* are not, there has been little formal use made of this distinction. Furthermore, it is interesting that the *fear* class introduces an intensional object, compared to an extensional subject introduced by *frighten* verbs. This distinction is shown in (40):

(40) a. Mary fears ghosts/big dogs.
b. Big dogs/*ghosts frighten Mary.

That is, Mary can fear something without there necessarily existing the object of her fears. Something which frightens Mary, however, must exist and be more than an intensional object.

Grimshaw's argument structure distinction between the two classes is supported if one assigns the *fear* class to states and the *frighten* class to transitions, as shown in (41):

(41) a. The movie frightened Mary.
b. Event structure:

ES: T → P, S

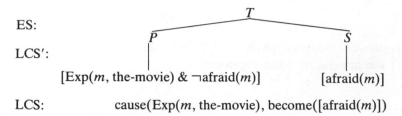

LCS′: P: [Exp(m, the-movie) & ¬afraid(m)] S: [afraid(m)]

LCS: cause(Exp(m, the-movie), become([afraid(m)])

The structure above suggests that the appropriate command relation which exists for verbs such as *frighten* derives from the underlying LCS′ relation of *experiencing*, within the initial event. For this example, the experiencer variable *Exp* might be filled by the binary predicate *see*(x, y). As Grimshaw argues, one possible effect of such "semantic dominance" within a predicate is the licensing of variable binding, for example, anaphora. Thus, the representation provides an explanation for certain syntactic effects which were problematic when analyzed in purely syntactic terms.

6. Adverbial modification

In this section we suggest that an event structure provides a natural representation for adverbs as event predicates. We will claim that there are two types of adverbs: *wide-scope* and *narrow-scope*. The ambiguity exhibited by an adverbial, in terms of behaving as a manner- versus speaker-oriented adverb, can be explained in terms of different scope assignments of the same adverb. Such a solution is possible only if we examine the finer structure of the event being modified.

Consider first the examples discussed in Cresswell (1985) and Higginbotham (1989) involving adverbs such as *fatally*:

(42) Mary fatally slipped.

Within a Davidsonian analysis, where adverbs are taken as event predicates, the intended interpretation for this use of the adverb is represented as (43):

(43) $\exists e[slipped(e, m) \wedge fatal(e, m)]$

where one can read this as, "there was a slipping event such that it was fatal to Mary". But there are more complicated examples where the adverb can also be interpreted as a manner adverbial. As McConnell-Ginet (1982) points out, the sentence in (44) has two readings: (a) it was rude of Lisa to depart, and (b) she departed in a rude manner:

(44) Lisa rudely departed.

The ambiguity arises from there being both a manner and a stative interpretation. McConnell-Ginet's solution involves adding an additional argument to the verb in order to derive the manner reading (45a), while adopting a more traditional Montagovian analysis for the stative interpretation, (45b):

(45) a. *depart*(*rude*, *lisa*)
     b. *rude*(*depart*(*lisa*))

We will not review the details of McConnell-Ginet's proposal here but, as Higginbotham (1989) points out, she has no natural way of accounting for the factivity of the construction under both interpretations.

Higginbotham (1989) proposes an analysis for such constructions in terms of an event semantics which overcomes some of the problems of McConnell-Ginet's solution. In the manner of Davidson (1980) and his own previous work (Higginbotham, 1985), he suggests that quantification over an event variable allows for a first-order treatment of such adverbs. Consider the representations he proposes for (44), illustrated below in (46):

(46) a. $\exists e[depart(e, Lisa) \wedge rude(e, \hat{e}'[depart_0(e')])]$
     b. $\exists e[rude(e, Lisa, \hat{e}'[depart(e', Lisa)]) \wedge depart(e, Lisa)]$

The first expression says that, compared to the set of departing events, Lisa's instance was a rude one. The reading in (46b), on the other hand, says that Lisa was being rude in that she departed (e.g. when she did). For Higginbotham, such modification is another example of *θ-identification*, which results in the conjunction of two attributes predicated of a single individual (or individual variable), and *θ-marking*, which applies the adverb as a function to its argument, the verb. The problem with this analysis is that it assumes a variable adicity for the adverb. That is, *rude* takes two arguments in one case and three in another. Assuming that there is some relationship between the two adverbs, Higginbotham (as well as McConnell-Ginet) must state it independently of the semantics of each lexical item. Following the general methodology outlined above, we show that the ambiguity results from a structural distinction and not from lexical polysemy. In fact, the adverbs in both interpretations are identical, and there is a scope distinction which gives rise to the ambiguity just discussed. To begin with, consider the event structure for a verb such as *depart*, given below:

(47) a.

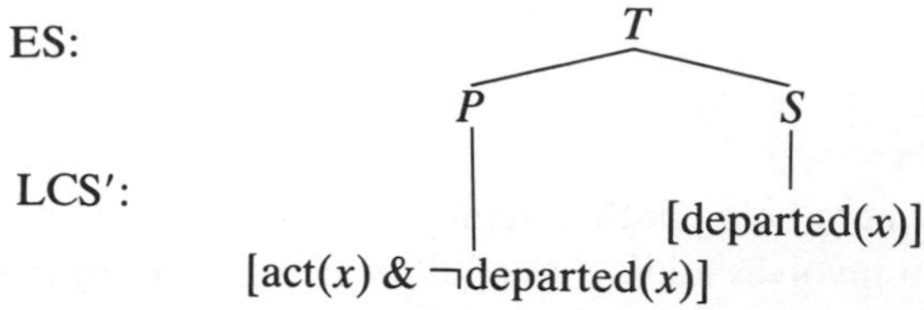

where we minimally distinguish between the action of departing and the resulting state of being departed. This is a transition, annotated by an *act* relation, making it behave like an accomplishment. We will suggest that adverbs such as *rudely*, traditionally termed *manner* adverbials, modify a semantic expression associated with an event structure or an action subevent. Since both the process of leaving and the entire transition are actions, there will be two interpretations possible, resulting from two distinct scopes: over the process (as in (48)); and over the transition (as in (49)). Thus, if one modifies the initial event by characterizing it as *rude*, we arrive at an event predication over the process, that is, a manner interpretation; namely, that the action was performed rudely for those types of actions. The representation for this is given below. In this representation the predicate modifies only the process of *leaving*, and not the state of *having left*:

(48)

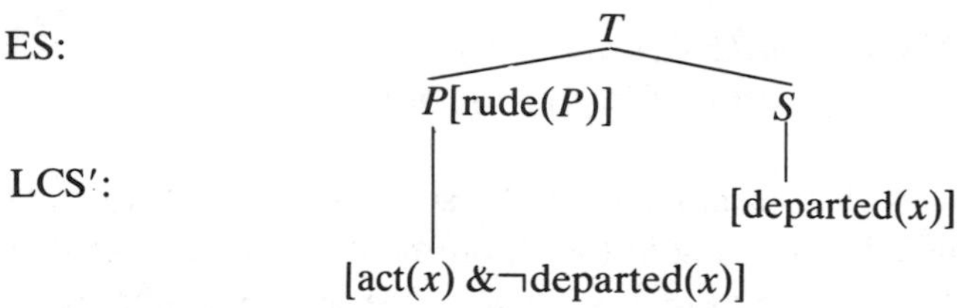

In this structure the adverbial *rudely* applies to the initial event, and behaves like a *narrow-scope* adverb, relative to the entire event structure. When *rudely* takes scope over the entire event as in (49), it is necessarily interpreted relative to the speaker and situation:

(49)

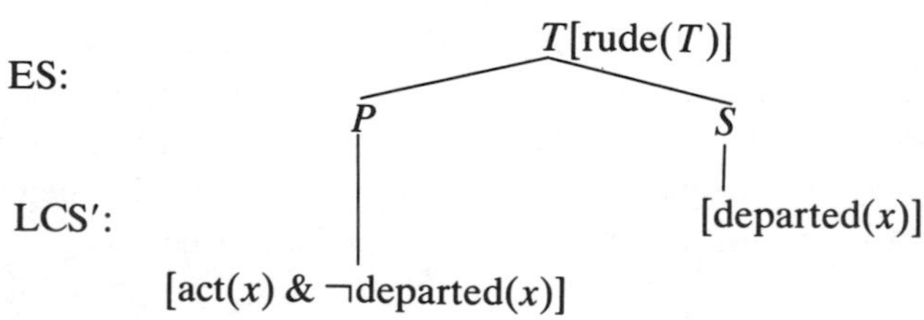

Thus, we can represent the ambiguity associated with the adverbial as one of a scope difference of the same lexical item; thus, this provides for a single one-place predicate treatment of the adverbial.

It is interesting to note that adverbs are idiosyncratic in their behavior as event predicates. For example, the adverbial *slowly* in both sentences in (50) refers to the action of walking, while *quickly* in (51) can refer either to the manner of action or to the duration of the entire event:

(50) a. Mary walked to the store slowly.
b. Mary slowly walked to the store.
(51) a. Mary walked to the store quickly.
b. Mary quickly walked to the store.

Such information must be associated with the individual adverb, where *quickly* may select for either reading. Notice that if *quickly* selects for a temporal interpretation, it must take wide-scope, since it requires a telic event to measure duration.

One of the diagnostics for aspectual classification discussed in the Introduction was the effect of modification by *almost*. We discovered that accomplishments allow two readings when modified by *almost* while non-accomplishments allow only one. For example, consider the sentences in (52):

(52) a. John almost built a house.
b. John almost ran.

Both sentences have an interpretation where the act is intended but never carried out, while (52a) carries the additional reading that the action is started but not fully completed. Why is it that *build* allows two interpretations while *run* allows only one?

Following the strategy introduced above, where an event structure allows for richer structural possibilities for adverbs as event predicates, we would expect a sentence to have as many interpretations for an adverbial as there are distinct predicates in the event structure. Since there are two distinct predicates involved in *build*, one within the initial event, and the other in the culminating event, there are two readings for the example in (52a), as illustrated in (53):

(53) a.

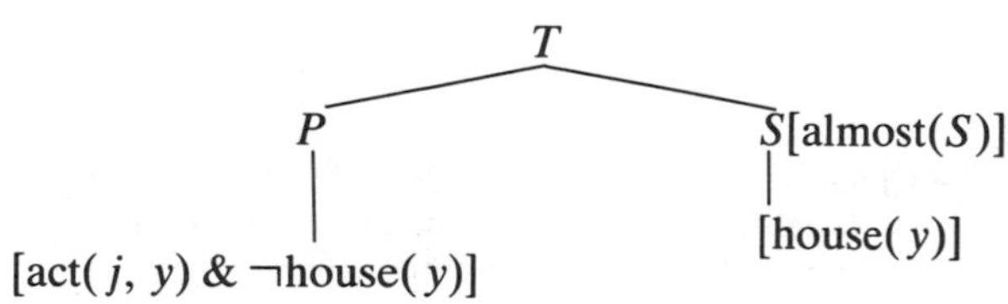

b.

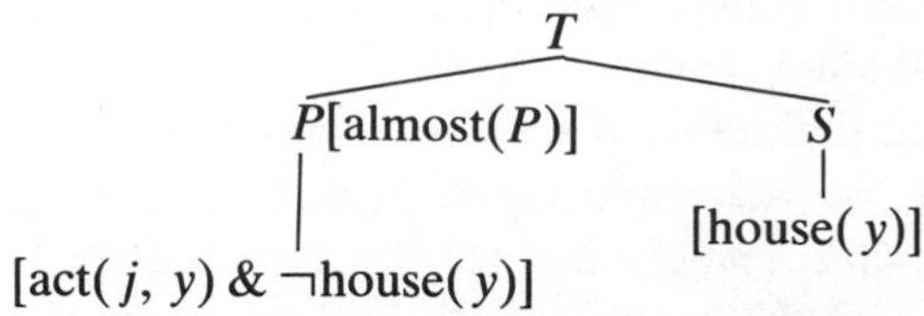

In (53a), by modifying the culmination event, *almost* prevents the assertability of the expression associated with the logical culmination of the event; namely that there exists a house. The other reading, that of intent, is represented as (53b). This is the same reading as that available to (52b), where the *almost* modifies the expression associated with the first event constituent (or the only one as in the case of (52b)):

(54)

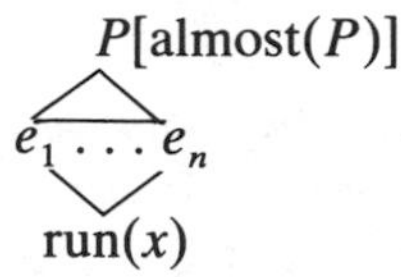

Assuming the proposal above to be correct, then we would assume that the other class of transitions, that is, achievements, should be unambiguous with respect to *almost*, since they involve only one distinct predicate in their event structure. As mentioned in the Introduction, this is in fact the case:

(55) a. John almost died.
b. Bill almost arrived.
c. Mary almost won the race.

The only reading available for these sentences is one where something has occurred without the terminus event being achieved (see (56)):[22]

(56)

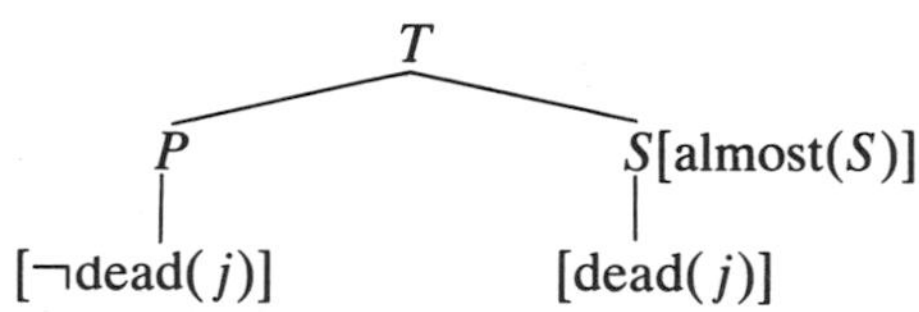

[22]Higginbotham (1989) proposes a scope analysis for the ambiguities involving "almost". His theory assumes a single event quantification, as proposed in Davidson (1980), and as a result is unable to capture the behavior of achievement verbs and adverbial scope.

This is the only interpretation available since non-agentive transitions refer to a single predicate and its opposition. Importantly, the privative term is considered a dependent predicate, and does not allow modification by the adverbial.

To close this section, let us return to the topic of temporal adverbials. It is interesting to see what further predictions are made by a subeventual analysis concerning the scope of temporal adverbial modification. With this analysis we would expect that a complex event structure would allow modification by a durative adverbial of one of its *subevents*. This prediction turns out to be correct, in fact, as we see from sentences such as (57):

(57) a. John gave Mary the record for the afternoon.
b. The company sent John the book for 10 days.
c. Mary ran into the house for 20 minutes. (See Fillmore, 1985.)

These examples illustrate how the adverbial can modify a subevent of the entire event. In (57a), for example, involving a transition, the interval *the afternoon* modifies only the state referring to Mary having the record, and not the actual act of giving. This distinction is made explicit using our representation of the lexical semantics for *give*:

(58)

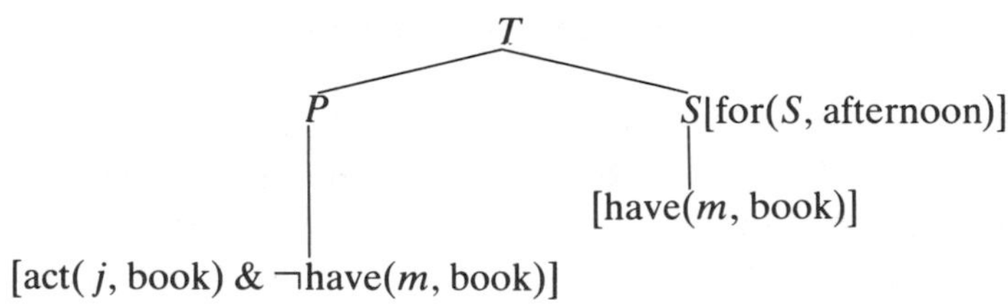

This structure states that the adverbial takes scope over the final event of the giving and not the act itself. In (57b), a similar modification occurs, where the expression *for* 10 *days* refers to the state of John having the book. Likewise, in (57c), the interval of 20 minutes denotes the time Mary spent inside the house rather than the duration of the act of running itself.

Other examples where the durative adverbial seems to modify the resulting state are given below:

(59) a. John left for a week.
b. John arrived for the day.
c. They entered the atmosphere for an hour.

What these examples seem to indicate is that duratives tend to take a narrow scope over any event type that predicates a single property (i.e., state) of an individual. If this is true, then what do we make of the obviously ungrammatical sentence in (60):

(60) *Mary died for two years.

Why is it not possible to apply the interval to Mary's state of being dead? In fact, it does seem that such cases are marginally permitted, as (61) shows:

(61) ?My terminal died for 2 days last week.

Apparently, the state that is delimited by an interval must be something that is potentially variable relative to the interpretation for the utterance. Thus, sentence (60) predicates *death* of an individual, which to our general mode of interpretation will not vary once predicated. A computer terminal, on the other hand, will allow for this predicate to be applied over and over again. This relates to the *persistence* of a property over an object, and is outside the scope of this discussion. It seems that a stage-level interpretation may be at play here as well (see Carlson, 1977).[23]

7. Interactions of event structure and argument structure

In this section we explore how a level of event structure can contribute to our understanding of the interactions between LCSs and their mappings to argument structure. We suggest that the distinctions provided by event structure are useful in determining how semantic participants in an LCS are realized syntactically. In fact, we argue that an event structure analysis gives further support to Rappaport and Levin's (1989) argument for deep unaccusativity. Much of our discussion, however, will be merely suggestive and must await further empirical investigations for support. For independent arguments in support of a level of event structure, see Grimshaw (1990) and Grimshaw and Vikner (1990).

We begin by discussing how the different event types translate to different verb classes as defined by their grammatical behavior. It is interesting to note that there is no direct or predictable behavior for the arguments of a verb as determined by its event type alone. For example, the verbs which are specified as transitions appear to form no equivalence class with respect to grammatical behavior. That is, all the verbs in (62) below are lexically transitions, but fall into distinct argument structure verb classes (see Levin, 1989):

[23]A reviewer has pointed out that what might be at play here is the "reversibility" of the final event. Thus, sentence (61) is more acceptable because the final event there, that is, the terminal being dead, is reversible, whereas in (60) it is not. The notion of reversibility does seem important here and is worth exploring. This issue is taken up in Pustejovsky (to appear).

(62) a. The bottle broke. (Unaccusative)
b. Mary broke the bottle. (Causative)
c. Mary built a table. (Creation)
d. The movie frightened Mary. (Psychological)

Similarly, those verbs which denote processes are associated with different verb classes, for example, those in (63):

(63) a. Mary slept. (Unergative)
b. John ran. (Manner of motion)

Using a level of event structure, we will argue that verb classes such as unaccusatives and unergatives correlate with independent principles of mapping from semantics to argument structure.

If we assume that for unaccusative verbs the subject is an underlying object (the "deep unaccusativity" analysis), then the first general behavior we see emerging from the sentences in (62) above is the following:

(A) The semantic participant involved in a predicate opposition is mapped onto the internal argument position of the lexical structure (roughly the d-structure object position).

That is, an event structure like that in (64a) is associated with an argument structure like (64b):

(64) a.

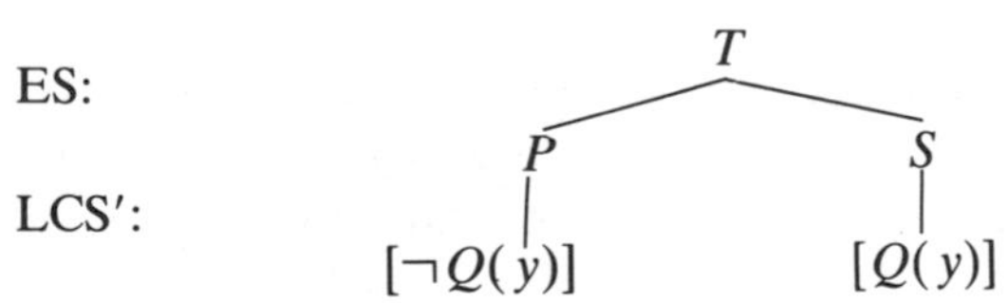

b. $V(y)$

As argued in previous sections, all transitions involve a predicate opposition of some sort. Yet, by itself, this property fails to distinguish adequately the verb classes in (62).

Independent of this principle, we argue, following Grimshaw (1990) and Pustejovsky (1989a), that the notions of causer and agent are somehow associated with the initial subevent of an event structure. More explicitly, let us propose the following principle:

(B) The agentive participant in the initial subevent of event structure is mapped onto the external argument position of the lexical structure (roughly the d-structure subject).

The result of both principles A and B applying in the structure in (65a) below is the argument structure in (65b) (where an external argument is marked with an asterisk):

(65) a.

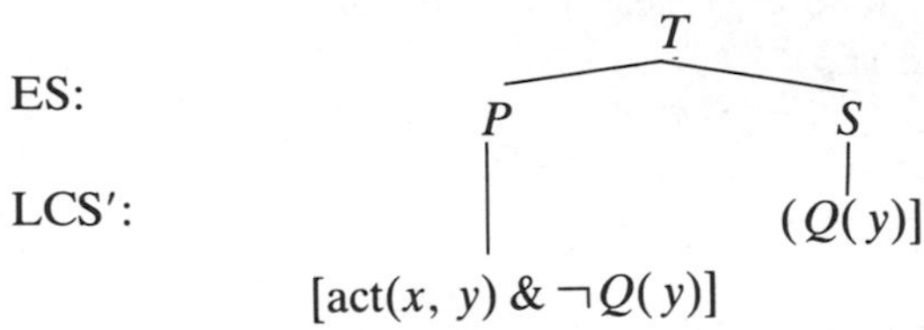

b. $V(x^*, y)$

An analysis in terms of event structure allows us to speculate on just what an unaccusative is, in terms of lexical semantic structure. Namely, *an unaccusative is a transition involving a unary predicate opposition, and nothing else*.

Above it was argued that resultative constructions are formed from processes in composition with a phrase denoting a state. Here we show that the apparent counterexamples to this generalization involving unaccusatives, discussed by Rappaport and Levin (1989), are not actually cases of the resultative construction at all, but involve the addition of emphatic (or manner) adjunct phrases. These cases are the following:

(66) a. The river froze solid.
b. The bottle broke open.

These are not true resultatives, for notice that the predication of the adjunct phrase is merely an attribute to the state introduced by the transition/unaccusative verb itself. This becomes clearer when we consider the following data:

(67) a. The river froze in 20 minutes.
b. The river froze solid in 20 minutes.

(68) a. The bottle broke suddenly.
b. The bottle broke open suddenly.

The events in both (67a) and (67b) and (68a) and (68b) are coextensive. That is, it is not the case that the event denoted in (a) is a subpart of that denoted in (b); rather they are the same event, with different information being expressed about it. That is, these are unlike the previous cases where a process shifted to a transition. Thus, in our terms, the examples mentioned in Rappaport and Levin (1989) as resultative constructions are not logically the same as the classic resultative construction. If this is the case, then the generalization that an unaccusative verb is a transition involving a unary predicate opposition strengthens Rappaport and Levin's argument for deep unaccusativity, assuming that only processes enter into resultative constructions.

To conclude this section, we simply state without motivation three final principles involved in mapping from event structure to argument structure. For more detailed discussion, the reader is referred to Pustejovsky (to appear).

(C) If the predicate opposition involves a relation, then both the participants are mapped onto internal argument positions of the argument structure. Otherwise, relational arguments are mapped directly as expressed at event structure; for example, *give* and *put* are examples where the culminating state is a relation, and both arguments are realizėd as internal arguments.

(D) Any participant in the initial event not expressed by principles (A) or (B) is mapped onto the external argument position.

(E) Each subevent must be associated with at least one argument position at lexical structure.

It is clear from the resultative data and the false reflexive data (e.g. *laugh herself silly*), that certain predicates require the expression of a separate, unsubcategorized argument while others do not, for example, *hammer the metal flat* (see Simpson, 1983). Principle (E) requires that every subevent (in this case, *silly* and *flat*) be associated with at least one argument position. In conjunction with principles (B) and (A), the false reflexive NP serves the function of representing the predicate opposition in the transition, while the external argument represents the causer in the initial event. Therefore, there must be both an internal argument (*herself*) and a unique external argument (*Mary*) to satisfy both conditions. Thus, the reflexive NP acts as a kind of argument epenthesis in the lexical structure:

(69)

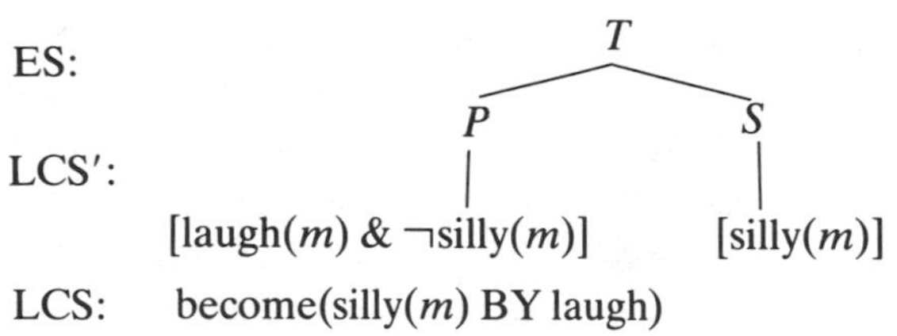

Notice that in the regular resultative cases the principles (A) and (B) are satisfied by the existing argument structure, obviating the need for argument epenthesis.

In this section, we have tried to give some indication of how event structure contributes to the understanding of the mapping between the lexical semantics and syntax, as represented at argument structure. We have glossed over many details and problems which might remain, but the general theme is quite clear:

the theory of grammar can be greatly enriched by representations such as those considered here for events. It remains to examine the limitations and further interactions of this system.

8. Conclusion

In this paper, we have tried to outline a partial theory of word meaning making use of a rich structural system for the subeventual properties of verbs. We have argued that words lexically specify a specific sequence of subevents organized by a well-defined geometry. Such configurations provide a very restrictive framework for partially defining the lexical semantics of words in the grammar. Metalogical notions such as *cause* and *become* are computed from the aspectual configuration associated with a lexical item and then a sentence.

By looking at the event structure of words in composition, we explained how the lexical specification of a verb's event-type can be overriden as a result of syntactic and semantic compositionality of the verb with other elements in the sentence.

Another advantage of proposing a richer subeventual structure for propositions is that we now have an analysis for the behavior of temporal adverbials, as well as adverbials such as *almost* and *rudely*. It was suggested that the reason accomplishments such as *build* allow two interpretations with such adverbs is due to the number of semantically specified event constituents for its event structure. Achievements, while having a very similar event constituency, have no unique semantic expression associated with the process preceding the culminating state. Finally, we examined briefly how the semantic participants in an event structure are associated with arguments in an argument structure representation. Following Grimshaw (1990), the notion of causer and "external" argument can be linked to a participant in the initial subevent within an event structure.

The purpose of this paper has been to show how verbs decompose into distinct event types with internal structure. Rather than examining the formal semantics of such structures, we have studied the effect that a level of event structure has on the grammar, and how it interacts with other levels of representation. In many ways, the proposal here is preliminary and merely suggestive, but we feel that an appreciation of the internal structure of events for word meaning is an important representational device for lexical semantics.

Bibliography

Bach, E. (1986). The algebra of events. *Linguistics and Philosophy*, *9*, 5–16.
Belletti, A., & Rizzi, L. (1985). Psych verbs and θ-theory. Manuscript, MIT.

Bennett, M., & Partee, B. (1972). Toward the logic of tense and aspect in English. Distributed by Indiana University Linguistics Club.

Brachman, R. (1979). On the epistemological status of semantic networks. In N. Findler (Ed.), *Associative networks: Representation and use of knowledge by computers*. New York: Academic Press.

Bresnan, J. (Ed.). (1982). *The mental representation of grammatical relations*. Cambridge, MA: MIT Press.

Burzio, L. (1986). *Italian syntax: A government-binding approach*. Dordrecht: Reidel.

Carlson, G. (1977). *Reference to kinds in English*. Doctoral dissertation, University of Massachusetts.

Carlson, L. (1981). Aspect and quantification. In P. Tedeschi & A. Zaenen (Eds.), *Syntax and semantics: Vol. 14, Tense and Aspect*. New York: Academic Press.

Carnap, R. (1956). *Meaning and necessity*. University of Chicago Press.

Chomsky, N. (1957). *Syntactic structures*. The Hague: Mouton.

Collins, A., & Quillian, M. (1969). Retrieval time from semantic memory. *Journal of Verbal Learning and Verbal Behavior*, *9*, 240–247.

Comrie, B. (1976). *Aspect*. Cambridge University Press.

Comrie, B. (1985). *Tense*. Cambridge University Press.

Cresswell, M. (1985). *Adverbial modification*. Dordrecht: Kluwer.

Croft, W. (1990). *Categories and relations in syntax: The clause-level organization of information*. Chicago: University of Chicago Press.

Davidson, D. (1980). *Essays on actions and events*. Oxford: Clarendon Press.

Dowty, D.R. (1979). *Word meaning and Montague grammar*. Dordrecht: Reidel.

Fillmore, C. (1968). The case for case. In E. Bach & R. Harms (Eds.), *Universals in linguistic theory*. Holt, Rinehart, and Winston: New York.

Fillmore, C. (1988). The mechanisms of construction grammar. Manuscript, University of California – Berkeley.

Foley, W.A., & van Valin, R.D., Jr. (1984). *Functional syntax and universal grammar*. Cambridge University Press.

Fodor, J. (1975). *The language of thought*. Cambridge, MA: Harvard University Press.

Graham, R. (1987). *Aristotle's two systems*. Oxford: Clarendon Press.

Green, G. (1974). *Semantics and syntactic regularity*. Bloomington: Indiana University Press.

Grimshaw, J. (1979). Complement selection and the lexicon. *Linguistic Inquiry*, *10*, 279–326.

Grimshaw, J. (1986). Nouns, arguments, and adjuncts. Manuscript, Brandeis University.

Grimshaw, J. (1990). *Argument structure*. MIT Press, Cambridge.

Grimshaw, J., & Vikner, S. (1990). Obligatory adjuncts and the structure of events. Manuscript, Brandeis University.

Gruber, J. (1965). Studies in lexical relations. Ph.D. thesis, MIT.

Hale, K., & Keyser, J. (1986). Some transitivity alternations in English. Center for Cognitive Science, MIT.

Hale, K., & Laughren, M. (1983). The structure of verbal entries. Walpiri Lexicon Project, MIT, Cambridge.

Higginbotham, J. (1985). On semantics. *Linguistic Inquiry*, *16*, 547–593.

Higginbotham, J. (1989). Elucidations of Meaning. *Linguistics and Philosophy*, *12*, 465–518.

Hinrichs, E.W. (1985). A compositional semantics for Aktionarten and NP reference in English. Ph.D. thesis, Ohio State University.

Horn, L. (1989). *A natural history of negation*. University of Chicago Press.

Ingria, R., & Pustejovsky, J. (1990). An active objects approach to syntax, semantics, and parsing. In C. Tenny (Ed.), *MIT working papers in parsing*. MIT.

Jackendoff, R. (1972). *Semantic interpretation in generative grammar*. Cambridge, MA: MIT Press.

Jackendoff, R. (1983). *Semantics and cognition*. Cambridge, MA: MIT Press.

Jackendoff, R. (1987). The status of thematic relations in linguistic theory. *Linguistic Inquiry*, *18*, 369–412.

Jackendoff, R. (1990). *Semantic structures*. Cambridge, MA: MIT Press.

Katz, J.J. (1972). *Semantic theory*. New York: Harper and Row.

Katz, J.J., & Fodor, J. (1963). The structure of a semantic theory. *Language*, *39*, 170–210.

Kenny, A. (1963). *Actions, emotions, and will*. New York: Humanities Press.

Keyser, S.J., & Roeper, T. (1984). On the middle and ergative constructions in English. *Linguistic Inquiry*, *15*, 381–416.

Klein, E., & Sag, I. (1985). Type-driven translation. *Linguistics and Philosophy*, *8*, 163–202.

Krifka, M. (1987). Nominal reference and temporal constitution. Manuscript, Tübingen.

Kunze, J. (1986). Phasen, Zeitrelationen und zeitbezogene Inferenzen. In *Probleme der Selektion und Semantik*. Berlin: Akademie-Verlag.

Lakoff, G. (1970). *Irregularity in syntax*. New York: Holt, Rinehart, and Winston.

Lakoff, G. (1971). On generative semantics. In D. Steinberg & L. Jakobovits (Eds.), *Semantics: An interdisciplinary reader*. Cambridge University Press.

Levin, B. (1989). Towards a lexical organization of English verbs. Manuscript, Northwestern University.

Levin, B., & Rapoport, T.R. (1988). Lexical subordination. *Proc. CLS*, *24*, 275–289.

Levin, B., & Rappaport, M. (1986). The formation of adjectival passives. *Linguistic Inquiry*, *17*, 623–662.

Levin, B., & Rappaport, M. (1988). On the nature of unaccusativity. In *Proc. NELS 1988*.

Levin, L. (1986). *Operations on lexical forms: Unaccusative rules in Germanic Languages*. Doctoral Dissertation, MIT.

Lloyd, G.E.R. (1968). *Aristotle: The growth and structure of his thought*. Cambridge University Press.

McConnell-Ginet, S. (1982). Adverbs and logical form: A linguistically realistic theory. *Language*, *58*, 144–184.

McKeon, R. (1941). *The basic works of Aristotle*. New York: Random House.

Modrak, D. (1987). *Aristotle: The power of perception*. Cambridge University Press.

Moravcsik, J.M. (1975). Aita as generative factor in Aristotle's philosophy. *Dialogue*, 622–638.

Mourelatos, A. (1978). Events, states, and processes. *Linguistics and Philosophy*, *2*, 415–434.

Parsons, T. (1985). Underlying events in English. In E. LePore & B. McLaughlin (Eds.), *Actions and events*. Blackwell, Oxford.

Parsons, T. (1990). *Events in the semantics of English*. Cambridge, MA: MIT Press.

Pelletier, J., & Schubert, L. (1989). Mass expressions. In D. Gabbay & F. Guenther (Eds.), *Handbook of philosophical logic, Vol. 4*.

Perlmutter, D. (1978). Impersonal passive and the unaccusative hypothesis. BLS 4, Berkeley, CA.

Pesetsky, D. (1987). Binding problems with experiencer verbs. *Linguistic Inquiry*, *18*, 126–140.

Pustejovsky, J. (1989a). Issues in computational lexical semantics. In *Proceedings of the European Association for Computational Linguistics* (pp. xvii–xxv). Manchester, UK, April 1989.

Pustejovsky, J. (1989b). The geometry of events. In C. Tenny (Ed.), *Generative Approaches to Aspect*. Cambridge, MA: MIT Lexicon Project.

Pustejovsky, J. (1991). The generative lexicon. *Computational Linguistics*, *17.4*.

Pustejovsky, J. (to appear). *The generative lexicon: A computational theory of lexical semantics*. Cambridge, MA: Bradford Books/MIT Press.

Pustejovsky, J., & Boguraev, B. (1991). Lexical knowledge representation and natural language processing. *IBM Journal of Research and Development*, *35*(4).

Quillian, M.R. (1968). Semantic memory. In M. Minsky (Ed.), *Semantic information processing*, Cambridge, MA: MIT Press.

Rapoport, T.R. (1990). Secondary predication and the lexical representation of verbs. *Machine Translation*, *5.1*.

Rapoport, T.R. (to appear). Verbs in depictives and resultatives. In J. Pustejovsky (Ed.), *Semantics and the lexicon*. Dordrecht: Kluwer.

Rappaport, M., Laughren, M., & Levin, B. (to appear). Levels of lexical representation. In J. Pustejovsky (Ed.), *Semantics and the lexicon*. Dordrecht: Kluwer.

Rappaport, M., & Levin, B. (1988). What to do with theta-roles. In W. Wilkens (Ed.), *Thematic Relations*. New York: Academic Press.

Rappaport, M., & Levin, B. (1989). Is there evidence for deep unaccusativity? An analysis of resultative constructions. Manuscript, Bar Ilan University and Northwestern University.

Reinhart, T. (1976). *The syntactic domain of anaphora*. Doctoral dissertation, MIT.
Rohrer, C. (Ed.). (1977a). *On the logical analysis of tense and aspect*. Tübingen: TBL Verlag Gunter Narr.
Rohrer, C. (1977b). Die Beschreibung einiger Spanischer Verbalperiphrasen im Rahmen eines Zeitlogischen Systems. In C. Rohrer (Ed.), *On the logical analysis of tense and aspect*. Tübingen: TBL Verlag Gunter Narr.
Ryle, G. (1949). *The concept of mind*. London: Barnes and Noble.
Scha, R., & de Bruin, J. (1988). The semantics of relational nouns. *Proceedings of 1988 Association for Computational Linguistics*.
Schank, R. (1975). *Conceptual information processing*. Amsterdam: North-Holland.
Simpson, J. (1983). Resultatives. In L. Levin & A. Zaenen (Eds.), *Papers in lexical-functional grammar*. Bloomington, IN: Indiana University Linguistics Club.
Talmy, L. (1985). Lexicalization patterns. In T. Shopen (Ed.), *Language typology and syntactic description*. Cambridge.
Tenny, C. (1987). Grammaticalizing aspect and affectedness. Ph.D. thesis, MIT, Cambridge, MA.
Tenny, C. (1989). The aspectual interface hypothesis. Lexion Project Working Papers 31, MIT.
Vendler, Z. (1967). *Linguistics and philosophy*. Ithaca: Cornell University Press.
Verkuyl, H. (1972). *On the compositional nature of the aspects*. Dordrecht: Reidel.
Verkuyl, H. (1989). Aspectual classes and aspectual distinctions. *Linguistics and Philosophy*, *12*, 39–94.
Vlach, F. (1981). The semantics of the progressive. In P. Tedeschi & A. Zaenen (Eds.), *Syntax and semantics*, *Vol. 14*, *Tense and Aspect*. New York: Academic Press.
Weinreich, U. (1972). Explorations in semantic theory. The Hague: Mouton.
Wilks, Y. (1975). A preferential pattern seeking semantics for natural language inference. *Artificial Intelligence*, *6*, 53–74.
Williams, E. (1981). Argument structure and morphology. *Linguistic Review*, 81–114.
Williams, E. (1987). Binding and linking. Manuscript, UMASS, Amherst.
Wright, G.H. von (1963). *Norm and action*. London: Routledge and Kegan Paul.

4

Learning to express motion events in English and Korean: The influence of language-specific lexicalization patterns*

Soonja Choi
Department of Linguistics, San Diego State University.

Melissa Bowerman
Max Planck Institute for Psycholinguistics.

English and Korean differ in how they lexicalize the components of motion events. English characteristically conflates Motion with Manner, Cause, or Deixis, and expresses Path separately. Korean, in contrast, conflates Motion with Path and elements of Figure and Ground in transitive clauses for caused Motion, but conflates motion with Deixis and spells out Path and Manner separately in intransitive clauses for spontaneous motion. Children learning English and Korean show sensitivity to language-specific patterns in the way they talk about motion from as early as 17–20 months. For example, learners of English quickly generalize their earliest spatial words – Path particles like up, down, *and* in *– to both spontaneous and caused changes of location and, for* up *and* down, *to posture changes, while learners of Korean keep words for spontaneous and caused motion strictly separate and use different words for vertical changes of location and posture changes. These findings challenge the widespread view that children initially map spatial words directly to nonlinguistic spatial concepts, and suggest that they are influenced by the semantic organization of their language virtually from the beginning. We discuss how input and cognition may interact in the early phases of learning to talk about space.*

*We would like to thank Herb Clark, Steve Pinker, Dan Slobin, and two anonymous reviewers for helpful comments on earlier drafts of this paper.

Introduction

In recent studies of lexical semantics, the expression of motion and location has played a central role (Jackendoff, 1983, 1990; Levin, 1985; Talmy, 1975, 1985). Spatial meanings are clearly fundamental to human cognition, and the system for encoding them is important not only in its own right but also because it provides the core structuring principles for many meanings that are not fundamentally spatial.

Although all languages seem to analyze motion/location events into components such as Motion and Path, they differ both in how they combine these notions into words (Talmy, 1975, 1985) and in the categories of spatial relations they distinguish (Bowerman, 1989, 1991; Casad & Langacker, 1985; Lakoff, 1987). The presence of both universality and language specificity allows us to raise basic questions about the relationship between nonlinguistic cognition and language input in children's acquisition of spatial expressions. Children are able to learn a great deal about space on a nonlinguistic basis (Gibson & Spelke, 1983; Piaget & Inhelder, 1956). But this nonlinguistic knowledge is not enough: children must still discover how spatial information is organized in their language. How do these two sources of structure interact in the course of language development?

Language specificity in semantic organization has rarely been considered in studies of the acquisition of spatial expressions. Most investigators have assumed that the meanings of spatial words like *in*, *on*, and *under* reflect nonlinguistic spatial concepts rather directly. This assumption has been a basis for a major hypothesis about the acquisition of spatial language: that children learn spatial terms by mapping them to concepts of space that they have formulated independently of language (e.g., H. Clark, 1973; Slobin, 1973).

The hypothesis of cognitive priority has found considerable support in research on the acquisition of spatial words. For example, children acquire English spatial prepositions and their counterparts in other languages in a relatively consistent order, and this order seems to reflect primarily the sequence in which the underlying spatial concepts are mastered (E. Clark, 1973; Johnston & Slobin, 1979). Also, when researchers have compared children's nonlinguistic grasp of spatial concepts directly with their knowledge of the words that encode these meanings, they have invariably found an advantage for nonlinguistic knowledge (e.g., Corrigan, Halpern, Aviezer, & Goldblatt, 1981; Halpern, Corrigan, & Aviezer, 1981; Levine & Carey, 1982). These findings have contributed not only to assumptions about spatial semantic development but also the rise of the more general "cognition hypothesis": that children initially identify words, inflections, and combination patterns with meanings formulated independently of language (see Cromer, 1974, for discussion). The findings are also consistent with Slobin's (1985) proposal that children map grammatical morphemes onto a starting set of universally shared meanings or "grammaticizable notions".

Nonlinguistic spatial understanding is, then, important in the development of spatial words. But there is reason to doubt whether, as claimed, it directly provides spatial concepts to which words can be mapped (see also Van Geert, 1985/6). In examining early vocabularies across languages, Gentner (1982) found that words for relational meanings are consistently learned later than words for concrete objects. After ruling out various other explanations (e.g., that adults model object words more often than relational words), she argued that this discrepancy reflects differences in the cognitive "naturalness" of the corresponding concepts: object concepts are more "given", whereas relational concepts are more imposed by the structure of language and so require additional time to be constructed. Schlesinger (1977) also rejected strong cognitive determinism and argued on theoretical grounds for an interaction in early language acquisition between children's own concepts and the semantic categories modeled in the input language. And Bowerman (1978a) and Gopnik (1980) proposed that children at the single-word-utterance stage generalize words to novel referents on the basis of not only their nonlinguistic concepts but also their observations of regularities across the situations in which adults use the words.

Existing cross-linguistic studies do not show which is more important in very young children's acquisition of spatial language: nonlinguistic spatial knowledge or the semantic organization of the input language. By age 3, English- and German-speaking children differ strikingly from Spanish- and Hebrew-speaking children in how they express spatial information in a story-telling task (Berman & Slobin, 1987). And 4- to 6-year-old children learning Warlpiri, an Australian language, differ from children learning English in the meanings they associate with spatial terms (Bavin, 1990). But it is not clear whether language specificity is present from the outset, as Gentner (1982) would predict, or emerges only gradually with divergence from a shared starting point, in line with Slobin (1985).

In this paper, we try to disentangle nonlinguistic spatial cognition from the structure of the linguistic input by comparing children acquiring English and Korean. We first contrast the way motion is lexicalized in the two languages, and then examine spontaneous speech from the period of one-word utterances and early word combinations.

The lexicalization of motion events in English and Korean

Semantic components of a motion event

In Talmy's analysis of how languages express motion, a "motion event" is defined as "a situation containing movement of an entity or maintenance of an entity at a stationary location" (1985, p. 60). By "movement" is meant a "directed" or "translative" motion that results in a change of location. By "location" is meant either a static situation or a "contained" motion that results in no overall change of location (e.g., jumping up and down, walking around in place). In this paper we focus on movement, along with a limited – although developmentally important – set of "contained" events, posture changes.

According to Talmy, a (dynamic) motion event has four basic components:

Motion: Presence of motion.
Figure: The moving object.
Ground: The reference-point object with respect to which the Figure moves.
Path: The course followed by the Figure with respect to the Ground.

These components can be identified in a straightforward way in the following English sentence:

(1) John went into the room .
[Figure] [Motion] [Path] [Ground]

A motion event can also have a "Manner" or a "Cause", which are analyzed as distinct external events. To this collection we will add "Deixis" (e.g., motion towards the speaker vs. away from the speaker), which seems to play a role in the lexicalization of motion events that is comparable to that of Manner or Cause (see DeLancey, 1985).[1]

According to Talmy, there are fundamental typological differences among languages in how a motion event is characteristically expressed in a sentence. In particular, he describes three patterns for what components are expressed by the main verb root and what is expressed by additional elements. We will be concerned with two of these: lexicalization or "conflation" in the main verb of Motion with either Manner or Cause, with path expressed separately, and conflation in the main verb of Motion with Path, with Manner or Cause expressed separately. (In the third, less common pattern, the main verb expresses Motion plus information about the Figure, with both Path and Manner or Cause expressed separately.)

English: Conflation of Motion with Manner or Cause

In English, as in most Indo-European languages and Chinese, Motion is characteristically conflated with Manner or Cause, and Path is expressed separately by

[1]Talmy (1985, p. 126) apparently regards Deixis (which he terms "Direction") as closely related to path in his analysis of the components of a motion event, and Aske (1989) treats it as a kind of Path. However, Deixis often patterns differently from other kinds of Paths in the way it is lexicalized (e.g., many languages express Deixis in main verbs like *come* and *go* even though they do not typically express other kinds of Paths in the verb system), so we distinguish it in this paper.

prepositions or particles (Talmy, 1975, 1985). The combination [Motion + Manner], for example, is found in *The rock SLID/ROLLED/BOUNCED down (the hill)*, *John WALKED/SKIPPED/RAN into the room*, and *John SLID/ROLLED/BOUNCED the keg into the storeroom*. The combination [Motion + Cause] is seen in *The wind BLEW the napkin off the table* and *John PUSHED/THREW/KICKED the keg into the storeroom*. The combination [Motion + Deixis] is also found in English, as in *John CAME/WENT into the room* and *John TOOK/BROUGHT the keg into the storeroom*.[2]

As these sentences illustrate, English uses the same verb conflations in both intransitive sentences expressing spontaneous motions and transitive sentences expressing motions caused by an agent. In addition, it marks Path in the same way in sentences of both types, using prepositions and particles like *in(to)*, *out (of)*, *on(to)*, *off*, *up*, *down*, and *away*. It also applies individual Path markers to a broad range of events within the domains of spontaneous and caused motion. For example, (put) *on* is used for the placement of clothing or other items onto all parts of the body, as well as for actions like putting a cup on a table, a lid on a jar, and a cap on a pen. Similarly, *up* and *down* are used not only for overall changes in the Figure's location (e.g., *go up*, *run down*) but also with posture verbs to indicate "in place" changes in the Figure's alignment or height with respect to the vertical axis, for example: *She suddenly SAT UP* (from a lying posture)/*SAT DOWN* (from a standing posture); she *LAY DOWN* (to take a nap); *He STOOD UP (and left the room)*. (Posture verbs plus *up* or *down* also sometimes express static postures, e.g., he SAT DOWN all during the concert; see Talmy, 1985).

Korean: Mixed conflation pattern

In the second class of languages in Talmy's typology, which includes Romance, Semitic, and Polynesian, Motion is characteristically conflated with Path in the main verb, and Manner or Cause is expressed separately with an adverbial. Spanish examples with [Motion + Path] verbs include *La botella ENTRÓ a la cueva (flotando)* "The bottle MOVED-IN to the cave (floating)" and *La botella SALIÓ de la cueva (flotando)* "The bottle MOVED-OUT from the cave

[2]All transitive verbs that express caused movement incorporate a causative meaning. This inherent causativity is distinct from the component "Cause" in Talmy's analysis. For example, although *bring* and *take* are inherently causative, they do not specify an independent event such as kicking or pushing that makes the Figure move, so they are not analyzed as conflations of Motion with Cause. Conversely, although intransitive *blow* is not inherently causative (cf. *the wind blew*), it can express the conflation [Motion + Cause], as in *The napkin blew off the table* (=the napkin moved off the table, from the wind blowing on it). The conflation of Motion with Cause in intransitive sentences is somewhat restricted in English and will not concern us further; this allows us to use the term "intransitive" to refer to constructions that express spontaneous motion by the Figure.

(floating)"; compare also SUBIR "move-up", BAJAR "move-down", and PASAR "move-past/through". Transitive Spanish verbs of the same type include METER "put in", PONER "put on", JUNTAR "put together" and SEPARAR "take apart" (Talmy, 1985).

Korean presents a mixed picture. In transitive clauses for caused motion, it conflates Motion with Path, like Spanish. But in intransitive clauses for spontaneous motion, it encodes Motion, Path and (optionally) Manner or Cause with separate constituents, a pattern not described by Talmy. In clauses of both types, Korean expresses most Path information with verbs; it lacks a system of morphemes dedicated to Path marking like the English spatial prepositions and particles. However, it does have three locative case endings, EY "at, to", -LO "toward", and -EYSE "from", which, when suffixed to a Ground nominal, function like the Spanish prepositions *a* "to" and *de* "from" in the examples above.

The basic word order of Korean is subject–object–verb. The verb phrase contains one or more "full" verbs; that is, verbs that can occur as the main verb or alone as a complete utterance (e.g., KA "go", imperative). The final verb of a sentence, which may be either a "full" verb or an auxiliary, bears all the inflectional suffixes such as tense (Lee, 1989). A pre-final verb is linked to the final verb by a "connecting" suffix such as -E or -A; the verbs together form a so-called compound verb.

Spontaneous motion

In expressions of spontaneous motion, the main (rightmost) verb is usually KATA "go" or OTA "come", in which motion is conflated with Deixis.[3] This verb is preceded by a Path verb, which in turn may be preceded by a Manner verb. The pattern is thus [Manner] [Path] [Motion + Deixis], as illustrated in (2):

(2) John-i pang-ey (ttwui-e) tul-e o-ass-ta.
J.-SUBJ[4] room-LOC (run-CONN) enter-CONN come-PST-DECL
[Figure] [Ground] ([Manner]) [Path] [Motion + Deixis]
"John came in(to) the room (running)."

[3]This verb can also be TANITA, which means "go and come repeatedly". However, TANITA does not combine with all Path verbs, and so is not as productive as the deictic verbs KATA "go" and OTA "come".

[4]The following abbreviations are used:

SUBJ – Subject marker
OBJ – Object marker
LOC – Locative marker
CONN – Connecting suffix
PST – Past tense marker
DECL – Declarative ending
CAUS – Causative suffix

Table 1. *Lexicalization of spontaneous changes of location in Korean*

Conflation pattern: [Path] – [Motion + Deixis] [Path]		[Motion + Deixis]
OLLA	"ascend"	
NAYLYE	"descend"	
TULE	"enter"	
NA	"exit"	KATA "go"
CINA	"pass"	OTA "come"
TTALA	"along"	
THONGHAY	"through"	
KALOCILLE	"across"	
TULLE	"via"	

Example: OLLA KATA (ascend go) "go up"

In this example, JOHN is the Figure, and PANG "room" is the Ground. The locative suffix -EY "to, at" on PANG indicates only that PANG represents the goal or location of the event specified by the verb. The fact that John changed his location is specified by the rightmost verb, O- "come". John's path with respect to the Ground is specified by the verb before O-: TUL- "enter". John's Manner of motion is specified by TTWUI- "run". Path verbs in addition to TUL- include NA- "exit", OLL- "ascend", and NAYLY- "descend"; a complete list is given in Table 1.

We translate intransitive Korean Path verbs with words like "enter" and "exit" instead of "in" and "out" to emphasize that they are verbs. But these translations are somewhat misleading, since they suggest that the verbs inherently conflate Motion with Path. In fact, the sense of motion in sentences like (2) comes primarily from the final verb, KATA "go" or OTA "come". If a Path verb is combined with ISSTA "be located" instead, it expresses static location. Path verbs can also be used as the main (rightmost) verb, in which case they express motion in a rather abstract, holistic way.[5]

[5]For example, in (1) below, TUL- "enter" is used with ISSTA "be located" to convey the static situation of the Figure. Similarly, in (2), OLL- "ascend" is the main verb. This sentence conveys the event of John's climbing the mountain as a whole; the fact that he had to move is backgrounded and not central to the meaning. In contrast, the sentence in (3), with the deictic verb KATA "go", expresses John's dynamic motion in climbing the mountain.

(1) cui-ka sangca-ey tul-e iss-ta.
mouse-SUBJ box-LOC enter-CONN be-DECL
"The mouse is in the box."

(2) John-i san-ey oll-ass-ta.
John-SUBJ mountain-LOC ascend-PST-DECL
"John climbed the mountain."

(3) John-i san-ey olla ka-ss-ta.
John-SUBJ mountain-LOC ascend go-PST-DECL
"John went up (onto) the mountain."

As noted earlier, the English Path particles *up* and *down* are used to express not only changes of location (with verbs like *go* and *run*), but also changes of posture (with verbs like *sit*, *stand*, and *lie*). Korean, in contrast, expresses posture changes with monomorphemic verbs, for example, ANCTA "sit down", NWUPTA "lie down", (ILE)SETA "stand up", ILENATA[6] "get up", KKWULTA "kneel down", KITAYTA "lean against". When these posture verbs are preceded by the Path verbs OLL- "ascend" and NAYLY- "descend", the resulting phrase does not have the same meaning as English *stand up*, *sit down*, etc.: it specifies that the Figure first gets up onto a higher surface or down onto a lower surface, and then assumes the indicated posture.

Caused motion

While spontaneous motion is encoded in "exploded" fashion in Korean, in that Motion, Path, and Manner are specified by separate words, caused motion is expressed quite compactly with inherently causative transitive verbs that conflate [Motion + Path]. Table 2 lists some frequent transitive Path verbs.

Recall that, in English, Path is marked the same way whether a motion is spontaneous or caused (cf. *The ball rolled INTO/OUT OF the box* vs. *John rolled the ball INTO/OUT OF the box*). For English speakers, it is so natural to think of these two Path meanings as "the same" that it is hardly worth remarking on. In Korean, however, Path is usually marked by different forms in the two cases; note that the only verb roots that appear in both Table 1 (intransitive Path verbs for spontaneous motion) and Table 2 (transitive Path verbs for caused motion) are OLL- "ascend" and NAYLY- "descend".[7] (These roots are inherently intransitive; the transitive forms are derived by adding the causative suffix -I.)

Not only are Path forms different for spontaneous and caused motion, but so are most of their meanings. Consider notions of joining and separation (bringing an object into or out of contact with another), which are typically expressed in English with phrases like *put in/on/together* and *take out/off/apart*. These are encoded in Korean with a variety of verbs, as shown in Table 2.[8] KKITA (glossable loosely as "fit", but used much more widely than English *fit*) is indifferent to whether the Figure goes into, onto, over, or together with the Ground, as long as it leads to a tight fit/three-dimensional meshing; hence, it is routinely used to express putting earplugs INTO ears and a cassette INTO a cassette case, one Lego piece ONTO or TOGETHER with another, and the top

[6] The morpheme ILE may have the meaning "ascend" but it occurs only with these two posture verbs, optionally with SETA "stand up", and obligatorily in ILENATA "get up".

[7] The two verbs TUL- "enter" and NA "exit" can also take the causative suffix. However, their causative forms are not productive spatial verbs because they cannot stand alone, and when they combine with other verbs they have idiomatic senses, e.g., SON-UL NA-I MILTA "hand-OBJ exit-CAUS push" (=put hand out to shake hands or receive something).

[8] If a Ground nominal is included in the sentence, it is marked with the suffix -EY "at, to" or -EYSE "from", as appropriate.

Table 2. *Korean transitive verbs for caused motion*

Verb	Meaning (Examples)
Cause to ascend/descend	
OLLITA	Cause something to ascend. (Move a poster upward on the wall)
NAYLITA	Cause something to descend. (Move a poster downward on the wall)
Join/separate	
KKITA /PPAYTA	"Fit"/"unfit" one three-dimensional object to/from another. (Lego pieces, ear plugs–ears, cassette–cassette case, top–pen, ring-finger)
NEHTA /KKENAYTA	Put/take things in/out of a loose container. (wallet–handbag, ball–box, furniture–room)
PWUTHITA /TTEYTA	Join/separate a flat surface to/from another flat surface. (sticker–book, poster–wall, two table sides)
KKOCTA	Put a solid object elongated in one dimension into/onto a base. (flower–vase, book–shelf, dart–board, hairpin–hair) /Separation: PPAYTA when the base holds the figure tightly, KKENAYTA when it holds it loosely
TAMTA /KKENAYTA	Put/take multiple objects in/out of a container that one can carry. (fruits–basket, candies–bowl, toys–box)
SITTA	Load something into/onto a vehicle. (hay–truck, package–car, car–boat) /Separation: NALUTA ("move an object from one place to another") when the object is moved to another place, but NOHTA (see below) when the object is put down on the ground
PWUSTA /PHWUTA	Pour liquid (or a large quantity of tiny objects) into/out of a container. (milk–cup, sand–pail)
NOHTA	Put something loosely on a surface. (pen–table, chair–floor) /Separation: TULTA for focusing on taking the object into the hand, CIPTA for focusing on picking it up.
KKATA	Take off a covering layer or wrapper. (shell–nuts, peel–banana, wrapper–candy) /Joining: SSATA for wrapping an object tightly.
KKAKTA	Take off a covering layer with knife. (skin–apple, planing a board, sharpening a pencil)
Put clothing item onto one's own body part	
IPTA	Trunk of body (dress, shirt, pants)
SSUTA	Head (hat, umbrella)
SINTA	Feet, legs (socks, shoes)
CHATA	Waist, wrist (belt, watch, diaper)
(PESTA is the reverse of all of these)	
Put something onto/into one's own body part in order to support or carry it	
ANTA	Arms (a person, an object, e.g., baby, package)
EPTA	Back (a person, e.g., a baby or child on mother's back)
CITA	Back (an object, if *not* also supported by shoulder)
MEYTA	Shoulder (an object hanging, e.g., backpack, bag over shoulder)
ITA	Head (an object, e.g., a pot)
TULTA	Hand (an object, e.g., briefcase, suitcase)
MWULTA	Mouth (an object, e.g., a cigarette)

of a pen ONTO (="OVER") the pen. The reversal of these actions is specified by PPAYTA "unfit". Because of the KKITA/PPAYTA Path category, Korean speakers must distinguish actions of putting in/on/together that result in a fitting relationship (KKITA) from those that result in loose containment (NEHTA) or surface contact (NOHTA, PWUTHITA); similarly, they must distinguish "taking out" of tight versus loose containment (PPAYTA vs. KKENAYTA) and "taking off" or removal from attached versus loose surface contact (PPAYTA or TTEYTA vs. CIPTA). These groupings and distinctions in Path meanings are not made in expressions for spontaneous movements into or out of a container, onto or off a surface, etc., since KKITA and PPAYTA do not have intransitive counterparts.

Transitive Path verbs of joining and separation also contrast with intransitive Path verbs in that they incorporate aspects of Figure and Ground as well as Path. For example, different verbs are used for solid versus liquid Figures, for three-dimensional versus flat versus elongated Figures, and for Ground objects that are conventionally used for carrying things versus vehicles versus other kinds of Grounds (see Table 2). Fine distinctions are made when the Ground is part of the human body: there are different verbs for putting clothing onto different body parts, and also for putting people or objects into/onto the arms, back, shoulder, head, mouth, and hand for purposes of support or carrying. Acts of putting a Figure onto the back are distinguished according to whether the Figure is animate or inanimate.

In Korean, expressions for caused motion also differ from those for spontaneous motion with respect to Deixis. Recall that intransitive expressions of spontaneous motion typically have as main verbs KATA "go" or OTA "come", which conflate Motion with Deixis. But for caused motion, Korean has no deictic transitive verbs comparable to English *take* and *bring*. Self-initiated changes of location by animate beings are consistently encoded with intransitive deictic verbs. When someone "takes" or "brings" something while moving, this can be expressed by combining KACY-E "have" with KATA "go" or OTA "come"; for example, *John took/brought a book to the library* is rendered as JOHN-I CHAYK-UL TOSEKWAN-EY KACY-E KA-/O-ASS-TA "John-SUBJ book-OBJ library-LOC have-CONN go-/come-PST-DECL" (=John went/came to the library having a book).

In transitive clauses, just as in intransitive clauses, Manner can be expressed with a verb preceding the Path verb, for example, TOLLY-E PPAYTA (turn "unfit"): "take Figure from its tightly fitting ground by turning it; twist out/off/apart". The pre-final verb can also express Cause, for example, MIL-E NEHTA (push put-in): "put something in a container by pushing it; push in".[9] However,

[9]Certain Path-conflating transitive verbs can also be used as Manner verbs in combination with a second Path-conflating transitive verb, because they express some Manner information in addition to Path information. For example, KKITA "fit" and PPAYTA "unfit" suggest that the action requires a bit of force; hence, one can say KKI-E NEHTA (fit put-in) to express shoving a block of a certain shape through a matching hole in a child's shape-fitting box so that the block falls down inside.

these combinations are less frequent than constructions like *twist/pull/cut/roll off* and *push/throw/kick/slide in* in English. This is because the two languages differ in what information must be expressed and what can be left to inference.

In English it is often obligatory to spell out Path rather completely, even when it can be readily inferred from context. If we heard "John threw his keys TO his desk/TO the drawer", we could reasonably suppose that the keys ended up ON the desk or IN the drawer. Still, these sentences sound odd: *on* and *in* are needed. Even when it is grammatical to specify Path less completely, fuller information is often given, especially in everyday speech; compare *John took his keys FROM his desk/FROM the drawer* (a bit formal or bookish) with *John took his keys OFF his desk/OUT of the drawer* (completely colloquial). In Korean, in contrast, a Path verb can often be omitted if a transitive verb expressing the Manner or Cause of the motion is supplied. As long as the Ground is specified and the relationship between Figure and Ground can be easily inferred, locative case endings such as -EY "to, at" or -EYSE "from" on the Ground nominal are sufficient, and a Path verb often sounds redundant.[10]

Summary of the lexicalization of motion events in English and Korean

To summarize, English uses the same verb conflation patterns in both intransitive clauses expressing spontaneous motion and transitive clauses expressing caused motion, and it encodes Path separately with the same Path markers (particles and prepositions) whether the clause is transitive or intransitive. Korean, in contrast, uses different lexicalization patterns for spontaneous motion and caused motion, and most of its Path markers (verbs) in the two cases are distinct. An overview of these patterns is given in Table 3. In addition, many Korean Path verbs have a

[10]For example, in (1) below, the Ground "desk" is specified with the locative marker (-ey), and the main verb is the Cause verb. In (2), both Cause (TENCY-) and Path (NOH-) verbs are present in addition to the Ground; to Korean speakers this seems redundant.

(1) John-i yelswey-lul chayksang-ey TENCY-ess-ta.
John-SUBJ key-OBJ desk-LOC throw-PST-DECL
"John threw keys TO desk."

(2) ? John-i yelswey-lul chayksang-ey TENCY-e NOH-ass-ta.
John-SUBJ key-OBJ desk-LOC throw-CONN put-on-PST-DECL
"John threw keys ONTO desk."

Fuller Path information can be supplied in sentences like (1) by a finer specification of the Ground object; for example:

(3) John-i yelswey-lul chayksang-wui-ey TENCY-ess-ta.
John-SUBJ key-OBJ desk-top-LOC throw-PST-DECL
"John threw keys TO desktop."

(4) John-i yelswey-lul selhap-an-ey TENCY-ess-ta.
John-SUBJ key-OBJ drawer-inside-LOC throw-PST-DECL
"John threw keys TO inside of drawer."

Table 3. *Comparison of English and Korean conflation patterns for motion events*

English		Korean		
		Spontaneous motion		
Verb	Particle	Verb	Verb	Verb
[Motion + Manner] [Motion + Cause] [Motion + Deixis]	[Path]	[Manner]	[Path]	[Motion + Deixis]
		Caused motion		
Verb	Particle	Verb	Verb	
[Motion + Manner] [Motion + Cause] [Motion + Deixis]	[Path]	[Manner] [Cause]	[Motion + Path + Ground][a]	

[a]These verbs are inherently transitive and causative.

narrower range of uses than the English Path markers that translate them. For example, OLL- "ascend" and NAYLY- "descend" are used only for changes of location and not posture, while English uses *up* and *down* for both. Similarly, Korean uses different verbs for putting clothing onto different parts of the body and for placing objects onto other surfaces, while English uses *on* across this whole range.[11]

[11]In addition to verbs conforming to the characteristic conflation pattern of English described by Talmy (1975, 1985), English has a number of intransitive and transitive Path-conflating verbs. Many of these, including *enter*, *exit*, *ascend*, *descend*, *insert*, *extract*, *join*, and *separate*, are borrowings from Romance. In Romance they represent the basic pattern, whereas in English they belong to a more formal register than their native counterparts *go in/out/up/down*, *put in/together*, *take out/apart*. A few path verbs, such as *fall*, *rise*, and *raise*, are native to English. Notions of Motion and Path and sometimes Figure or Ground also seem to lurk in the more complex meanings of a variety of other verbs such as *pluck*, *stuff*, *jam*, *peel*, *load*, *fit*, and *unwrap*. In light of such verbs, Steve Pinker (personal communication) has suggested to us that the differences between English and Korean might be "more in the number and frequency of verbs used than in some major typological parameter of the entire language". But we believe that the differences are more fundamantal. In Korean, Path meanings are expressed almost exclusively by Path verbs (only "at/to" and "from" are expressed separately, and only if the Ground object is mentioned). In English, however, most native Path verbs may or even must combine with a separate preposition or particle that either marks the incorporated Path meaning redundantly or specifies it more precisely; compare *fall DOWN*, *rise/raise UP*, *stuff/jam X INTO Y*, *pluck X OFF/OUT of Y*, *peel X OFF Y/X and Y APART*, *load X ONTO/INTO Y*, *fit X INTO/ONTO/TOGETHER with Y*. This is true even of some of the Romance borrowings, e.g., *insert X INTO Y*, not simply *...TO Y*. Candidate Path verbs may be absorbed into the basic English pattern of marking Path separately because they often incorporate elements of Manner as well as Path and so can be treated as [Motion + Manner] conflations; for example *fall* means something like "to go down in an uncontrolled manner", *insert* suggests "to put in in a controlled way" (e.g., because the space is small), *stuff* suggests the use of force, and *peel* specifies a particular manner in which two surfaces separate.

Development of motion expressions in English and Korean

Children learning English and Korean must, then, master different systems for lexicalizing motion events. How do they approach this task? The English data we use to investigate this question come from Bowerman's diary records of her two daughters, C and E. Data collection began when the children were about 1 year old and cover the period of one-word utterances and early word combination in rich detail. Aspects of the expression of motion in these records have been discussed in Bowerman (1976, 1978a, 1978b, 1980). The data can be compared with information given in a number of studies of children learning English, including Bloom (1973), Farwell (1977), Gopnik (1980), Greenfield and Smith (1976), McCune-Nicolich (1981), and Tomasello (1987).

Our main set of Korean data was collected longitudinally by Choi, who visited four children in their homes every three to four weeks from age 14 to 24–28 months (group I). At each session, she and the mother played with the child for 60–90 minutes. All sessions were video-taped and transcribed. Choi also elicited mothers' reports on their children's uses of spatial expressions. These data are supplemented by data collected from four other Korean children every two to four weeks from 19–20 months to 25–34 months (group II).[12]

Early in language development, most references to action take place in the immediate context of the action. In this study we consider only utterances produced while a motion event was taking place, just after it had occurred, or just before it occurred as a statement of intention, desire, or expectation. Both the English- and Korean-speaking children began to use words to encode motion in such situations in the same age range – around 14 –16 months.

The motion events referred to by the two sets of children were remarkably similar. For example, they commented on their own changes of posture or location, such as sitting down, standing up, or climbing up onto chairs or laps; they appealed to adults for help in changing location or to go outside; they asked to be picked up or carried; and they referred to donning and doffing clothing and to object manipulations of many kinds, for example, putting things into a bag and taking them out and putting Lego pieces or Popbeads together and taking them apart. Some examples are shown in Table 4. These similar preoccupations – also shown by Dromi's (1987) Hebrew-speaking daughter at the one-word stage – are apparently driven by shared aspects of children's general cognitive development, including what they are interested in talking about (Gopnik & Choi, 1990; Gopnik & Meltzoff, 1986).

Underlying the impression of similarity between the two sets of children there are important differences. We look first at the children learning English and then

[12]Pat Clancy collected the data from two of these children, and Young-Joo Kim from one; the fourth was studied by Choi. We would like to thank Clancy and Kim for their generous permission to use their data.

Table 4. *Words produced in similar contexts by learners of English and Korean between 14 and 21 months*

Context	English	Korean[a]
Wanting to go outside	out	pakk-ey "outside-LOC"
Asking M to pick her up	up	anta "pick up and hold in arms"
Sitting down	down	ancta "sit down"
Asking M to get up in the morning	up	ilenata "get up"
Joining two Lego pieces	on	kkita "fit"
Separating Popbeads	off	ppayta "unfit"
Putting coat on	on	ipta "put clothes on trunk"
Putting toys in container	in	nehta "put in loosely"
Putting a small object into a hole or a crack	in	kkita "fit"

[a]The verb ending -TA on all but the first example is the citation form. Endings actually produced by the children include various modals like -E (or -A) for requests or assertions (e.g., *an-a* for *an-ta* "pick up and hold in arms" and *anc-a* for *anc-ta* "sit down"), and -TA for certain types of assertions (Choi, 1991).

at the children learning Korean, focusing on spontaneous versus caused motion, motion "up" and "down", and how Path morphemes combined with verbs.[13]

English

Words used for motion events

It is well known that words like *down*, *up*, *in*, *out*, *on*, *off*, *back*, and *away* play a central role in the early expression of motion by children learning English, first appearing as single-word utterances and later figuring in early word combinations (Bloom, 1973; Farwell, 1977; Gopnik, 1980, Greenfield & Smith, 1976; Gruendel, 1977a; McCune-Nicolich, 1981; Miller & Ervin, 1964; Tomasello, 1987). This is true also for our two diary subjects, C and E (Bowerman, 1976, 1978a, 1980). In adult speech, these words often appear as verb particles in sentence-final position with heavy stress, which may make them especially salient to children (Brown, 1973; Slobin, 1973; Tomasello, 1987). Many of them also serve as prepositions in adult English, and can express static location, as in *The book is IN the bookcase*. However, children at first use them primarily or exclusively for motion. C and E began to use them for static location in the second half of the second year; for

[13]See Bowerman (1989) and Bowerman and Choi (in preparation) on the expression of caused motion, especially how children categorize manipulations like putting things into/onto/together with other things and taking them out/off/apart.

example, *in* produced while peeking into the bag in which a hamburger had just arrived in a restaurant (E, 19 months). Other words that C and E used for motion events between 14 and 18 months include *go, come, sit, walk, run, jump, ride, fall, push, pull, and throw*.

Spontaneous versus caused motion

Table 5 shows the emergence of Path particles and verbs for spontaneous versus caused motion in C's and E's speech. Utterances are classified according to

Table 5. *Early words for spontaneous and caused motion events in C's and E's speech*[a]

C: Age in months	Spontaneous motion	Caused motion
14–16	down[b], out	on[c], off[c]
		open[d]
17–18	up, down, out, on	up, down, on, off
	come, fall, walk, run, sit, ride	open
19–20	up, down, in, out, away	up, down, in, out, on, off, back
	go, come, walk, fall, sit, lie	open, close, hold, fall
	go away	
21–22	up, down, in, out, back, away	up, down, in, out, on, off, back, away
	go, come, walk, jump, fall, sit, ride	open, close, push, turn, pour, carry, come, put, take
	come down, sit down, get down, fall down, lie down, get/got up, sit up, come out, get/got out, fall out, sit on, come back, go away	fall down, lie down, help down, sit up, get up, go in, pour in, get out, pour out, keep out, come out, come out, fall out, take off, clean off, dry off, put back, throw away, take away, put away, get away
23–24	up, down, in, out, on, back	up, down, in, out, on, off, away
	go, come, run, jump, fall, sit, ride	open, close, push, throw, put, take, give, spill, pour
	fall down, sit down, lie down, get down, get/got up, get in, go out, come out, fall off, come back, go away	get down, push down, get up, pick up, pull up, bring in, do in, take out, pour out, blow out (=deflate), put on, take off, brush off, came off, take away, put away, throw away, put together

Table 5 continued.

E: Age in months	Spontaneous motion	Caused motion
14–16	up, down, out	down, off, back
	go, come	open, close, push, pull, throw
17–18	out[e]	up, on, off, in, back
	go, walk, jump, fall, sit	open, close, push, pull, throw, sit, fall
19–20	up, down, in, out, on, off, back, away	up, down, in, out, on, off, back, away
	go, come, walk, run, fall, ride	open, close, push, pull, spill, pour, kick, throw, take, come, carry, fit
	come up, get up, stand up, step up, sit down, lie down, fall down, run down, come in, come out, get out, going on, come/came off, get off, come back, get away	stand up, get down, pour in, close in, came on, came off, take off, fall off, get off, throw away
21–22	up, down, in, out, on, off, back, away	up, down, in, out, on, off, back, away
	go, come, run, walk, fall, climb, ride	open, close, push, pull, take, put, bring, give, turn, kick, carry, fall, spill, pour
	get up, stand up, came up, reach up, play up, go up and down, come down, fall down, get down, lie down, come in, get in, sit in, come out, fall out, get out, stick out, blow out (i.e., go out of window), get on, come/came off, come/came back, going away, going around	carry up, get up, pull up, put down, push down, pull down, pour down, put in, get in, push in, fit in, pour in, dip in, take out, pull out, get out, carry out, put on, get on, take on, take off, get off, push off, came off, fell off, put back, give back, throw away.

[a]Particles and verbs are listed only if they were produced spontaneously (i.e., not imitated) at least three times during the period shown, either in isolation or in combination with other words. All non-imitated verb + particle combinations are listed.

[b]Most uses of *down* in this period were for getting off a rocking horse, sometimes with an adult's help. One instance was for going downstairs.

[c]Until 18 months C pronounced both *on* and *off* as /a/ (final consonants in general were missing), so it is unclear whether she had two words or one.

[d]Although *open* and *close* are not used in adult English for caused motion (i.e., change of location), the children often overextended them to contexts in which adults would say *take off/out/apart* or *put on/in/together* (see Bowerman, 1978a).

[e]E often said *up* and *down* for static position in this period (e.g., *up* while looking at something high on a shelf.)

whether the motion was (or would be, in the case of anticipated events) spontaneous, or required an agent's causal action. Most utterances classified under "spontaneous motion" were used for self-initiated motion by animate beings, usually the child herself (see Huttenlocher, Smiley, & Charney, 1983). They also included uses of *up* and *down* for changes of location that the child initiated and was active in pursuing, even though she was helped by an adult, for example, *up* as the child clambered up on a chair with a boost. (*Up* or *down* as requests to be picked up or lifted down, or comments on these actions, were classified as caused motion.)

Utterances were classified under "caused motion" when they referred to a motion brought about by an external agent. When a child says "in" while putting a ball into a box, we cannot be certain whether she intends to refer to the agent's action ("put in"), or only to the motion of the Figure ("go in"). Adult English often allows the speaker to focus only on the Figure's motion, leaving the agent out of perspective (Talmy, 1985), and children in the early period of word combining say both "put X in" and "X goes in" (for example) in the context of caused motion (Bloom, Lightbown, & Hood, 1975). Our classification thus uses the nonlinguistic context as a guide – imperfect in the case of caused motion – to the child's likely intentions.

In the age period 14–16 months, C and E produced only a few Path particles. All but one (E's *down*) were applied to either spontaneous motion or caused motion, but not both. In some cases this reflected the child's initial restriction of the form to specific contexts; for example, at first C said *out* only for going outdoors (spontaneous) and E said *off* only for removing clothing and other objects from the body (caused). In other cases, however, the child used the form quite productively within the limits of spontaneous or caused motion (see Bowerman, 1978a, 1980, on C's extensive use of *on* and *off*).

Over the next few months, however, the children used Path particles increasingly often for both spontaneous and caused motion. By 19–20 months, they used almost all Path particles in both ways, and for a wide variety of spontaneous and caused motion events. For example, they used *on* for sitting or standing on things and for putting on clothing of all kinds, attaching tops to pens and stickers to surfaces, and putting objects down on surfaces, and *off* for the reverse of these actions. They used *in* for going into houses, rooms, bathtubs, and the child seat of a shopping cart and for putting things into various containers (e.g., pieces into puzzles, noodles into bowl, riding toys into house), and *out* for the reverse of these actions (see Gopnik, 1980, and Gopnik & Meltzoff, 1986, for similar uses by other children). They used *back* for their own or another person's spontaneous return to an original location, for putting objects back where they were usually kept (e.g., watch on arm, books on shelf), and for rejoining parts of an object (e.g., top on pen, lid on bottle). Between 17 and 20 months they also used many of the particles for static spatial relations, for example, *in* when looking at a box with crackers in it or a picture of a bear in a helicopter.

Combining Path with Manner/Cause/Deictic verbs

By 19 months (E) and 21 months (C), the children began to combine Path particles with a variety of verbs specifying the Manner, Cause, or Deictic aspect of a motion event (see Table 5) (combinations with nouns naming the Figure started earlier). Many of the children's verb–particle combinations are also common in adult speech, but there is evidence that they understood the underlying combinatorial principle and were not simply imitating. First, they produced novel combinations such as "carry up" (picking up and righting a fallen-over stool; E, 21 months), "sit in" (after another child got into a bus and sat down; E, 21 months), "close in" (trying to stuff jack-in-the-box down into box and shut lid; E, 20 months), "catch in" (asking M to capture her between two boxes; E, 24 months), "do it in" (=put it in; C, 23 months), and "blow out" (a) holding hand out of open car window; E, 22 months; (b) asking F to deflate a beach ball; C, 24 months). Second, the particle and the verb in the children's combinations factored motion events appropriately into an independent Path and Motion; for example, *out* expressed a Figure's exit from containment regardless of whether the action was specified as *fall*, *pour*, or *take*, while the use of *pull*, *push*, *fall*, etc., was indifferent to whether the Path followed by the Figure was specified as *up*, *down*, *in*, *out*, *on*, *off*, or *back*.

DOWN and UP

We will illustrate English-speaking children's use of Path morphemes more closely with *down* and *up*. These are typically among the first words used for motion events: one or both sometimes appear as early as 12–14 months (e.g., Farwell, 1977, Greenfield and Smith, 1976; Gruendel, 1977a; Nelson, 1974), and they are often present by 16 or 17 months (Bloom, 1973; Gopnik, 1980; Ingram, 1971; Tomasello, 1987). In E's speech, *down* appeared at 13 months and *up* at 16 months; in C's it was 16 and 17 months. Both children occasionally overextended *down* to "up" situations before learning *up*, an error also reported by Greenfield and Smith. In Table 6, we show representative uses in chronological order for each child.

Like many children reported in the literature, C and E at first said *up* and/or *down* primarily or exclusively for movements of their own bodies, either spontaneous (including assisted) or caused by an adult. But they soon became more flexible. Between 16 and 20 months, both children said *up* and *down* for their own and other people's spontaneous vertical motions, including both changes of location like falling and getting on or climbing off raised surfaces such as chairs, couches, riding toys, and laps, and changes of posture like sitting down, standing

Table 6. *Examples of DOWN and UP in C's and E's early speech*

	Spontaneous motion (age in months)	Caused motion (age in months)
	DOWN	
C:	Wanting M to help her get down from rocking horse (16)	
	Climbing down from doll's crib (17)	Pushing cat's head down (17)
		Taking cow down out of crib (17)
	Sliding down off bed (18)	Wanting M to take her out of Roc-n-Spin chair (18)
	Coming downstairs (18)	
	Climbing down out of washtub (19)	Wanting M to take her down from dressing table (19)
	Watching squirrel come down tree (20)	
	Coming downstairs (21)	
E:	Trying to climb down off counter (13)	Wanting M to take C down from chair (13)
	At top of slide wanting to slide down (14)	Asking M to take her down from counter (14)
	Wanting C to come down from counter (15)	
	Asking M to sit down (16)	Dumping an armload of yarn into her wagon (16)
	Sitting down in car (16)	
	Climbing down from chair (16)	Setting books on the floor (16)
		Wanting to take chair down from on table (16)
	Asking F to sit down (17)	Wanting M to put beads down on the floor (17)
		Wanting M to put her cup down on saucer (18)
	After getting from chair to floor (19)	
	Getting down from high chair (20)	Wanting M to take cup down from desk (20)
	UP	
C:	Climbing up steps (17)	
	Wanting to get on upper bunk bed (18)	Trying to get her walker up onto the couch (18)
	Wanting to climb on counter (18)	
	Climbing onto the couch (18)	
	Wanting to get into M's lap (18)	
	Wanting M to stand up by the crib (19)	
	Wanting F to get out of bed (19)	

Table 6 continued.

	Spontaneous motion (age in months)	Caused motion (age in months)
	UP (continued)	
C:	Wanting M to get out of bed (20)	Picking up crayons from the floor (21)
		When somebody picks up a baby (21)
		Picking up a piggy bank and taking it to a pile of toys she's making (21)
E:	Standing up in the car (16)	
	Climbing up the slide (16)	
	Standing up in her crib (16)	
	Climbing up on her horse (16)	
	Trying to lift herself up on the counter (16)	
	Re: M who just climbed up on a chair (17)	Putting a tiny figure on a toy tree (17)
	Sitting up after lying on her back (19)	Putting something on coffee table (19)
	Climbing up on a chair (19)	Putting a peg doll on top of toy fire engine (19)
	Trying to climb on M's lap (20)	Picking up a newspaper (20)
	Standing up in high chair (20)	Wanting Mary to lift her onto a bed (20)
	When C arrives at top of stairs (21)	Wanting M to pick her up (21)

Note: utterances were produced just before, during, or just after the events indicated. M = Mother, F = Father, C = Child's sister.

up, and getting up in the morning. They also said *up* and *down* for caused motions, for example, when they wanted an adult to lift them up onto a higher surface or take them down from it, for picking up objects from the floor or putting them on raised surfaces, pushing or pulling things downward, and putting things down on the floor or other low surfaces. They also used *up* as a request to be picked up and held or carried, and both *up* and *down* for static situations, for example, *up* when pointing to the upper branches of a tree in a picture, and *down* when looking at a doll floating head down in the tub. This range of uses is consistent with that reported for other children in this age period.

English-speaking children acquire *up* and *down* so early, and extend them so readily to many situations of vertical motion or orientation, that many investigators have assumed that vertical motion "up" and "down" are nonlinguistic notions. For example, Nelson (1974), reporting on a year-old child who extended *up* on the first day of its use "to all vertical movement of the child himself or of objects", proposed that "there is a core representation of this action concept . . .

something like Vertical Movement" (p. 281). Similarly, Bloom (1973, p. 70) suggested that the early uses of *up* reflect the "notion of 'upness'" and Gruendel (1977a) concluded that uses of *up* in her data support Bloom's proposal that "'upness' is itself a true early-cognized or conceptualized relation". In a study of the development of relational words at the one-word stage, McCune-Nicolich (1981) found that *up* and *down*, along with several other words, emerged somewhat abruptly in the speech of five children, spread rapidly to a variety of contexts, and were less likely to be imitated than other words. She proposed that these early-learned relational words code "pre-established cognitive categories" – in particular, operative knowledge of the late sensorimotor period to do with space, causality, sequence, and the like. She predicted that "since operative intelligence is a universal aspect of cognition, the same categories of meaning would be expected for all children, although various lexical items might be used to encode these" (p. 18).

When our attention is confined to English, it is plausible to think that children generate notions of vertical motion nonlinguistically and simply map them directly to *up* and *down*. But in cross-linguistic perspective, it is sobering to realize how neatly tuned these meanings are to the requirements of what is, after all, a language-specific system of expressing Path. Let us turn now to Korean to see whether children exposed to a different system express the same meanings, albeit mapped to different words.

Korean

Words used to express motion

Because we have fewer data from each Korean child than from our English-speaking subjects, we will often consider the children of a particular age period together. A summary of pooled data is presented in Table 7.

Like our English-speaking subjects, our Korean subjects began to refer to motion events between 14 and 16 months. The first productive words for motion of all four children in group I were the transitive Path verbs KKITA "fit" and/or PPAYTA "unfit".[14] Typical contexts of use included putting Lego pieces together or taking them apart, and fitting plastic shapes into the holes of a shape box. By 17–18 months a number of other transitive Path verbs emerged: PWUTHITA "put one surface to another", which the children used for stickers and bandaids, KKA(K)TA "peel off",[15] NEHTA "put into a loose container", KKENAYTA "take out of loose container", and some "carrying" and "clothing" verbs. By

[14]The ending -TA marks the citation form of a verb in Korean. Verbs in the children's speech were suffixed instead with various modal endings, most typically -E (or -A), which is used in adult speech for requests or assertions. Thus, a child's rendering of KKITA "fit" would typically be KKI-E.

[15]At this early stage of development, the children did not differentiate phonologically between KKATA "take off covering layer or wrapper" and KKAKTA "take off covering layer with knife".

Table 7. *Early words for spontaneous and caused motion events in Korean children's speech*[a]

Age in months	Spontaneous motion	Caused motion
14–16 ($N = 4$)		O.M.:[b] kkita (1) "fit", ppayta (3) "unfit", yelta (1) "open", tatta (1) "close"
17–18 ($N = 4$)	DEIXIS: kata (1) "go"	O.M.: kkita (4) "fit", ppayta (4) "unfit", yelta (1) "open", tatta (1) "close", pwuthita (1) "juxtapose two surfaces", kka(k)ta (3) "peel off", nehta (1) "put in", kkenayta (1) "take out", ollita (1) "cause to go up"
	POSTURE: ancta (2) "sit down"	CARRYING: anta (2) "in arms", epta (1) "on back"
		CLOTHING: pesta (1) "take off"
		MANNER/CAUSE: tollita (1) "turn"
19–20 ($N = 4$)	DEIXIS: kata (3) "go", ota (1) "come"	O.M.: kkita (4) "fit", ppayta (4) "unfit", yelta (3) "open", tatta (1) "close", pwuthita (1) "juxtapose two surfaces", kka(k)ta (3) "peel off", nehta (1) "put in", nohta (1) "put on surface", ollita (1) "cause to go up", kkocta (1) "put elongated object to base", kkenayta (1) "take out"
	POSTURE: ancta (2) "sit down", ilenata (3) "get up"	CARRYING: anta (2) "in arms", epta (2) "on back"
	PATH + DEIXIS: na kata (1) "go out"	CLOTHING: pesta (1) "take off", ipta (1) "on trunk", sinta (1) "on feet"
	MANNER: ttwuita (1) "run"	MANNER/CAUSE: tollita (1) "turn"
21–22 ($N = 8$)	DEIXIS: kata (4) "go", ota (4) "come"	O.M.: kkita (6) "fit", ppayta (6) "unfit", yelta (3) "open", tatta (2) "close", pwuthita (3) "juxtapose two surfaces", kka(k)ta (7) "peel off", nehta (3) "put in", kkenayta (3) "take out", ollita (3) "cause to go up", naylita (1) "cause to go down", kkocta (1) "put elongated object to base"
	POSTURE: ancta (4) "sit down", ilenata (3) "get up", nwupta (2) "lie down", ileseta (1) "stand up"	
	PATH + DEIXIS: na kata/ota (4) "go/come out", tule kata/ota (1) "go/come in", olla kata/ota (3) "go/come up", naylye kata/ota (1) "go/come down", ttele kata (1) "fall–go"	CARRYING: anta (5) "in arms", epta (5) "on back"
	MANNER: ketta (1) "walk", ttwuita (1) "run", naluta (1) "fly"	CLOTHING: pesta (4) "take off", ipta (4) "on trunk", sinta (4) "on feet", ssuta (3) "on head"
	MANNER + DEIXIS: nalla kata (1) "fly–go" (change of location by flying)	MANNER/CAUSE: ssotta (1) "pour carelessly", chata (1) "kick", milta (3) "push", nwuluta (1) "push down", tollita (1) "turn", tencita (1) "throw"

Table 7 continued.

Age in months	Spontaneous motion	Caused motion
23–24 ($N = 8$)	DEIXIS: kata (7) "go", ota (5) "come" POSTURE: ancta (7) "sit down", ilenata (4) "get up", nwupta (3) "lie down", ileseta (1) "stand up" PATH + DEIXIS: na kata/ota (5) "go/come out", tule kata/ota (4) "go/come in", olla kata/ota (5) "go/come up", naylye kata/ota (2) "go/come down" MANNER: ttwuita (2) "run", ttuta (1) "float", ttelecita (1) "fall"	O.M.: kkita (6) "fit", ppayta (6) "unfit", yelta (7) "open", tatta (3) "close", pwuthita (4) "juxtapose two surfaces", kka(k)ta (7) "peel off", nehta (4) "put in", kkenayta (3) "take out", ollita (2) "cause to go up", naylita (2) "cause to go down", nohta (3) "put on surface", kkocta (1) "put elongated object to base" CARRYING: anta (6) "in arms", epta (4) "on back", tulta (1) "in hands" CLOTHING: pesta (6) "take off", ipta (5) "on trunk", sinta (4) "on feet", ssuta (2) "on head" MANNER/CAUSE: tollita (1) "turn", nwuluta (2) "push down", tencita (2) "throw", kkulta (1) "pull", capta (2) "hold/catch"

[a]Numbers in parentheses refer to the number of children who produced the word during the period shown. ($N = 4$) refers to group I, ($N = 8$) refers to groups I and II combined. For group I, each verb listed was produced by the child at least once during the recording session, and the mother reported that the child produced it more than once during the age period indicated. For group II, the verb was produced by the child at least once during the recording session.

[b]O.M. = verbs of object manipulation.

19–20 months, NOHTA "put on surface", KKOCTA "put elongated object to base", and OLLITA "cause to go up" were added, along with additional clothing verbs.

Spontaneous versus caused motion

As Table 7 shows, the Korean children used transitive Path verbs only for caused motion and never overgeneralized them to spontaneous motion; for example, they never said KKITA "fit" when they crept into a narrow space or KKENAYTA "take out of a loose container" when they got out of the bathtub. In fact they never violated the distinction between spontaneous and caused motion along a Path throughout the entire developmental period observed: no verb was used in contexts of both kinds. In comparison, recall that our English-speaking subjects used some Path particles for both spontaneous and caused motion by as early as 14–16 months, and many by 20 months.[16] A major

[16]The English-speaking children did discriminate well between transitive and intransitive verbs. They never used a transitive verb such as *take* for spontaneous motion. Occasionally they used intransitive verbs for caused motion (see Table 5), but mostly in contexts where this is also acceptable in adult speech, e.g., *fall* when a Figure is dropped or knocked over and *come* (*out/off*, etc.) for manipulations of small objects (cf. adult utterances like "Will it come out?"). Errors such as "I come (=bring) it closer" (Bowerman, 1974) did not start until about age 2, and can be attributed to a learned rule, not ignorance that a verb is basically intransitive (Bowerman, 1974; Pinker, 1989).

difference between children learning English and Korean, then, is in their willingness to extend Path words across the transitivity boundary.

Unlike English-speaking children, our Korean subjects at first focused almost exclusively on caused motion. In C's and E's speech, expressions for spontaneous and caused motion developed in parallel. In the Korean children's speech, intransitive motion verbs appeared much later than transitive motion verbs. As Table 7 shows, the children produced no intransitive verbs for Motion or Path at all between 14 and 16 months. At 17–18 months KATA "go" was used by one child. Two others may have also said KATA at this age according to their mothers, but, if so, it was far less productive than transitive motion verbs: the children did not say it during the recording sessions and the mothers' reports were not consistent from one session to the next. KATA "go" and OTA "come" became productive only at 19 months. One child combined KATA with the Path verb NA "exit" (NA KATA "exit go; go out") during this period as a request to go outside. The other children began to combine KATA and OTA with Path verbs only at 21 months.

As discussed earlier, many transitive motion verbs of Korean conflate Motion not only with Path but also with information about Ground and sometimes Figure. The children's use of these verbs was generally appropriate, showing that they were sensitive to the incorporation of these elements. The sense that ground may be a component of a motion verb's meaning seemed to become particularly strong between 17 and 20 months. At this time the children distinguished two verbs of supporting/carrying according to the body part that serves as Ground (ANTA "put into arms to support/carry" vs. EPTA "put on back to support/carry"), and they also began to distinguish clothing verbs according to the Ground body part: IPTA "put clothes on trunk", SINTA "put clothing (e.g., shoes, socks) on feet". SSUTA "put clothing on head" appeared at 21 months.

Combining Path verbs with Manner and Cause verbs

Our Korean subjects were rather slow to learn verbs like TENCITA "throw" and MILTA "push", which in adult speech can be used either alone or in combination with transitive Path verbs to express the Manner or Cause of a caused motion event. Only one such verb, TOLLITA "cause to turn", is attested up through 20 months, and it was produced by only one child. More verbs of this type began to come in at 21–22 months (see Table 7). But they were not combined with Path verbs, even though the children produced word combinations of other kinds. Caused motion events were expressed either with Path verbs or with Manner/Cause verbs, but not with both at once – a pattern characteristic of adult Korean as well, as discussed earlier.

Our Korean subjects contrast sharply with our English-speaking subjects in their slow acquisition of Manner/Cause verbs and their failure to combine them with Path verbs. Recall that in the age range 17–20 months, C and E expressed motion events with both Path particles and many different Manner/Cause verbs, and from 19–21 months they often combined the two elements, particularly when expressing caused motion (see Table 5). Such combinations are, of course, characteristic of English and other languages of its conflation type, as described by Talmy (1975, 1985).

Motion "down" and "up"

As discussed earlier, English-speaking children learn *down* and *up* so early, and extend them so readily to many events involving downward and upward motion, that many investigators have supposed that they are mapped directly to nonlinguistic sensorimotor notions of vertical motion "downward" and "upward". If this is so, Korean children – presumably equipped with similar nonlinguistic concepts – should seize on Korean words produced frequently in contexts involving vertical motion, and extend them freely to other events involving vertical motion regardless of whether the motion is spontaneous or caused or whether it involves a change of location or posture. For example, they might initially say either OLLA KATA "go up" or OLLITA "cause to go up" for both spontaneous upward motions, including posture changes, and for caused upward motions. Similarly, they might say either NAYLYE KATA "go down" or NAYLITA "cause to go down" for getting down, sitting or lying down, putting things down, and as requests to be put down. Alternatively, they might select ANTA "pick up and support/carry in arms" to mean "up" in general, or ANCTA "sit down" to mean "down" in general.

This does not occur. Although ANTA "pick up and hold/carry in arms" and ANCTA "sit down" were produced by some of the children from 17–18 months, they were never overextended to other situations involving vertical motion. The intransitive and transitive causative forms of OLL- "up" and NAYLY- "down" emerged very late compared to *up* and *down* in the speech of children learning English. The development of our four youngest subjects (group I) is shown in Table 8.

Among the children of group I, SN was, at 18 months, the youngest to produce one of these words – OLLITA "cause to go up". However, he made an intriguing error in the meaning he first assigned to it. When he was 17 months old his mother had said OLLITA when she was putting plates back in a kitchen cabinet high above the counter. SN apparently overlooked the "up" information embedded in this complex event and inferred that the word meant "put something in the location where it belongs"; for a month, he used the verb only for "putting away" events of many sorts, regardless of directionality, for example, putting a toy back in a container on the floor. He made this error at a time when he was learning a variety of transitive verbs – for example, clothing verbs – that include a Ground component. The acquisition of Ground-incorporating verbs may sensitize Korean children to the possibility that Ground may be relevant to the meaning of a new transitive motion verb. Only at 19 months did SN begin to use OLLITA for caused upward motion, for example, to ask his mother to lift him up onto a step.

Table 8. *Examples of NAYLY- ("descend") and OLL- ("ascend") in four Korean-speaking children*

	Spontaneous motion (age in months)	Caused motion (age in months)
	NAYLYE KATA (descend–go)	NAYLY-ITA (descend–causative)
AN:	Getting down from her high chair (24)	Taking a plate down from table (24)
	Getting down from counter (24)	
MK:	–	Taking an object down from counter (25)
		Taking an object down from shelf (25)
SN:	–	–
YN:		Asking M to pull her pants down (23)
		Asking M to pull her pants down (25)
		Asking M to take her down from her high chair (25)
	Getting down from her high chair (26)	
	Going downstairs (26)	
	Getting down from a step (26)	
	OLLA KATA (ascend–go)	OLL-ITA (ascend–causative)
AN:		Putting an object up on the table (21)
		Putting a toy on her leg while seated (22)
	Climbing up on couch (24)	Putting her plate up on the counter (24)
	Climbing onto her bed (24)	
	Climbing up in her high chair (24)	
MK:	–	Putting an object on the counter (26)
		Putting a toy car up on the shelf (27)
SN:		Putting toys back in their usual place (18) (not necessarily "up", see text)
		Wanting M to put him in high chair (19)
		Wanting M to lift him onto the step in the bathroom (19)
		Putting an object on the chair/ kitchen counter (20)
	Going upstairs (22)	
	Climbing up on a chair (22)	
YN:		Asking M to pull her pants up (26)
	Climbing up in her high chair (26)	Asking M to lift her up onto a stool (26)

At 22 months he finally also began to say OLLA KATA "go up" in connection with spontaneous motions like getting on a chair.

OLLITA and OLLA KATA emerged even later in the speech of the other three children. The development of NAYLITA "cause to go down" and NAYLYE KATA "go down" is similar to that of OLLITA "cause to go up" and OLLA KATA "go up", but still slower, as shown in Table 8. Although the Korean children were slow to use words comparable to *up* and *down*, this does not mean that they did not talk about events involving upward and downward motion. They did – but using verbs that classify these events on the basis of criteria other than their shared Path.

The late appearance of intransitive Path verbs is not restricted to OLLA KATA "go up" and NAYLYE KATA "go down", nor to these four youngest children of our sample. Of the eight children whose data at 21–22 months are shown in Table 7, only three said OLLA KATA/OTA "go/come up", only one said NAYLYE KATA "go/come down", only four said NA KATA/OTA "go/come out", and only one said TULE KATA/OTA "go/come in". We return to the question of why these verbs are so late in the discussion section.

Discussion

Although children learning English and Korean talk about similar motion events in the second year of life, they do not do so in similar ways. English-speaking children rely heavily on Path particles. They start out using some of these in restricted or idiosyncratic ways, but soon extend them to a wide range of spontaneous and caused motion events that share similar abstract Paths. By about 20 months they begin to combine them productively with verbs that specify the Manner, Cause, or Deictic aspects of the motion event.

Korean children use no words in these ways. Like Korean adults, they distinguish strictly between words for spontaneous and caused motion. Concentrating first on caused motion, they learn a variety of transitive verbs that conflate Path with notions of Figure and especially Ground, and extend them to different classes of motion events than are picked out by English-speaking children's Path particles.[17] Their intransitive Path verbs are limited for many months to verbs of

[17]For example, they use the same verb (KKITA "fit") for putting a Figure into a tight container and attaching it to an outside surface (*in* vs. *on* for learners of English), and the same verb (PPAYTA "unfit") for the reverse of these actions (*out* vs. *off*). But they use different verbs for putting objects into tight versus loose containers (KKITA vs. NEHTA; both *in* for learners of English) or taking them out (PPAYTA vs. KKENAYTA; both *out*), for joining three-dimensional (KKITA), flat (PWUTHITA), or elongated (KKOCTA) Figures to a Ground (all *in* or *on* for learners of English, depending on whether there is containment), for putting clothing on the head (SSUTA), trunk (IPTA), or feet (SINTA; all *on*), and for being supported or carried in the arms (ANTA) or on the back (EPTA) (both *up* or *carry*).

posture change. They do not acquire intransitive Path verbs for spontaneous motion "in", "out", "up", and "down" until long after English learners begin to use Path particles for spontaneous motion, and they are just as late on transitive verbs for caused motion "up" and "down". Once they do learn verbs for "up" and "down", they never overgeneralize them to posture changes or use them as requests to be picked up and carried, both favorite uses of *up* and *down* by English-speaking children.

These findings challenge the widespread view that children map spatial morphemes directly to their sensorimotor concepts of space, and suggest instead that children are guided in constructing spatial semantic categories by the language they are exposed to. We will elaborate on this interpretation shortly. But first let us try to rule out alternative interpretations that do not require crediting such young children with a language-specific semantic organization of space.

Context-bound learning and homonyms

Perhaps the look of language-specific semantic organization is an illusion. Maybe children just imitate the words they hear in particular contexts, and see no relationship between them. For instance, our subjects may have simply learned what to say when climbing onto a chair, when wanting to be picked up, and when getting into a standing posture. Learners of Korean would use three different verbs, while learners of English would say *up* in each case, but for both sets of children the word said in each context would be independent.

This hypothesis is easy to rule out. First, our subjects used spatial words creatively, extending them to many events for which they had never heard adults use them. Many of their novel uses were completely appropriate; for example, 1–11 and 17–24 in Table 9. Others were errors from the adult point of view, for example, 12–16 and 25–34. Errors show particularly clearly that children are not simply imitating what they have heard in particular contexts. They have often been interpreted as evidence that children rely on meanings generated independently of language (e.g., Nelson, 1974; see Bowerman, 1989, for discussion). But our subjects' errors seem to reflect problems of detail within spatial semantic systems that, in broad outline, were already language specific. For example, our Korean subjects knew that PPAYTA "unfit" had to do with taking something from a position of tight fit or attachment, but they sometimes overextended it to attachments of the wrong kind, for example, those involving flat surfaces (e.g., 32 in Table 9) or tight clothing or embrace (e.g., 25–28, 31). Similarly, our English-speaking subjects knew that *in* applied generally to "containment", but they tended to assimilate "position between" to this category (14–15).[18]

[18]See also Bowerman (1978a, 1980) on overextensions of *open* and *close* to actions that adults would encode with *on* and *off* or *together* and *apart*.

Table 9. *Examples of novel uses of spatial words by learners of English and Korean between 15 and 25 months (age in months; errors are starred)*

ENGLISH	
1. ON	Putting a ladybug magnet on a can opener, C 16.
2. ON + negative head shake.	Has just been told not to pull off a bit of paper stuck to M's leg, but she wants it off, E 18.
3. OFF	Asking M to remove a (nonremovable) upright pole from back of her riding toy, C 17.
4. IN. TOY IN	Trying to fit piece of camera into loop formed by pull-handle of drawer, C 21.
5. IN 'GAIN	Trying to shove piece of toy furniture through door in doll house, E 18.
6. OUT	Has just dipped hand into her glass of milk and taken it out again; is now inspecting it, C 17.
7. OUT	Trapped behind toys in her room, she wants help in getting out, E 17.
8. SMOKE OUT	Watching steam coming out of vent in the ground, E 21.
9. DOWN	Pushing down head of neighbor's cat, C 17.
10. DOWN	Asking M to move chair from table to floor, E 16.
11. UP, DOWN	"Walking" her fingers up to her neck and back down, E 19.
12. *OPEN	Trying to separate two Frisbees, C 16.
13. *CLOSE KNEES	Asking M to put her knees together, E 21.
14. *MONIES ... IN	Looking for coins she'd just stuffed down between two couch cushions, E 19.
15. *IN	Putting ping-pong ball between knees, E 20.
16. *OFF	Asking M to unfold a newspaper, C 15.
KOREAN	
17. PPAYTA	Trying to pull out the string from the end of the toy fire hose, AN 15.
18. PPAYTA	Trying to take out Investigator's (Inv.'s) jigsaw puzzle game from tight-fitting box, AN 15.
19. PPAYTA	Asking Inv. to take lid off her (Inv.'s) pill box, SN 19.
20. PPAYTA	Taking flute apart, HS 22.
21. PPAYTA	Trying to take out pencil stuck through paper, HS 22.
22. KKITA	Putting doll into tight-fitting seat of small horse, AN 17.
23. KKITA	Fitting a train into its wooden base (Inv.'s new toy), MK 17.
24. KKITA	Watching Inv. put video cassette in camcorder, TJ 23.
25. *PPAYTA	Trying to take bib/shirt off, AN 16. (PESTA is appropriate.)
26. *PPAYTA	Asking M to take his bib/shirt off, SN 18. (PESTA)
27. *PPAYTA	Asking M to take her shirt off, TJ 18. (PESTA)
28. *PPAYTA	Wanting to get toy away from sister, HS 22. (CWUTA "give")
29. *PPAYTA	Asking someone to peel a banana, HS 25. (KKATA)
30. *KKITA	Sticking fork into apple, TJ 23. (KKOCTA)
31. *KKITA	Re: Being held tight by an adult, PL 22. (ANTA)
32. *KKITA	Attaching magnetic fish to magnetic mouth of duck, TJ 25. (PWUTHITA)
33. *OLLITA	Putting toys back in place, SN 18. (KACTA TWUTA "bring/take back")
34. *KKOCTA	Putting a Lego piece onto another, SN 20. (KKITA)

Second, the "context-bound" explanation flies in the face of much work on early word use by other investigators. Although many researchers have noted that first words are often tied to specific contexts, most assume that this phase is short-lived. According to some, there is a shift to a more symbolic basis for word meanings around the middle of the second year (e.g., McShane, 1979; Nelson & Lucariello, 1985); others argue that many or most words are never significantly context bound at all (Barrett, Harris, & Chasin, 1991; Harris, Barrett, Jones, & Brookes, 1988; Huttenlocher & Smiley, 1987). The move away from context-based word use is often assumed to show that the child has come to rely on her own nonlinguistic conceptualizations of objects and events (e.g., Barrett et al., 1991; Nelson & Lucariello, 1985). Our subjects began to use a variety of spatial words in flexible and context-free ways between 16 and 20 months. Ironically, though, this development went paired with striking language specificity, which clashes with the hypothesis that the children were now starting to rely on their own nonlinguistic conceptions of space.

But perhaps we can reconcile evidence for creativity with the idea that children learn words for rather specific meanings. Suppose children share a repertoire of nonlinguistic spatial concepts that, although narrow, are broad enough to accommodate new instances. And suppose they associate each concept with a different word. For the hypothetical concepts "sitting down", "lying down", "going down", and "putting down", Korean children would learn four different words, while English speakers would learn four words all pronounced *down*, perhaps as reduced versions of more complete English verb phrases like *sit down*, *lie down*, *go down*, and *put down*. Let us call this the "homonym" hypothesis.[19]

This hypothesis requires a close look. Even for adult English speakers, some uses of the same Path particles are probably unrelated, and other uses only loosely related via a network of polysemes (see Brugman, 1981; Herskovits, 1986; Lakoff, 1987; Langacker, 1987; Lindner, 1981). And some uses that are related for adults might well start out as distinct for children, only coming together later as learners discover abstract similarities across situations to which the same particles are applied. We ourselves have assumed that English-speaking children's uses of *on* and *off* for actions with light switches and water faucets are independent of the spatial uses of these morphemes, and so have left them out of our analyses. But most of the differences we have found between children learning English and Korean do not submit easily to the homonym hypothesis.

The hypothesis requires us to assume that whenever learners of one language use a single word for situations that learners of another language distinguish with two or more words, the single word actually has two or more independent meanings. Sometimes this seems plausible; for example, it is not too jarring to

[19]We are grateful to Eve Clark for making us worry about this possibility, and for her insightful feedback on our attempts to deal with it.

posit homonymous *downs* for "sitting down" and "lying down". But do we really want to have to separate *down* for climbing down from a chair from *down* for being lifted down from the chair, and *in* for climbing into a tub from *in* for putting something into the tub? (Recall that the Korean children used different path verbs for spontaneous and caused motion events.) And do we feel comfortable with homonymous *ins* for putting a book in a tight-fitting box versus a looser box (KKITA vs. NEHTA for Korean children), and homonymous *outs* for the reverse of these actions (PPAYTA vs. KKENAYTA)?[20] These uses are so consistent with the central spatial meanings of these particles that it has never occurred to previous investigators that they might be independent acquisitions.

In fact there are good reasons to believe they are not. Once particular spatial words emerge in children's speech they often spread rapidly to new uses, which supports the intuition that they are interrelated. For example, our subject C first said *in* at 19 months for coming indoors (="come/go in"). Within a few days she also used it for "put in" actions like putting a sock in the laundry basket and a bead in a container, and for static containment, as when playing with an unopened thermometer package. E first said *up* at 16 months when she stood up in the car (="stand up"); within a few days she also used it for "go/get up" events like climbing up a slide, stepping up on a little chair, and trying to pull herself up by the kitchen counter, as a request to be lifted (="pick up"), and for static "upness", for example, for a picture of a cat sitting on a broomstick at a higher angle than a witch. Similar rapid extension patterns for *up* have been reported by Bloom (1973, p. 88), Leopold (1939), and Nelson (1974). Children's speed in generalizing especially *up* and *down* across diverse contexts is well recognized, and has often been cited to support the hypothesis that these words are mapped to unitary concepts of vertical motion (e.g., McCune-Nicholich, 1981). While we disagree that the route between nonlinguistic concepts and spatial word meanings is as direct as this, we concur that core uses (though not necessarily every use) of the various Path particles are related for the child.

Language-specific semantic learning

The differences we have found between learners of English and Korean cannot be ascribed to word meanings that are highly context bound or based on very narrow nonlinguistic spatial concepts. They constitute real differences in the children's

[20]Note also that adult English routinely applies *put in* and *take out* to most "tight" and "loose" manipulations with containers, so learners of English are probably not relying on distinct underlying verb phrases when they say *in* or *out* for these acts. If English speakers find it strange to split up the core meanings of *in* and *out*, Korean speakers find it equally strange to imagine that when a child says KKITA for fitting a figure "into" or "onto" a tight ground, or PPAYTA for taking it "out of" or "off", these uses are independent for him.

semantic organization – differences that correspond directly to the way spatial meanings are structured in the language the children are learning.

English isolates Path as a recurrent component of motion events in an exceptionally clear and consistent way. With its system of Path particles, it encourages learners to identify abstract notions of Path that are indifferent to whether the Figure moves spontaneously or is caused to move, and to details about the shape or identity of the Figure and Ground objects. Korean does not single out Path as a separate component of motion events as clearly and consistently as English. It uses Path verbs that differ in both form and meaning for spontaneous and caused motion (except for motion "up" and "down"), and – for caused motion and posture verbs – it combines information about Path with information about the shape or identity of the Figure and Ground objects. Korean children, then, are not prompted to analyze out Path as an abstract component of motion events as strongly as are learners of English, and this may account for their delay in acquiring those Path verbs that do express Path in relatively pure form. Instead, they are encouraged to classify motion events on the basis of Path meanings admixed with causativity and properties of the Figure and Ground.[21]

In rejecting the hypothesis that children's early spatial words are mapped to nonlinguistic concepts, we do not mean that nonlinguistic spatial cognition plays no role in spatial semantic development. Clearly it does. For example, across languages, children learn words for topological relationships (e.g., *on* and *in*) before words for projective relationships (e.g., *in front of* and *behind*) (Johnston & Slobin, 1979). This bias – also shown by our subjects – presumably reflects the order of emergence of nonlinguistic spatial understanding. Children also make certain errors even on words for topological relationships (see Table 9), which suggests that some topological distinctions are more difficult than others, presumably for cognitive reasons. We must, then, posit an interaction between language input and cognitive development. But how does this interaction take place?

More than thirty years ago Brown proposed that for language learners, "a speech invariance is a signal to form some hypothesis about the corresponding invariance of referent" (1958, p. 228). Our findings confirm this. Even very young children must be sensitive to the way adults use spatial words across contexts – otherwise they could not learn to classify spatial referents in a language-specific way so early. But we still know little about how children track uses of the same form over time, and how they generate and modify hypotheses about the adult's intended "invariance of referent".

[21] These claims are intended to apply only to children's organization of space *for purposes of talking about it* ("thinking for speaking", to borrow a phrase from Slobin, 1991). We take no stand here on whether the proposed semantic differences between learners of English and Korean have any Whorfian consequences for nonlinguistic spatial thought. Such effects would be compatible with our findings, but are not entailed by them.

A prerequisite for generating hypotheses about spatial words is to have some system for representing space. But "both the nature of the initial system for internally describing space and the way in which such a system can be modified by experience . . . remain as mysterious as ever" (Pylyshyn, 1977, p. 174). Many researchers have approached this problem by positing a set of semantic primitives or "privileged notions": an inborn mental vocabulary of distinctions or components drawn on in acquiring spatial words, such as verticality, region, inclusion, support, contact, attachment, Figure, Ground, Path or direction, and object dimensionality (point, line, plane, or volume) (Bierwisch, 1967; H. Clark, 1973; Jackendoff, this issue; Jackendoff & Landau, 1991; Miller & Johnson-Laird, 1976; Olson & Bialystok, 1983; Talmy, 1983). Spatial primitives would no doubt interact with other privileged notions such as, for verbs, causality and manner (Gropen et al., this volume; Jackendoff, 1983, 1990; Pinker, 1989). The repertoire of primitives would be the same for all languages, although they might be combined in different ways.

This approach has a number of advantages. Most important for us, it can help explain how children home in so quickly on language-specific spatial meanings: they do not need to generate endless hypotheses about what aspects of spatial relationships might be relevant in their local language, but only to choose and combine primitives in the right way. The approach also allows us to reconcile language specificity with errors: by hypothesis, children are relatively accurate on words based on (combinations of) features that are highly accessible, but make errors on words with features that are less salient or emerge only later in cognitive development (Bowerman, 1985; Slobin, 1985).[22] But it will take serious work to make the semantic primitives approach truly explanatory rather than simply programmatic.

One problem is that it may be difficult to make principled distinctions between meanings that are "privileged" for space (or any other semantic domain) and other conceptual distinctions a speaker can make (see also Bolinger, 1965; E. Clark, 1983). For instance, notions like "verticality", "inclusion", and "support" make plausible-sounding spatial primitives, whereas notions like "arms", "head", "back", "feet", and "clothing item" do not. But notions of both kinds played a role in the meaning of our subjects' earliest spatial words.

One attempt to get a better grip on what components should be considered "privileged" has been to restrict the notion of primitives to the "grammaticized" portion of language. According to this approach, open-class words like nouns and verbs may incorporate any kind of meaning, no matter how idiosyncratic or culturally specific. In contrast, closed-class morphemes like inflections, particles,

[22]Of course, this explanation is circular unless we can find some independent way to predict how accessible a feature is. See Bowerman and Gentner (in preparation) for a cross-linguistic (Dutch–English) test of the prediction that the ease of spatial semantic distinctions for children is linked to the frequency with which the distinctions are marked in the world's languages.

and prepositions draw on a much more restricted set of meanings (Slobin, 1985; Talmy, 1983, 1985). In particular, closed-class spatial morphemes are insensitive to most properties of the Figure and Ground objects, such as exact shape, angle, and size, and instead schematize spatial situations in terms of more abstract topological properties (Talmy, 1983; see also Jackendoff & Landau, 1991).[23] If information of this kind comes built in, English learners will not waste time hypothesizing that closed-class items like *up* or *on* apply only to Figures or Grounds of a certain kind (Landau & Stecker, in press). Korean learners, however, cannot rule out this possibility when they meet open-class items like the verb SINTA "put a clothing item on the feet or legs".

But this solution raises new problems. First, if meanings like "clothing item" and "feet" are not semantic primitives but have to be constructed from experience, it should take longer for Korean children to acquire spatial verbs that incorporate them than for English-speaking children to acquire Path particles that do not. But this is not the case. Second, we would need to explain how children between about 17 and 20 months – the period when our subjects were acquiring language-specific meanings for spatial morphemes – determine whether a morpheme is a member of an open or a closed class, and so decide on what kinds of hypotheses they should consider.

Finally, the semantic primitives approach probably underestimates what the child must learn about meaning. When meaning components are assumed to be built in, there is no need to explain them further (except, of course, at the genetic level). For some candidate primitives, this may be correct. For example, both English and Korean learners seem to recognize that different expressions may be needed for spontaneous and caused motion, and they do not extend words across this boundary unless – as for English particles – this use is demonstrated in the input. This is consistent with reports that children learning Japanese (Rispoli, 1987) and Quiché Mayan (Pye, 1985) identify verbs as transitive or intransitive from the start, and suggests that a full-blown sensitivity to caused versus spontaneous (or to transitive vs. intransitive) may be present in children from the outset of language acquisition. For other candidate primitives, however, experience may have significant "sharpening" effects (along lines discussed by Bornstein, 1979, for perceptual features). Let us consider the notion "Path" as an example.

We assume that learners of English and Korean have the same prelinguistic *potential* for identifying Path as an independent component of motion events. But

[23]Levinson (1991) has challenged this argument with data from Tzeltal. In this Mayan language, spatial relationships comparable to *in* and *on* are expressed with a closed-class set of "positional" verbs that predicate "to be located" of Figures of different types. Far from being abstract and purely topological, these verbs distinguish Figures on the basis of shape, size, and in some cases identity; for example, different verbs are needed for predicating spatial location of a wide-mouthed vessel, a narrow-mouthed vessel, an inverted object with flat side down (e.g., a lump of dough), a small sphere, a large sphere, things sitting bulging in a bag, objects leaning at various angles, and so on.

we have suggested that the structure of English encourages children to *develop* this potential more than the structure of Korean – to actually carry out this kind of analysis. Why should we think this? Why not simply assume that both sets of children have a fully developed notion of Path from the beginning, along with some candidate instantiations of it like motion "up" and "down"? Our reason for doubt is that our Korean subjects were so late to acquire "pure" Path markers of Korean like the intransitive verbs OLL- "ascend", NAYL- "descend", TUL- "enter", NA "exit", and the transitive verbs OLLITA and NAYLITA "cause to ascend/descend". They began to use these verbs only several months after acquiring verbs in which Path is conflated with information about the Figure and/or the Ground, and months after our English learners had acquired words like *up*, *down*, *in*, and *out*.

This delay is hard to explain if we assume that Korean and English learners both begin with a fully developed ability to isolate Path from complex motion events.[24] However, it is interpretable if we assume that children do not have a fully developed notion of Path, but rather are selectively prompted by the structure of the input to develop their skill at this analysis. Children learning English are systematically shown how to isolate a few recurring kinds of Path, and they learn how to do this quickly. Children learning Korean, in contrast, meet Path mostly conflated with notions of spontaneous or caused motion and often with specific properties of the Figure and Ground as well, so it takes them longer to realize that Path can sometimes be extracted and receive its own marking. If this analysis is correct, a danger of the "semantic primitives" approach is that by supplying the child with components that are "ready to go", it may cause us to overlook subtle learning processes promoted by the structure of the language being acquired.

In conclusion, we have shown that the meanings of children's early spatial words are language specific. This means that language learners do not map spatial

[24]One attempt to do so would be to say that Korean learners are just as sensitive as English learners to path, but that they have more trouble with the superficial problem of identifying the morphemes to express it with (we are following the logic of Slobin, 1973, here). In particular, English Path particles often occur sentence-finally and can receive heavy stress, both properties known to facilitate acquisition of a form. In contrast, the Korean intransitive "pure" path verbs are usually pre-final, followed by KATA "go" or OTA "come". This account does not go through, however. Most critically, it does not explain why the transitive "pure" path verbs OLLITA and NAYLITA "cause to ascend/descend" are just as delayed as the intransitive "pure" path verbs, even though they are not followed by deictic verbs and are identical in their positioning to KKITA "fit" and other transitive path verbs that are learned much earlier. It is also doubtful whether the intransitive "pure" path verbs are perceptually less salient than early-learned transitive path verbs. In caregivers' speech, verbs of both kinds receive major stress and are typically followed by further unstressed morphemes such as the modal markers CWE "do something for someone" or PWA "try". For example, OLL- "ascend" might appear in a phrase like [ólaka] (OLL-A KA) "ascend go; go up" or [ólakapwa (OLL-A KA PWA) "try to go up", and KKITA "fit" in a phrase like [kkíepwa] (KKI-E PWA) "try to put it in" or [kkíecwe] (KKI-E CWE) "shall I put it in for you?" In both cases, the path verbs are stressed but nonfinal, which makes them similar in perceptual salience.

words directly onto nonlinguistic spatial concepts, as has often been proposed, but instead are sensitive to the semantic structure of the input language virtually from the beginning. How children figure out language-specific spatial categories remains a puzzle. Although an appeal to semantic primitives offers some help, it leaves many questions unanswered. One thing seems clear, however: children could not learn language-specific spatial meanings as quickly as they do unless they have some good ideas about what to look for.

References

Aske, J. (1989). Path predicates in English and Spanish: A closer look. *Berkeley Linguistics Society Papers*, *15*, 1–14.

Barrett, M., Harris, M., & Chasin, J. (1991). Early lexical development and maternal speech: A comparison of children's initial and subsequent uses of words. *Journal of Child Language*, *18*, 21–40.

Bavin, E. (1990). Locative terms and Warlpiri acquisition. *Journal of Child Language*, *17*, 43–66.

Berman, R., & Slobin, D.I. (1987). Five ways of learning how to talk about events: A crosslinguistic study of children's narratives. *Berkeley Cognitive Science Report*, *46*: Berkeley, CA.

Bierwisch, M. (1967). Some semantic universals of German adjectivals. *Foundations of Language*, *3*, 1–36.

Bloom, L. (1973). *One word at a time*. The Hague: Mouton.

Bloom, L., Lightbown, P., & Hood, L. (1975). Structure and variation in child language. *Monographs of the Society for Research in Child Development*, *40* (serial no. 160).

Bolinger, D. (1965). The atomization of meaning. *Language*, *41*, 555–573.

Bornstein, M.H. (1979). Perceptual development: Stability and change in feature perception. In M.H. Bornstein & W. Kessen (Eds.), *Psychological development from infancy: Image to intention*. Hillsdale, NJ: Erlbaum.

Bowerman, M. (1974). Learning the structure of causative verbs: A study in the relationship of cognitive, semantic, and syntactic development. *Papers and Reports on Child Language Development*, *8*, 142–178.

Bowerman, M. (1976). Semantic factors in the acquisition of rules for word use and sentence construction. In D.M. Morehead & A.E. Morehead (Eds.), *Normal and deficient child language*. Baltimore: University Park Press.

Bowerman, M. (1978a). The acquisition of word meaning: An investigation into some current conflicts. In N. Waterson & C. Snow (Eds.), *The development of communication*. New York: Wiley.

Bowerman, M. (1978b). Systematizing semantic knowledge: Changes over time in the child's organization of word meaning. *Child Development*, *49*, 977–987.

Bowerman, M. (1980). The structure and origin of semantic categories in the language-learning child. In M.L. Foster & S.H. Brandes (Eds.), *Symbol as sense*. New York: Academic Press.

Bowerman, M. (1985). What shapes children's grammars? In D.I. Slobin (Ed.), *The cross-linguistic study of language acquisition. Vol. 2: Theoretical issues*. Hillsdale, NJ: Erlbaum.

Bowerman, M. (1989). Learning a semantic system: What role do cognitive predispositions play? In M.L. Rice & R.L. Schiefelbusch (Eds.), *The teachability of language*. Baltimore: Brooks.

Bowerman, M. (1991). The origins of children's spatial semantic categories: Cognitive vs. linguistic determinants. Paper presented at Wenner-Gren symposium "Rethinking linguistic relativity", Ocho Rios, Jamaica. (To appear in J.J. Gumperz & S.C. Levinson (Eds.), *Rethinking linguistic relativity*.)

Bowerman, M., & Choi, S. (in preparation).

Bowerman, M., & Gentner, D. (in preparation).

Brown, R. (1958). *Words and things*. New York: Free Press.

Brown, R. (1973). *A first language: The early stages*. Cambridge, MA: Harvard University Press.

Brugman, C. (1981). Story of *over*. M.A. thesis, University of California at Berkeley. Available from the Indiana University Linguistics Club.

Casad, E., & Langacker, R. (1985). "Inside" and "outside" in Cora grammar. *International Journal of American Linguistics*. *51*. 247–281.

Choi, S. (1991). Early acquisition of epistemic meanings in Korean: A study of sentence-ending suffixes in the spontaneous speech of three children. *First Language*, *11*, 93–119.

Clark, E.V. (1973). Non-linguistic strategies and the acquisition of word meanings. *Cognition*, *2*, 161–182.

Clark, E.V. (1983). Meanings and concepts. In J.H. Flavell & E.M. Markman (Eds.), *Mussen handbook of child psychology. Vol. 3: Cognitive development*. New York: Wiley.

Clark, H.H. (1973). Space, time, semantics, and the child. In T. Moore (Ed.), *Cognitive development and the acquisition of language*. New York: Academic Press.

Corrigan, R., Halpern, E., Aviezer, O., & Goldblatt, A. (1981). The development of three spatial concepts: In, on, under. *International Journal of Behavioral Development*, *4*, 403–419.

Cromer, R.F. (1974). The development of language and cognition: The cognition hypothesis. In B. Foss (Ed.), *New perspectives in child development*. Harmondsworth, Middlesex: Penguin.

DeLancey, S. (1985). The analysis–synthesis–lexis cycle in Tibeto-Burman: A case study in motivated change. In J. Haiman (Ed.), *Iconicity in syntax*. Amsterdam: Benjamins.

Dromi, E. (1987). *Early lexical development*. Cambridge, UK: Cambridge University Press.

Farwell, C. (1977). The primacy of "goal" in the child's description of motion and location. *Papers and Reports on Child Language Development*, *16*, 126–133.

Gentner, D. (1982). Why nouns are learned before verbs: Linguistic relativity versus natural partitioning. In S.A. Kuczaj II (Ed.), *Language development. Vol. 2: Language, thought, and culture*. Hillsdale, NJ: Erlbaum.

Gibson, E.J., & Spelke, E.S. (1983). The development of perception. In J.H. Flavell & E.M. Markman (Eds.), *Mussen handbook of child psychology. Vol 3: Cognitive development*. New York: Wiley.

Gopnik, A. (1980). *The development of non-nominal expressions in 12–24 month old children*. Unpublished doctoral dissertation, Oxford University.

Gopnik, A., & Choi, S. (1990). Do linguistic differences lead to cognitive differences? A cross-linguistic study of semantic and cognitive development. *First Language*, *10*, 199–215.

Gopnik, A., & Meltzoff, A. (1986). Words, plans, things, and locations: Interaction between semantic and cognitive development in the one-word stage. In S.A. Kuczaj II & M.D. Barrett (Eds.), *The development of word meaning*. Berlin: Springer-Verlag.

Greenfield, P., & Smith, J. (1976). *The structure of communication in early language development*. New York: Academic Press.

Gruendel, J. (1977a). Locative production in the single word utterance period: A study of *up–down*, *on–off*, and *in–out*. Paper presented at the Biennial Meeting of the Society for Research in Child Development, New Orleans, 1977.

Gruendel, J. (1977b). Referential extension in early language development. *Child Development*, *48*, 1567–1576.

Halpern, E., Corrigan, R., & Aviezer, O. (1981). Two types of "under"? Implications for the relationship between cognition and language. *International Journal of Psycholinguistics*, *8-4*(24), 36–57.

Harris, M., Barrett, M., Jones, D., & Brookes, S. (1988). Linguistic input and early word meaning. *Journal of Child Language*, *15*, 77–94.

Herskovits, A. (1986). *Language and spatial cognition: An interdisciplinary study of the prepositions in English*. Cambridge, UK: Cambridge University Press.

Huttenlocher, J., & Smiley, P. (1987). Early word meanings: The case of object names. *Cognitive Psychology*, *19*, 63–89.

Huttenlocher, J., Smiley, P., & Charney, R. (1983). Emergence of action categories in the child: Evidence from verb meanings. *Psychological Review*, *90*, 72–93.

Ingram, D. (1971). Transitivity in child language. *Language*, *47*, 888–909.
Jackendoff, R. (1983). *Semantics and cognition*. Cambridge, MA: MIT Press.
Jackendoff, R. (1990). *Semantic structures*. Cambridge, MA: MIT Press.
Jackendoff, R., & Landau, B. (1991). Spatial language and spatial cognition. In D.J. Napoli & J. Kegl (Eds.), *Bridges between psychology and linguistics: A Swarthmore Festschrift for Lila Gleitman*. Hillsdale, NJ: Erlbaum.
Johnston, J., & Slobin, D.I. (1979). The development of locative expressions in English, Italian, Serbo-Croatian and Turkish. *Journal of Child Language*, *6*, 547–562.
Lakoff, G. (1987). *Women, fire, and dangerous things: What categories reveal about the mind*. Chicago: University of Chicago Press.
Langacker, R.W. (1987). *Foundations of cognitive grammar. Vol. 1: Theoretical prerequisites*. Stanford, CA: Stanford University Press.
Landau, B., & Stecker, D.S. (in press). Objects and places: Syntactic geometric representations in early lexical learning. *Cognitive Development*.
Lee, H.B. (1989). *Korean grammar*. New York: Oxford University Press.
Leopold, W. (1939). *Speech development of a bilingual child* (Vol. 1). Evanston, IL: Northwestern University Press.
Levin, B. (1985). Lexical semantics in review: An introduction. In B. Levin (Ed.), *Lexical semantics in review*. Lexicon Project Working Papers, No. 1. Cambridge, MA: MIT Center for Cognitive Science.
Levine, S.C., & Carey, S. (1982). Up front: The acquisition of a concept and a word. *Journal of Child Language*, *9*, 645–657.
Levinson, S.C. (1991). Relativity in spatial conception and description. Paper presented at Wenner-Gren symposium "Rethinking linguistic relativity", Ocho Rios, Jamaica. (To appear in J.J. Gumperz & S.C. Levinson (Eds.), *Rethinking linguistic relativity*.)
Lindner, S. (1981). A lexico-semantic analysis of verb–particle constructions with *up* and *out*. Unpublished doctoral dissertation, University of California at San Diego. Available from the Indiana University Linguistics Club.
McCune-Nicolich, L. (1981). The cognitive bases of relational words in the single-word period. *Journal of Child Language*, *8*, 15–34.
McShane, J. (1979). The development of naming. *Linguistics*, *17*, 879–905.
Miller, G.A., & Johnson-Laird, P.N. (1976). *Language and perception*. Cambridge, MA: Belknap Press of Harvard University Press.
Miller, W., & Ervin, S. (1964). The development of grammar in child language. In U. Bellugi & R. Brown (Eds.), The acquisition of language. *Monographs of the Society for Research in Child Development*, *29.92*, 9–34.
Nelson, K. (1974). Concept, word, and sentence: Interrelations in acquisition and development. *Psychological Review*, *81*, 267–285.
Nelson, K., & Lucariello, J. (1985). The development of meaning in first words. In M.D. Barrett (Ed.), *Children's single-word speech*. New York: Wiley.
Olson, D.R., & Bialystok, E. (1983). *Spatial cognition: The structure and development of the mental representation of spatial relations*. Hillsdale, NJ: Erlbaum.
Piaget, J., & Inhelder, B. (1956). *The child's conception of space*. London: Routledge & Kegan Paul.
Pinker, S. (1989). *Learnability and cognition: The acquisition of argument structure*. Cambridge, MA: MIT Press.
Pye, C. (1985). The acquisition of transitivity in Quiché Mayan. *Papers and Reports on Child Language Development*, *24*, 115–122.
Pylyshyn, Z.W. (1977). Children's internal descriptions. In J. Macnamara (Ed.), *Language learning and thought*. New York: Academic Press.
Rispoli, M. (1987). The acquisition of the transitive and intransitive action verb categories in Japanese. *First Language*, *7*, 183–200.
Schlesinger, I.M. (1977). The role of cognitive development and linguistic input in language acquisition. *Journal of Child Language*, 4, 153–169.
Slobin, D.I. (1973). Cognitive prerequisites for the development of grammar. In C.A. Ferguson &

D.I. Slobin (Eds.), *Studies of child language development*. New York: Holt, Rinehart & Winston.

Slobin, D.I. (1985). Crosslinguistic evidence for the language-making capacity. In D.I. Slobin (Ed.), *The crosslinguistic study of language acquisition, Vol. 2: Theoretical issues*. Hillsdale, NJ: Erlbaum.

Slobin, D.I. (1991). Learning to think for speaking: Native language, cognition, and rhetorical style. Paper presented at Wenner-Gren symposium 'Rethinking linguistic relativity", May, Ocho Rios, Jamaica. (To appear in J.J. Gumperz & S.C. Levinson (Eds.), *Rethinking linguistic relativity*.)

Talmy, L. (1975). Semantics and syntax of motion. In J. Kimball (Ed.), *Syntax and semantics*. New York: Academic Press.

Talmy, L. (1983). How language structures space. In H. Pick & L. Acredolo (Eds.), *Spatial orientation: Theory, research, and application*. New York: Plenum.

Talmy, L. (1985). Lexicalization patterns: Semantic structure in lexical forms. In T. Shopen (Ed.), *Language typology and syntactic description, Vol. III: Grammatical categories and the lexicon*. Cambridge, UK: Cambridge University Press.

Tomasello, M. (1987). Learning to use prepositions: A case study. *Journal of Child Language*, *14*, 79–98.

Van Geert, P. (1985/6). In, on, under: An essay on the modularity of infant spatial competence. *First Language*, *6*, 7–28.

5

Wiping the slate clean: A lexical semantic exploration*

Beth Levin
Department of Linguistics, Northwestern University.

Malka Rappaport Hovav
Department of English, Bar Ilan University.

This paper presents a case study in lexical semantic analysis aimed at uncovering syntactically relevant components of verb meaning. Our strategy is to investigate the nature of the lexical knowledge that a speaker of English possesses with respect to certain apparently semantically related verbs: a set of verbs that might as a first approximation be classed as verbs of removal. However, a closer examination of these apparently semantically related verbs reveals that their syntactic properties diverge. An exploration of the patterns of behavior of the verbs suggests that the initial class includes three linguistically significant subclasses. The components of meaning that are relevant to characterizing each subclass are identified by isolating those components of meaning that the members of each subclass share. The conclusion considers the implications of the meaning components identified in this study for a lexical semantic representation.

*This paper grew out of earlier work on locative alternation verbs; see Rappaport and Levin (1988). We would like to thank Sue Atkins, Mary Laughren, Betsy Ritter, and two reviewers for their comments on earlier drafts of this paper. We are also grateful to Donald Hindle for searching the AP news wire for instances of many of the verbs we discuss here; these examples have been helpful in developing our analysis. This research was supported in part by NSF Grant BNS-8919884.

1. Introduction

The lexicon has recently assumed an increasingly central place in many syntactic theories, as more and more facets of the syntactic configurations that verbs and other argument-taking elements are found in are seen to be projections of their lexical properties. Consequently, much effort has been devoted to investigating the nature of their lexical representation. Ideally, a lexical entry should minimize the amount of information necessary for any given word. This goal can be achieved by factoring any predictable information out of lexical entries. The meaning of a word must be part of its lexical entry, since an important part of knowing a word is knowing its meaning. The question is whether this is all that needs to be learned and, more specifically, whether a word's syntactic properties (i.e., the syntactic configuration(s) it can appear in) are predictable from its meaning. Chomsky (1986), for example, speculates that only the meaning of a verb needs to be learned. Much research has focused on precisely this issue by exploring to what extent the syntactic properties of verbs – the lexical category with the most complex properties – can be derived from their lexical semantic properties.

That the meaning of a verb plays a large part in determining its syntactic properties is clear from a variety of facts concerning the syntactic expression of arguments to verbs. To take a simple example, consider the frequently made observation that verbs that denote an agent acting on and causing an effect on a patient, such as *cut* or *destroy*, figure among the transitive verbs of any given language. Observations such as these indicate that the meaning of a verb plays some role in determining its syntactic properties. There are two open questions: first, how much does the meaning of a verb determine its syntactic properties; and, second, a question which will be the focus of this paper, to the extent that syntactic properties are predictable, what components of verb meaning figure in the relevant generalizations?

These two questions cannot be approached independently. There are many ways verbs can be potentially classified according to their meaning, and the wrong classification might well preclude the statement of the correct generalizations in the semantics to syntax mapping, suggesting that the relation between the two is more idiosyncratic that it actually is. Some illustrations will help to clarify this point.

To begin with a rather extreme example, a natural class of verbs from the point of view of meaning might be the set of verbs that describe things that can be done to books (essentially, the set of verbs that take the word *book* as one of their typical objects). An investigation of machine-readable dictionaries (Boguraev, 1991; Boguraev, Byrd, Klavans, & Neff, 1989), followed up by an investigation of on-line text corpora (Klavans, personal communication), reveals that this is quite a large class of verbs. Among its members are the verbs *abridge*, *autograph*, *ban*, *borrow*, *bowdlerize*, *catalogue*, *censor*, *commission*, *consult*, *entitle*, *print*, *publish*, *read*, *remainder*, *review*, *write*. However, as far as we can tell, there is no evidence that this set of verbs is linguistically significant.

Recently the question of the extent to which the syntactic properties of verbs are semantically determined has also been debated in the linguistics literature in the context of the unaccusative hypothesis: a hypothesis concerning the nature of the intransitive verb class, first proposed by Perlmutter (1978) and later adopted and extended by Burzio (1986). This hypothesis concerns the syntactic configurations that intransitive verbs are found in. The proposal is that the single argument of some intransitive verbs, the unaccusative verbs, is an underlying object, while the single argument of others, the unergative verbs, is an underlying subject. Some researchers, including Perlmutter in his original paper on the unaccusative hypothesis, have argued that the status of an intransitive verb as unergative or unaccusative can be determined from its meaning. However, other researchers, including Rosen (1984), have concluded that the distinction between unaccusative and unergative verbs cannot be characterized in terms of meaning alone. To support her view, Rosen points out that, for example, Italian verbs of bodily processes show variable behavior: *russare* ('snore') manifests unergative properties, while *arrossire* ('blush') manifests unaccusative properties.

However, this particular example need not argue against the semantic determination of syntactic properties; rather it emphasizes the importance of identifying the appropriate semantic components. The verbs *russare* ('snore') and *arrossire* ('blush') would only be expected to show similar behavior if the semantic notion "bodily process" is relevant to determining the status of verbs with respect to the unaccusative hypothesis; if it is not, then similar behavior is not necessarily expected. Some bodily process verbs, including those Rosen cites, are open to more than one semantic characterization. The concept denoted by English *snore* can be classified as an activity, while that denoted by English *blush* is open either to an activity or to a change of state interpretation. Interestingly, Italian *arrossire* ('blush') literally means "become red", suggesting that in Italian this verb probably ought to be considered a change of state verb. There is evidence, in fact, that the semantic notions of activity and change of state, rather than the semantic notion of bodily process, are the aspects of meaning that figure in the determination of a verb's status (Levin & Rappaport Hovav, 1991; McClure, 1990; Tenny, 1987; Van Valin, 1990; Zaenen, in preparation).

As this example illustrates, it is not easy to uncover the components of meaning that figure in the statement of generalizations such as the one just discussed. Some of the problems said to face attempts to determine syntactic behavior from meaning might simply stem from the use of the wrong facets of meaning in the statement of generalizations. Given that regularities exist, it is important to determine the components of meaning that figure in determining a verb's syntactic properties, even if ultimately it turns out that not all of these properties of a verb are fully predictable from its meaning (for some discussion see Jackendoff, 1990).

This paper presents a case study in lexical semantic analysis aimed at uncovering syntactically relevant components of verb meaning. Our strategy is to investigate the nature of the lexical knowledge that a speaker of English possesses with respect to certain apparently semantically related verbs: a set of verbs that might as a first approximation be classed as verbs of removal. However, the syntactic properties of these apparently semantically related verbs turn out on further examination to diverge. An exploration of the patterns of behavior of different verbs with respect to these syntactic properties suggests that the initial class includes three linguistically significant subclasses of verbs. The components of meaning that are relevant to characterizing each of the subclasses are identified by isolating those components of meaning that verbs in each subclass share. In the Conclusion we consider the implications of these meaning components for a lexical semantic representation.

2. Introducing the verbs

Our major focus throughout this paper is a variety of verbs that can be used to express the semantic notion of removal. We begin our investigation of such verbs by taking a detailed look at two verbs, the verbs *clear* and *wipe*, which can describe the removal of a substance or physical object – the *locatum* – from a *location*,[1] as in (1):

(1) a. Doug cleared dishes from the table.
 b. Kay wiped the fingerprints from the counter.

As the examples below show, the verbs *clear* and *wipe* seem to express their arguments in the same way: the agent is expressed as the subject of the verb, the locatum is expressed as the direct object, and the location from which the locatum is removed is expressed via a prepositional phrase headed by one of the prepositions typically used to indicate sources in English. This set of prepositions includes *from, out (of),* and *off (of)*, as well as combinations of *from* and other locative prepositions (e.g., *from under*, *from behind*). All these possibilities are attested with the verbs *clear* and *wipe*:

(2) a. Doug cleared the dishes out of the cupboard.
 b. Doug cleared the dishes off of the shelf.
 c. Doug cleared the dishes from under the sink.

[1]These terms are taken from Clark and Clark (1979).

(3) a. Kay wiped the fingerprints out of the cupboard.
b. Kay wiped the fingerprints off of the wall.
c. Kay wiped the fingerprints from behind the stove.

The similar expression of the arguments of the verbs *clear* and *wipe* is perhaps not unexpected given their similar meanings. Moreover, it is precisely the way the verb *remove* itself expresses its arguments:[2]

(4) Monica removed the groceries from the bag.

We might then assume that the lexical semantic representations associated with both *clear* and *wipe* identify them as verbs of removal, whatever form this representation takes. Linking rules (Carter, 1976, 1988; Ostler, 1979) – the rules that determine the mapping from the lexical semantic representation to the syntax – would then be responsible for associating the syntactic frame "NP V NP FROM NP"[3] with these and other verbs of removal. We refer to this syntactic frame, which is characterized by a locatum expressed as direct object and a location expressed in a source prepositional phrase, as the *locatum-as-object variant*. Linking rules would specify which argument of a verb is associated or "linked" with which syntactic position in this frame.

The verbs *clear* and *wipe* share an alternative way of expressing their arguments. Both verbs also allow the location argument to be expressed as the direct object of the verb, as in (5), rather than via a source prepositional phrase as in (1). We refer to this alternative expression of the arguments as the *location-as-object variant*:

(5) a. Doug cleared the table.
b. Kay wiped the counter.

The alternation in the expression of arguments shown by the verbs *clear* and *wipe* might on an initial analysis be attributed to membership in the class of verbs of removal. However, the verbs *clear* and *wipe* diverge from the verb *remove* with respect to their ability to be found in the location-as-object variant. The verb *remove* does not allow this option, as shown in (6), which cannot mean "Monica

[2]There appears to be some variability among the *remove* verbs – the set consisting of the verb *remove* and other verbs that pattern like it such as those listed in (12) below – concerning which of the set of prepositions used to express the notion of source they allow. The verb *remove*, for example, is not found with *out (of)* and *off (of)*. We do not address this issue further here, but see Ostler (1980) for some relevant discussion of similar constraints.

[3]We use "FROM" to represent the set of prepositions used to indicate sources in English. Although we have only included NP as the object of "FROM" in this frame, when the preposition heading the PP is *from* itself, the object of the preposition can be either an NP or a PP, as shown by examples like (2c) and (3c).

emptied the bag". This property is unexpected if the alternate realization of arguments is a property of verbs of removal:

(6) *Monica removed the bag.

Furthermore, the parallels in the expression of arguments do not carry through completely even for the verbs *clear* and *wipe*: these verbs differ from each other with respect to whether the locatum argument can still be expressed when the location is expressed as the object. With the verb *clear*, this is possible: the locatum argument can be expressed in a prepositional phrase headed by the preposition *of*, as in (7a). But the verb *wipe*, unlike *clear*, only marginally, if at all, allows the locatum argument to be expressed in an *of* phrase, thus the contrast in (7):

(7) a. Doug cleared the table of dishes.
b. *Kay wiped the counter of fingerprints.

The set of contexts that the verbs *clear* and *wipe* are found in are repeated below to highlight the similarities and differences between these two verbs:

(8) a. Kay wiped the fingerprints from the counter.
b. Kay wiped the counter.
(9) a. Doug cleared dishes from the table.
b. Doug cleared the table (of dishes).

The fact that the verb *remove* does not show alternate expressions of its arguments, when taken together with the fact that the verbs *clear* and *wipe* do not show uniform syntactic behavior, suggests that even if the notion "removal" is a syntactically relevant meaning component, it alone is not sufficient to explain the behavior of these three verbs. Furthermore, the differences in the verbs' syntactic behavior cannot simply reflect idiosyncratic properties of the individual verbs, since there are other verbs which behave like each of the three verbs considered. Specifically, we find a few other verbs that behave like *clear*; these are listed in (10).[4] Many verbs behave like *wipe*, among them those in (11). And the verbs in

[4]The class of verbs that express their arguments like *clear* is sometimes taken to be larger than the class listed in (10), as in Fraser (1971) and Hook (1983), among others. For instance, the verbs *drain* and *strip* have been associated with this class. We believe that previous studies have grouped too large a class of verbs together, and that some of the additional verbs are actually somewhat different from the more narrowly defined *clear* class we identify here. For purposes of exposition, we use the more restricted conception of this class and return to the other verbs that have been included in the class in the appendix.

(12) behave like *remove* in not allowing alternative expressions of their arguments:

(10) *Clear* verbs: clear, clean, empty
(11) *Wipe* verbs: buff, brush, erase, file, mop, pluck, prune, rake, rinse, rub, scour, scrape, scratch, scrub, shear, shovel, sponge, sweep, trim, vacuum, wipe, . . .
(12) *Remove* verbs: dislodge, draw, evict, extract, pry, remove, steal, uproot, withdraw, wrench, . . .

As the list of class members shows, the *clear* class is much smaller than the other two. We attribute this difference in size to the absence of a productive process that allows new members to be added to this class; see section 3 for discussion.

The attested patterns of behavior exhibited by these three types of verbs should receive a principled and systematic account. The alternations in the expression of arguments shown by the *clear* verbs and the *wipe* verbs (as well as the more general alternation these are considered to be instances of the locative alternation; see section 7) have sometimes been likened to the dative alternation – the alternation in the expression of arguments manifested by verbs such as *give* or *sell*:

(13) a. Carla gave a present to Tina.
b. Carla gave Tina a present.

Some accounts have assumed that a verb showing such an alternation has a single lexical semantic representation but allows alternate syntactic realizations of its arguments. Our approach will be that such a verb has two distinct but related lexical semantic representations and that the alternate expressions of arguments reflect the different meanings associated with these representations.

An examination of the meaning of the members of the three verb classes shows that each pattern of argument expression is restricted to a semantically coherent class of verbs and thus is clearly tied to verb meaning. Our next step, then, is to set out the components of meaning that are shared by verbs which pattern like *clear*, verbs which pattern like *wipe*, and verbs which pattern like *remove*.

3. A closer look at the meaning of the verbs

Although both the *clear* verbs and the *wipe* verbs appear to denote actions that involve the removal of a substance from a location, a closer examination of these two classes reveals a systematic difference in the meaning of their members. Each of the *clear* verbs specifies the state of the location as a result of the action denoted by the verb. The *clear* verbs differ from each other simply with respect to the resultant state: being clean is different from being clear, which, in turn, is different from being empty. None of the *clear* verbs makes explicit how the resultant state is achieved. For instance, it is possible to clear an obstructed path in various ways: by raking, sweeping, or shovelling it. All that matters is that the path ends up unobstructed. Similarly, a blackboard can be cleaned in a number of ways: by erasing it, wiping it, washing it, and so on. As long as the erasing, wiping, or washing results in the removal of any writing or other marks from the blackboard's surface, the action can be described as cleaning the blackboard. We can say that the meaning of the *clear* verbs includes a resultant state, or, borrowing a term used by Talmy (1975, 1985), that these verbs *lexicalize* a resultant state.

Consistent with their meaning, the *clear* verbs are deadjectival;[5] the adjectives that these verbs are derived from name the state that results from the action denoted by the *clear* verb: if someone clears a road, then the result is that the road is clear. However, while the action denoted by the verb necessarily implies the resultant state, the state denoted by the related adjective does not have to be the result of a specified or unspecified action or event. A clear blackboard does not have to be one which has been cleared:

(14) a. clean the blackboard; a clean blackboard
b. clear the road; the road is clear
c. empty the drawer; an empty drawer

In contrast, none of the *wipe* verbs are zero-derived from adjectives, although they do have related adjectival passive participles: **the wipe table* versus *the wiped table*; **the sweep floor* versus *the swept floor*.

While the meaning of a *clear* verb does not make explicit how the removal of a substance from a location is effected, the meaning of a *wipe* verb does. Wiping a blackboard is not the same as washing or erasing it, even if all three actions can result in the blackboard being clean. The *wipe* verbs further differ from the *clear* verbs in not specifying the effect that the action they denote has on the location. Although the action of wiping a blackboard might typically result in cleaning it, it is possible to wipe a blackboard without making it clean. In contrast, a blackboard is always clean as a result of being cleaned.

[5]It is likely that the verbs *clear*, *clean*, and *empty* are derived from the adjectives with the same names (rather than the adjectives being derived from the verbs) since the meaning of each adjective is simpler and included within the meaning of the corresponding verb. Furthermore, there are pairs of verbs and adjectives that show the same semantic relation although the verb in the pair is more complex morphologically than the adjective, as we discuss in section 4 (e.g., *deepen/deep*; see (19)). We use the term *zero-derived* to indicate that the verb and adjective are identical in form; however, we do not take a position as to whether the derivational process involves a "zero" morpheme or no morpheme at all.

The *wipe* verbs fall into two subclasses according to whether their meaning specifies a manner, as in (15a), or an instrument, as in (15b):

(15) a. buff, erase, pluck, prune, rinse, rub, scour, scrape, scratch, scrub, shave, skim, trim, wipe, . . .
b. brush, file, mop, rake, shear, shovel, sponge, vacuum, . . .

The meanings of the manner subclass verbs *wipe* and *rub* make explicit the way in which the action the verbs denote is performed: these two verbs involve different types of moving contact with a surface. In contrast, the instrument subclass verbs *rake* and *mop* are denominal, denoting actions performed with the instruments from which these verbs take their names.[6] The verb *mop* patterns like the verb *wipe* with respect to the expression of its arguments, as the following examples show:

(16) a. Sylvia mopped the spots from the floor.
b. Sylvia mopped the floor.
c. *Sylvia mopped the floor of spots.

This similarity is not surprising since the instrument restricts the action denoted by the verb in the same way that a manner does. That is, each instrument implies an action of a certain sort: the action required to use the instrument to perform its intended function. We continue to refer to the larger class of verbs that includes both the manner and instrument subclasses as the *wipe* verbs, referring to the specific subclasses when necessary. We will say that the property that characterizes the *wipe* verbs is that they lexicalize a means component, where means component refers to either a manner or an instrumental component.[7]

This examination of the *clear* verbs and the *wipe* verbs can help explain the difference in size between the two classes. In their survey of the process of coining new zero-derived verbs from nouns in English, Clark and Clark (1979) note that this word-formation process is particularly productive with nouns referring to

[6]Some members of the manner subclass have associated zero-derived result nominals; these nominals are typically used in light verb constructions (*give the table a wipe*). As Sue Atkins has pointed out to us, it appears that the manner verbs that have zero-derived nominals are those where the action denoted by the verb need not necessarily be iterative, so that *buff* and *erase*, which involve several iterated small movements, do not produce **give something a buff/an erase*.

[7]Resultant state and means are better described as components of meaning than as features because each has multiple instantiations. It is the presence or absence of a particular type of meaning component that is syntactically relevant, rather than its particular instantiation. These meaning components may turn out not to be primitive elements of the lexical semantic representation, but rather may be notions defined over the elements of a more complex representation. Furthermore, we do not claim that these meaning components necessarily exhaust the meaning of these verbs; they simply number among the linguistically relevant components of verb meaning.

instruments. A verb derived from such a noun denotes the typical action involving the use of the instrument the noun refers to. If we were to coin an innovative verb from a newly invented instrument used for removal, we would predict that this verb will behave like the verb *mop*. And the verb *vacuum*, which could only have been coined after the invention of the vacuum cleaner, shows precisely this behavior. The small size of the *clear* class, when compared with the *wipe* class, probably reflects the fact that this very productive strategy for adding to the verb lexicon does not create verbs of the *clear* type. Assuming these verbs are deadjectival, it could be attributed to the absence of a productive process of creating verbs from adjectives. And furthermore, even if such a process were available, there is not continuing extensive growth in the adjective lexicon the way that there is in the noun lexicon.

Although we have referred to the *clear* and *wipe* verbs as verbs of removal, we have seen that these verbs do not consistently pattern like either the verb *remove* – arguably the prototypical verb of removal – or the other verbs of removal listed in (12). Furthermore, the difference extends to their meaning. Unlike the *clear* and *wipe* verbs, the *remove* verbs simply describe the removal of something from a location. The *remove* verbs do not specify how the action of removing was performed. For example, it is possible to remove snow from a road in a variety of ways: by shovelling, raking, sweeping, etc. Nor do the *remove* verbs specify what effect the removal has on the location: snow can be removed from a road without clearing the road. Thus the *remove* verbs lexicalize neither a means nor a resultant state. Rather these verbs mean roughly "cause an entity not to be at a location" and nothing more.

4. Reassessing the classification of the verbs

In the previous section we argued that the *clear* and *wipe* verbs lexicalize the meaning components resultant state and means, respectively. In this section we begin to investigate the part that these meaning components play in determining the semantic class membership of these verbs and, hence, their syntactic behavior. Our basic claim is that verbs often have "basic" and "extended" meanings. We suggest that the component of meaning lexicalized in the verb determines its basic meaning. The basic meaning of a lexical item is its simplest meaning, reflecting little more than the lexicalized meaning components. Extended meanings are more complex meanings that are built on other meanings. This section will focus on the basic meaning of the *clear* and *wipe* verbs; extended meanings will be discussed in following sections. We propose that the use of the *clear* and *wipe* verbs in the location-as-object variant involves the basic meaning of these verbs, and, that on this meaning these verbs are not verbs of removal, but rather belong to other well-defined classes of verbs. As evidence for this proposal, we show that the *clear* and *wipe* verbs manifest properties associated with the members of these other verb classes when they are found in the location-as-object variant.

There is evidence that the *clear* verbs are basically change-of-state verbs, and that the meaning that they manifest in the location-as-object variant is roughly "cause an entity to come to be in the resultant state lexicalized by the verb". In this variant, these verbs denote causing a change of state in what we have called the location argument, so that the label "location argument" is something of a misnomer, and this argument is more appropriately viewed as the entity that undergoes the change of state. As such, the location argument is expressed as a direct object – the typical expression of an argument that denotes an entity undergoing a change of state. The state is the state lexicalized in a *clear* verb.

Support for this suggestion comes from the fact that the verbs *empty* and *clear* can undergo the causative/inchoative alternation, as illustrated below:[8]

(17) a. Martha emptied the tub.
b. The tub emptied.

(18) a. The strong winds cleared the skies.
b. The skies cleared.

This alternation, where the semantic role of the subject of the intransitive use of a verb is the same as that of the object of the transitive use of the same verb, is characteristic of most verbs of change of state, such as those listed in (19)

[8]Despite the fact that the verb *clean* does not show the causative/inchoative alternation, we believe it is a change-of-state verb. If a verb is found in the causative/inchoative alternation, then it is a change-of-state verb (or at least a verb of change, since verbs of change of position such as *move* and *bounce* also show this alternation). However, not all change-of-state verbs show this alternation. For instance, the verbs *pasteurize* and *homogenize* are change-of-state verbs, but they have only transitive, and not intransitive, uses (*The farmer pasteurized/homogenized the milk; *The milk pasteurized/homogenized*). We do not understand the conditions that prevent certain change-of-state verbs from having intransitive as well as transitive uses, but we suspect that these verbs are basically two-argument verbs meaning "cause to come to be in state". In contrast those verbs with both transitive and intransitive uses are basically one-argument verbs meaning "come to be in state", with the transitive use having a meaning "cause to come to be in state". It appears that a verb can show both transitive and intransitive forms if the change of state can come about "naturally" (as if without the direct intervention of an animate causer). Homogenization, pasteurization, and cleaning all involve changes of state that as we know them require the intervention of an agent, and hence the verbs naming these actions are only found as two argument verbs. Although we are aware of studies that address the issue of why some verbs do not have transitive uses (Hale & Keyser, 1986, 1987; Smith, 1970), we do not know of studies directly addressing the opposite question: why some change-of-state verbs do not have intransitive uses, although the paper by Brousseau and Ritter (1991) begins to look at some relevant issues.

We assume that such studies will also clarify why the set of objects that some verbs of change of state, including the verb *clear*, permit in their transitive use is more restricted than the set of subjects they take in their intransitive use. For example, compare *Susan cleared the table/*The table cleared* with *The wind cleared the sky/The sky cleared*. See Brousseau and Ritter (1991) for some other minimal pairs and for a discussion of factors that enter into these differences.

(Fillmore, 1967; Guerssel, Hale, Laughren, Levin & White Eagle, 1985; Hale & Keyser, 1986, 1987; among others). Furthermore, many change-of-state verbs, like the *clear* verbs, are deadjectival; they are either zero-derived from adjectives or formed from adjectives by the suffixation of *−en*, as the two subclasses in (19) show:

(19) a. cool, dim, dry, narrow, open, shut, slow, steady, thin, warm, . . .
  b. broaden, darken, deepen, harden, redden, ripen, soften, thicken, . . .
(20) a. Francesca cooled the coffee.
  b. The coffee cooled.
(21) a. Jane thickened the sauce.
  b. The sauce thickened.

Many change-of-state verbs, particularly those whose name is related to an adjective, have a sense in which they function as predicates whose single argument is the entity that undergoes a change of state and comes to be in the state lexicalized in the verb; this state is the one that the related adjective also describes. On this sense these verbs mean "come to be in state". These verbs also have a second sense that could be paraphrased as "cause to come to be in state"; this sense involves two arguments: one denoting the entity that undergoes the change of state, and the other denoting the agent/cause of the change of state. (Some change-of-state verbs, however, have only one of these two senses; see footnote 8.) We are claiming that the verb *empty*, as used in (17a), is a causative change-of-state verb, and that all that this sentence denotes is the causation of a specific change in the state of the tub (to a state where its contents are gone). Thus what sets verbs like *clean*, *clear*, and *empty* apart from other verbs of change of state is that they denote a change of state in an entity that typically is brought about by removing something from that entity. Other changes of state are brought about in different ways; for instance, by changes in chemical composition, structure, etc.

In may seem odd to claim that a verb like *clear*, which denotes an action which necessarily involves removal, is not classified as a verb of removal. However, this aspect of the real-world event denoted by a verb does not necessarily have to be reflected in its linguistic characterization. The evidence from the syntactic behavior of the *clear* verbs indicates that these verbs in the location-as-object variant are linguistically classified as change-of-state verbs and not as verbs of removal. A single real-world event may be described in different ways, necessitating the use of verbs from different linguistically significant semantic classes.

What about the *wipe* verbs? We propose that like the *clear* verbs, they too are not verbs of removal in their basic sense (see also Jackendoff, 1990, p. 296, who makes a similar claim). However, the *wipe* verbs are not change-of-state verbs either. We take the sense of *wipe* in the location-as-object variant (*Kay wiped the counter*) to be its basic sense, as we do with the *clear* verbs, although we take the principle which determines the expression of a location argument as object to be different in the two instances. The *wipe* verbs can be characterized in terms of their aktionsart – the inherent temporal structure of the events they denote. Each of the *wipe* verbs is an activity verb in the sense of Vendler (1957). Activity verbs denote events that, in the absence of a specific goal or temporal endpoint, have indefinite duration. The *wipe* verbs, like activity verbs in general, can be subdivided into a number of syntactically relevant semantically coherent subclasses. We discuss two subclasses that account for many of the *wipe* verbs.

Many members of the manner subclass of the *wipe* verbs are verbs denoting contact with a surface through motion of some entity, as also proposed by Jackendoff (1990); among them are the verb *wipe* itself, as well as the verbs *rub*, *scrape*, and *scrub*. Each verb in this subclass describes a particular type of surface contact that involves moving an entity against a surface. The surface is what we have called the location argument, while the moved entity is only optionally expressed with these verbs via an instrumental phrase (*Kay wiped the counter with a wet sponge*). The verbs is this subclass differ from each other in the specific type of motion that is involved in the surface contact, and, if an instrument is involved, in the type of instrument used. For instance, wiping usually involves a cloth or a sponge, but a cloth would not be a possible instrument for scraping.

A property that suggests that some *wipe* verbs are verbs of surface contact through motion is that many of them are found in the conative construction illustrated in (22b), as well as in the locatum-as-object variant (22a):

(22) a. Kay rubbed/scraped the counter.
b. Kay rubbed/scraped at the counter.

The conative construction is characterized by a change in the transitivity of the verb (the verb is used intransitively in the conative construction, with the noun phrase that was the direct object when the verb was used transitively expressed in a prepositional phrase headed by the preposition *at*), as well as by a slight change in meaning. This construction is attested with verbs whose meaning includes notions of both movement and contact (Guerssel et al., 1985; Laughren, 1988). The verbs found in this construction are drawn from several semantic classes; they include verbs of impact by contact, such as *hit* or *kick*, and verbs of contact and effect, such as *cut* or *hack*. Simple verbs of contact and simple verbs of motion are not found in this construction (**Terry touched at the cat*, **Nina moved at the table*). The conative construction is also not found with verbs of change of state, including the *clear* verbs (**Francesca cooled at the coffee*, **Martha emptied at the tub*), since they lack the appropriate meaning components. As expected, there are verbs that qualify as verbs of contact through motion but which are not understood as verbs of removal; for example, the verb *dab*, which like other verbs of contact through motion, undergoes the conative alternation (*Shelly dabbed at her face*).

As Jackendoff (1990) points out, it is possible to wipe a table even if its surface is already clean and clear so that there is nothing to remove from it. This property is consistent with the characterization of the verb *wipe* as a verb of surface contact through motion rather than as a verb of removal. In fact, this observation can be taken further. There is another property of the *wipe* verbs that receives a natural explanation if these verbs are not verbs of removal in their basic sense: some of these verbs are used not only as verbs of removal but also as verbs of putting, as shown in (23):

(23) a. Kay wiped the polish onto the table.
b. Lynn scraped the leftovers into a bowl.

This property is problematic if these verbs are basically verbs of removal since putting and removing are opposite activities. But if the putting and removal senses of these verbs are both extended senses of these verbs, as we will suggest in section 5, then no problem arises.

The verb *shovel* and the other members of the instrument subclass of the *wipe* verbs are again activity verbs. They simply denote the activity typically performed with the instrument from which the verb takes its name (see Clark & Clark, 1979, for discussion). These verbs also are not necessarily verbs of removal. As illustrated in (24) and (25), some of them can also be used as verbs of putting:

(24) Sylvia shovelled the snow onto the lawn.
(25) Kelly raked the leaves into the gutter.

It appears that whether a verb that takes its name from an instrument can be used as a verb of removal or as a verb of putting depends on the nature of the instrument involved. Thus there are verbs that take their names from instruments that are not understood as either verbs of removal or verbs of putting, such as *microwave* and *saw*.

The *wipe* verbs also contrast with the *clear* verbs in not participating in the causative/inchoative alternation. A similar contrast can be observed elsewhere in the English lexicon. Consider the verbs *cut* and *break*, which both appear to denote actions that involve a "separation in the material integrity" of some entity (Hale & Keyser, 1986, 1987). The verb *cut* lexicalizes a means component (the use of a sharp instrument). The verb *break* does not lexicalize a means component – entities can be broken in a variety of ways – but it does lexicalize a resultant state. Thus the meanings of the verbs *cut* and *break* contrast in much the same way as those of *wipe* and *clear*. Furthermore, the verb *cut* is not found in the causative/inchoative alternation (*Kelly cut the cake/*The cake cut*), though the verb *break* is (*Sharon broke the glass/The glass broke*).

It appears that verbs that lexicalize a means components cannot be used intransitively in the sense associated with the inchoative variant of the causative/inchoative alternation (see also Guerssel et al., 1985). We attribute this property to the means component, whose presence requires the verb to select an explicit agent or cause as an argument. This requirement cannot be met in the inchoative variant, which simply describes a change of state without specifying its cause. The causative construction must be used when the cause must be expressed.[9]

In this section we have argued that the *clear* and *wipe* verbs in their basic sense are not verbs of removal. Rather the *clear* verbs are verbs of change of state, and the *wipe* verbs are activity verbs. The elements of meaning which are lexicalized in these verbs determine the basic classification of the verbs and their behavior. What we have called the location-as-object variant is simply the way these two types of verbs express their arguments. The *clear* verbs and the *wipe* verbs might appear to be verbs of removal even in the location-as-object frame, but this impression results from real-world knowledge associated with the events these verbs denote and is not part of their linguistic classification. The analysis of the meaning of the *clear* and *wipe* verbs proposed in this section explains why these verbs behave differently from verbs of removal. In section 6 we show that these classifications also account for the differences between the *clear* and *wipe* verbs with respect to the possibility noted in section 2 of expressing the locatum argument in an *of* phrase. But first we turn to the question of why these verbs, if they are not verbs of removal, are found in the syntactic frame associated with verbs like *remove*.

5. The locatum-as-object variant again

Suppose we take the expression of arguments manifested by the verb *remove* to be that characteristic of verbs of removal. That is, verbs of removal express their arguments as in the locatum-as-object variant ("NP V NP FROM NP"). We could propose that when verbs such as *clear* and *wipe* express their arguments like *remove* they are indeed verbs of removal, even though when found in the location-as-object variant they belong to another semantic class. Thus the *clear* and *wipe* verbs would have several distinct but related meanings. Is there evidence for this approach? And is there a way to explain the multiple classification of these verbs?

In English, verbs may systematically acquire additional meanings through a process of *lexical extension*, described in detail by Levin and Rapoport (1988). This process systematically creates extended senses of a verb in a regular manner

[9]This property is consistent with our suggestion in footnote 8 that when a verb denotes an action in which an agent is inherently implicated the verb cannot show an inchoative form.

from its basic sense. For example, lexical extension would relate the basic sense of the verb *bake* as a change-of-state verb (*Tracy baked the potatoes*) to its extended sense as a verb of creation (*Tracy baked a cake*), where the verb means roughly "create by means of change of state *bake*" (see Atkins, Kegl, & Levin, 1988). Similarly, verbs of sound emission manifest a wide range of extended senses, including an extended sense as verbs of motion – "move while emitting the characteristic sound" – as in *The bullet whistled by her* or *A large truck rumbled down the street* (Levin, 1991).[10]

Knowledge of possible extended senses and the factors that license them are an important part of the lexical knowledge of a speaker of English. Such systematically related extended senses are typically licensed by a combination of necessary conditions (the word's basic semantic class membership) and sufficient conditions (properties related to those aspects of a word's meaning that set it apart from other class members). For example, belonging to one of several semantic classes, including the class of verbs of sound emission, is necessary for a verb to show an extended sense as a verb of motion; the sufficient condition that a verb of sound emission must meet is that the sound is one that is emitted as the movement happens. Thus the verb *purr* only has an extended sense as a verb of motion for certain choices of subject. Contrast **The cat purred down the street*, which is unacceptable since purring is not a necessary concomitant of a cat's motion, with *The beautiful new Mercedes purred along the autobahn*,[11] where the motion of a car is necessarily accompanied by the sound of its engine. Consider also *The bullet whistled by her*, where whistling is the sound emitted as a bullet moves.

Levin and Rapoport (1988) represent lexical extension as a process of subordination which relates lexical semantic representations of verb meaning that take the form of predicate decompositions (see also Laughren, 1988). When a verb undergoes lexical subordination, the lexical semantic representation associated with its basic meaning is subordinated under a newly introduced primitive predicate using a subordinating function. For instance, a subordinating function "by means of" is used in deriving creation *bake*, which means roughly "create by means of change of state *bake*", from change of state *bake*.[12] A verb's semantic class membership will shift when it manifests an extended meaning, and the verb will take on the behavior appropriate to the semantic type of the extended meaning. As a consequence, a verb's syntactic behavior will be different in its basic and extended meanings. (See Atkins et al., 1988; Laughren, 1988; and

[10]Lexical extension is not restricted to the verb lexicon. For example, nouns like *reel* or *cup*, which refer to a container, can be used to refer to the quantity of material held in such a container (*a reel of thread* or *a cup of milk*) For further discussion, see Apresjan, 1973; Atkins, 1991; Brugman and Lakoff, 1988; Cruse, 1986; Leech, 1981; Norvig, 1989; among others.

[11]We thank a reviewer for pointing this example out to us.

[12]See Levin and Rapoport (1988) for explicit lexical semantic representations. See Pustejovsky (1989) for a somewhat different approach to the relation between change of state *bake* and creation *bake*.

Levin, 1991, for some discussion.) For instance, as discussed by Atkins et al., only change of state *bake*, and not creation *bake*, shows the causative/inchoative alternation typical of change-of-state verbs; creation *bake* shows properties that are appropriate to verbs of creation, such as the benefactive alternation (*bake a cake for someone/bake someone a cake*).

Let us look now at the *wipe* verbs. We suggest that when a *wipe* verb is found in the syntactic frame associated with verbs of removal ("NP V NP FROM NP"), it is manifesting an extended use as a verb of removal. Although the *wipe* verbs are basically various types of activity verbs such as verbs of surface contact through motion, those *wipe* verbs that denote activities that can effect the removal of something from a location can take on an extended sense as verbs of removal. Removal *wipe* would mean "remove by means of surface contact through motion *wipe*". As a verb of removal, *wipe* would be expected to express its arguments like other verbs of removal. Furthermore, removal *wipe* should show the properties associated with verbs of removal and not those associated with verbs of surface contact through motion. For instance, verbs of removal are not found in the conative construction, as shown in (26), and, in fact, the conative construction is not possible with those *wipe* verbs that are otherwise found in the conative alternation when they are used in the removal sense, as shown in (27) (compare (22b)):

(26) a. Monica removed the groceries from the bag.
b. *Monica removed at the groceries from the bag.

(27) a. Kay rubbed the fingerprints from the counter.
b. *Kay rubbed at the fingerprints from the counter.

As mentioned in the previous section, the *wipe* verbs can be used either as verbs of putting or as verbs of removal. The putting and removal senses of the *wipe* verbs share the same component of meaning lexicalized in the verb: the means component. However, the verb *wipe* would mean "remove by means of surface contact through motion *wipe*" in its removal sense, and "put by means of surface contact through motion *wipe*" in its putting sense. The means component determines the basic sense of the *wipe* verbs, as well as their possible extended senses. Our knowledge of the potential real-world uses of the means lexicalized in these verbs determines which of the extended senses of the *wipe* verbs are possible. The option of demonstrating removal and putting senses seems to be available when the means can effect either removing or putting, as with the verbs *wipe*, *scrape*, and *shovel*. When the means can be used only to remove something or only to add something, then the dual senses are not found. For example, the verb *vacuum* can only have the verb of removal extended sense and not the verb of putting extended sense (*Andrea vacuumed the sand off the floor/*Andrea vacuumed the sand into the corner*).

A lexical extension analysis can also be applied to the *clear* verbs to explain their use in the locatum-as-object variant. We might propose that removal *clear* means something like "remove by means of change of state *clear*".[13] Again, due to the class shift associated with the extended meaning, the *clear* verbs in their removal sense should show the properties of verbs of removal and not those of verbs of change of state. Evidence in favor of this comes from examining the behavior of *clear* verbs in the middle construction (Keyser & Roeper, 1984; Hale & Keyser, 1987; among others). This construction resembles the inchoative (intransitive) variant in the causative/inchoative alternation superficially, but differs from it in several respects. Sentences (28b) and (28c) illustrate, respectively, inchoative and middle uses of the verb *dry*:

(28) a. Tony dried the cotton clothes.
b. The cotton clothes dried.
c. Cotton clothes dry easily.

First, the middle construction, unlike the inchoative construction, does not denote an event. Second, the middle construction may imply an agent, but the inchoative construction need not. Third, the middle construction typically includes an adverbial phrase such as *easily*. Finally, the middle construction is found with some verbs that are not found in the causative/inchoative alternation, such as *cut* (*Freshly baked bread cuts easily*/**The freshly baked bread cut.*)

Change-of-state verbs are among the types of verbs found in the middle construction (Hale & Keyser, 1987), but removal verbs are not, as shown by the contrast in (29). The *clear* verbs are only found in the middle construction on their change-of-state sense, as shown by (30a) and (31a), and not on their removal sense, as shown in (30b) and (31b):[14]

(29) a. Cotton clothes dry easily.
b. *Groceries remove from bags easily.
(30) a. This new oven cleans without any trouble.
b. *Even the toughest grease spots clean with no bother from this oven.
(31) a. This new type of bathtub empties in a flash.
b. *Even the dirtiest water empties easily from this new bathtub.

[13]It is likely that the subordinating function "by means of" is not quite appropriate here, and that the list of subordinating functions needs to be expanded. See Laughren (1988), for discussion of a range of subordinating functions found in the Australian language Warlpiri.

[14]Some speakers have said that the verb *remove* might be found in the middle construction in sentences such as ?*Some ink spots remove easily*, but this sentence involves a different, change-of-state, sense of *remove*, which might be paraphrased as "cause to disappear" rather than "cause to change location". Notice that the example degrades with the addition of a *from* phrase, as in ??*Some ink spots remove easily from cotton fabrics*, since the presence of this phrase favors the removal interpretation.

6. The *of* phrase

As discussed in section 2, the *clear* verbs are set apart from the *wipe* verbs with respect to the syntactic frames they are found in. Only the *clear* verbs are found in the *of* variant:

(32) Doug cleared the table of dishes.

This property of the *clear* verbs can be explained in part by noting that the set of adjectives related to the *clear* verbs can each take a complement expressed by means of an *of* phrase:

(33) clear of snow, clean of bugs, empty of water

The ability of these adjectives to take a complement can be attributed to the type of state they denote: it is a state that is characterized by a lack of something. Adjectives denoting such states are basically two-place predicates. Like all adjectives, one of their arguments is the entity that the state denoted by the adjective is predicated of: the "subject" of the adjective. Their second argument, expressed in the *of* phrase, is the thing with respect to which this state of being without holds. For example, if a table is clear of dishes, then the state of being clear holds with respect to dishes, and the table itself may not be totally clear.

The use of an *of* phrase is not restricted to the *clear* verbs and related adjectives. Such *of* phrases are also found with other adjectives that are similar in meaning to those in (33), even though not all of these adjectives have similarly related verbs:[15]

(34) bare of furniture, bereft of friends, devoid of content, free of debts

These *of* phrases also occur with some verbs that are found only in the "NP V NP *of* NP" frame that characterizes the *of* variant; that is, they do not show the alternate expressions of arguments available to the *clear* verbs:

[15]The verbs *bare* and *free* are deadjectival, although they do not behave like the *clear* verbs. We assume that they exemplify the idiosyncrasies that are associated with the lexicon. Specifically, as a reviewer points out, the meaning of the verb *bare* has become more lexicalized than that of some of the other verbs examined; its meaning is something like "reveal" or "expose", rather than "cause to be bare", the sense that would be parallel to the *clear* verbs. The verb *free* is found in the same syntactic frames as *clear*, but never with a single set of noun phrases filling the argument slots (*free a bird from a cage/*free a cage of a bird*; *free a man of responsibilities/*free responsibilities from a man*). We believe that there are different senses of the verb *free* involved in the different syntactic frames, and that these senses can be shown to have meanings compatible with the syntactic frames they are found in. However, showing this would require an extensive and detailed study of the meaning of this verb that would go beyond the scope of this paper.

(35) *Deprive* verbs: bilk, cheat, defraud, denude, deprive, dispossess, fleece, rid, rob, . . .

(36) a. The government cannot deprive the accused of the right to a fair trial.
b. *The government cannot deprive the right to a fair trial from the accused.

Like the *clear* verbs when they are found in the *of* variant, the meaning of these verbs, which we refer to as the *deprive* verbs, is roughly "cause to come to be in a state of being without". These verbs differ from the *clear* verbs in one other fundamental respect: they are not found in the causative/inchoative alternation. It is possible that they lack this property because they denote events in which agents are inherently implicated (see footnote 8).

It is difficult to characterize precisely the relationship that holds between the locatum and location arguments in the "NP V NP *of* NP" syntactic frame associated with both the *clear* verbs and the *deprive* verbs. This relationship is different from the one in the locatum-as-object variant, where it is simply a relationship of location: the locatum is located at the location. The relationship in the *of* variant involves something more; there must be some sort of "inherent" connection between the locatum and location. This relationship might be compared to the relationship that holds between the first object and the second object when *give* and other dative alternation verbs are found in the double object variant, (37b), but not in the *to* variant, (37a):[16]

(37) a. Carla gave a present to Tina.
b. Carla gave Tina a present.

With dative verbs, the double object variant is used to express the notion "cause to have", which could involve a transfer of possession (*give someone a present*), but might also involve a more abstract notion of "cause to have" which does not actually involve a transfer of possession (*give someone a headache*, *give someone an idea*). Semantically, the *of* variant of the *clear* verbs appears to be the inverse of the double object variant of the dative alternation verbs. Just as the double object variant is used to express "cause to have", the *of* variant is used to express "cause not to have". The parallel is particularly strong as the *of* variant is used to express a range of meanings: from instances where "cause not to have" could involve actual removal from a location (*clear the table of dishes*) to instances where a more abstract sense of "cause not to have" is involved, one that involves no actual physical movement (*clear someone of guilt*).

The fact that the "NP V NP *of* NP" construction is used to express more than simple location is reflected in the fact that with the *clear* verbs not all instances of

[16]See studies of the dative alternation such as Green (1974) or Oehrle (1976) for more discussion of this relationship.

the *of* variant can be paraphrased by a locatum-as-object variant involving the same *clear* verb, just as it has been noted that not all instances of the double object variant with dative alternation verbs can be paraphrased by the *to* variant (*give someone a headache* but **give a headache to someone*). Consider the following example:

(38) a. The judge cleared the accused of guilt.
b. *The judge cleared guilt from the accused.

Guilt is an abstract property that must be associated with a person; the relationship between the two is not one of location. Such properties are frequently expressed in *of* phrases, both with *clear* verbs, as in (39), and *deprive* verbs, as in (40); some of the *deprive* verbs are almost exclusively found with such *of* phrases:

(39) a. . . . an initial probe had cleared him of wrongdoing. (Example from the AP news wire)
b. Under cross-examination, Jefferies testified that on March 30, 1987, he emptied his office of notes on his daily activities after October 1986. (Example from the AP news wire)

(40) a. . . . the plan deprived them of political power and fair representation. (Example from the AP news wire)
b. . . . they were being robbed of their civilized values . . . (Example from the AP news wire)

An examination of naturally occurring instances of the *clear* and *deprive* verbs in the AP news wire[17] confirms that there is an inherent connection between the location and locatum in the syntactic frame "NP V NP *of* NP". The most prevalent examples of the verb *clear* in the *of* variants take the following form: clearing people, companies, or governments of wrongdoing, allegations, charges, suspicion, complicity. These examples all involve abstract properties. Other examples include: clearing a complex of militants, a building of personnel, a mine of fumes, a ship of debris, and a patient of port wine stains. All these examples could be viewed as instances of inalienable possession, where inalienable possession is interpreted in a broad sense.

The fact that an *of* phrase cannot appear with the *wipe* verbs can be attributed to the fact that these verbs do not lexically specify a resultant state, let alone a resultant state that the *of* phrase can be associated with. However, if an appropriate resultant state could be added to the meaning of a *wipe* verb then we might expect an *of* phrase to appear. The state that results from the action denoted by a *wipe* verb can be introduced periphrastically using the resultative

[17]These examples were provided by D. Hindle of AT&T Bell Laboratories.

construction, as in (41):

(41) a. Kay wiped the counter clean.
b. Sylvia shovelled the walk clear.

When a *wipe* verb is used as the main verb in a resultative construction, the state of the location argument that results from the action denoted by the verb can be expressed explicitly in an adjective phrase predicated of this argument. For instance, in (41a) the counter becomes clean as a result of being wiped, while in (41b) the walk becomes clear as a result of being shovelled. When adjectives like *clear* are used in the resultative construction, they can still take an *of* phrase which describes the element with respect to which the state holds. In this way the locatum argument of a *wipe* verb can be expressed when the location is expressed as the object:

(42) a. Kay wiped the counter clean of fingerprints.
b. . . . it was said she had worked like a Trojan to scrub the house clean of decades of muddy boot-prints . . . (S. Webster, *Small Tales of a Town*, 1988, p. 19)
c. Army troops shovelled Pennsylvania Avenue clear of snowdrifts. (Example from the AP news wire)

The asymmetry in the way that the *clear* and *wipe* verbs express the locatum argument is tied to the fact that the *wipe* verbs do not lexically encode a resultant state. The nature of this difference confirms the characterization of the basic meaning of the members of the two verbs classes proposed in section 3.

However, occasionally *wipe* verbs are found taking an *of* phrase directly, as in the following examples:

(43) a. Although this year the school was shorn of his name and the Marxist curriculum, Karl Marx remains in the glass-covered courtyard. (A. Shelley, "Behind the Facades, Surprises in Budapest", *NYT Travel Section*, 22 July, 1990, p. 29)
b. . . . but Uncle Mosin, who skimmed the city of scandal and news, had warned that there were rumours of riots. (A. Hosain, *Sunlight on a Broken Pillar*, Virago, London, 1988, p. 71)
c. . . . the palm trees are trimmed of unsightly brown fronds . . . (S. Grafton, "*A*" *is for Alibi*, Bantam, New York, 1987, p. 8)

We suggest that when a *wipe* verb is used in this way, it manifests a sense that is consistent with the meaning we have previously seen to be associated with the frame "NP V NP *of* NP". That is, the verb means "cause something to come to be in a state of being without". In fact, the means component becomes almost incidental in the examples in these uses of the *wipe* verbs and sometimes even disappears completely. For instance, (43a) simply means that the school was deprived of its name; there is no sense in which the school lost its name through the use of shears. Such uses of the *wipe* verbs may come about since the action denoted by each of the *wipe* verbs in its basic sense may result in a change in the state of the locatum arguments – often a change into a state of being without. It is significant that the verbs are in the adjectival passive form in several of the examples in (43), since the adjectival passive necessarily focuses on the state that results from an action. As in the other instances of the "NP V NP *of* NP" syntactic frame, there is an inherent connection between the location and locatum. For instance, a frond is an inalienable part of a palm tree and a name must be attached to a person, animal, or place. The existence of such a sense of the *wipe* verbs gives the impression that the *wipe* verbs pattern like *clear* verbs, although they are not inherently change-of-state verbs in their basic sense.

7. The locative alternation revisited

The verbs *clear* and *wipe*, as well as other verbs that pattern like them, have sometimes been considered a subclass of the larger class known as the *locative alternation verbs* (see, for example, Fraser, 1971; Hook, 1983; Rappaport & Levin, 1988), a set of verbs whose best-known members are the much discussed *spray/load* verbs (Anderson, 1971; Jackendoff, 1990; Jeffries and Willis, 1984; Rappaport & Levin, 1988; Schwartz-Norman, 1976; among others). The *clear* verbs and the *wipe* verbs have been grouped with the *spray/load* verbs because, as shown in a squib by Fraser (1971), the two classes of verbs share a variety of properties, including the ability to participate in a comparable alternation in the expression of arguments. The alternation shown by the *spray/load* verbs is illustrated in (44):

(44) a. The farmer loaded hay on the truck.
     b. The farmer loaded the truck with hay.
(45) a. Phyllis sprayed the wall with paint.
     b. Phyllis sprayed paint on the wall.

From the perspective of meaning, the *clear* and *wipe* verbs could be considered inverses of the *spray/load* verbs. The *spray/load* verbs describe the putting of a locatum at some location; as mentioned, the *clear* and *wipe* verbs can be roughly characterized as describing the removal of a locatum from a location. The ability to express the location either as direct object or via a prepositional phrase is probably the most important of the properties that the verbs *clear* and *wipe* share with the *spray/load* verbs. The property has led to the suggestion that *clear* and *wipe*, as well as *spray* and *load*, are part of a larger set of locative alternation verbs.

We now briefly consider the implications of our lexical semantic analysis of the *clear* and *wipe* verbs for the nature of the locative alternation. We have proposed that each alternate expression of arguments of these verbs is associated with a distinct sense of the verb and is determined by that sense of the verb. The verb senses in the different variants are related by the process of lexical extension and, therefore, share certain components of meaning, which create a relationship between the variants. As mentioned in section 2, we claim that the locative alternation as manifested by the *clear* and *wipe* verbs is not a simple alternation in the expression of the arguments of verbs that each have a single sense.

Our analysis of the *clear* and *wipe* verbs raises the question of whether the range of data grouped under the label "locative alternation" constitutes a unified phenomenon. On this analysis, the relationship between the variants of the *clear* and *wipe* verbs is different from the relationship between the variants of the *spray/load* verbs, as characterized in Rappaport and Levin (1988). Although our account of the *spray/load* verbs also appealed to the notion of lexical extension to explain the relationship between the variants, we proposed that the sense of a *spray/load* verb in the locatum-as-object variant, (44a), is basic, while that in the location-as-object variant, (44b), is derived via lexical extension. We assume that in the locatum-as-object variant these verbs denote a simple change of location, and in the location-as-object variant these verbs denote a change of state brought about by means of the change of location.[18]

A comparison of this analysis of the *spray/load* verbs with that of the *clear* and *wipe* verbs shows that the two analyses reverse which of the variants is associated with the basic sense of the verb and which with the extended sense. For the *clear* and *wipe* verbs, we claim that the locatum-as-object variant involves the extended sense of the verbs, while the location-as-object variant involves the basic sense. However, with both types of verbs, each variant realizes its arguments in accordance with independently necessary linking rules, given the semantic type of the verb sense in that variant.[19]

[18]In Rappaport and Levin (1988), we offer some justification for this choice of which variant reflects the basic sense of the verb and which the extended sense, using considerations other than lexicalization. But the component of meaning lexicalized can also be used to make this decision: the means/manner lexicalized by the *spray/load* verbs often imposes strict selectional restrictions on the locatum, but not on the location.

[19]The locative alternation verbs have attracted attention because they demonstrate what has become known as the holistic/partitive effect: when the location argument is expressed as the object of the verb, there is an implication that the location is wholly affected by the action denoted by the verb that does not necessarily hold when the location is expressed via a prepositional phrase. For example, in *clear dishes from the table*, some dishes may still be left on the table, while in *clear the table of dishes*, it is unlikely that any dishes are left on the table. There is much debate concerning the characterization and nature of this effect; see Anderson, 1971; Jeffries and Willis, 1984; Schwartz-Norman, 1976; among others for discussion. The holistic/partitive effect as manifested with the *clear* verbs might well be linked to the nature of the *of* variant and the location-as-object variant: both denote a change of state in the location argument. A similar suggestion is made by Rappaport and Levin (1988) to account for the effect as it is found with *spray/load* verbs.

8. Conclusion

This study shows how a careful examination of verb meaning reveals that what at first might appear to be idiosyncratic properties concerning the expression of the arguments of a variety of verbs reflect differences in their meaning. We started by examining a set of verbs that all appeared to be associated with the notion of removal. We identified various semantically coherent subclasses among these verbs, each with distinctive behavior, and we showed that the members of two of these classes, the *clear* and *wipe* verb classes, were not inherently verbs of removal. Two components of meaning were shown to be important in the characterization of the meaning of the members of these classes: means and resultant state.

This observation is significant because other lexical semantic investigations suggest that essentially the same meaning components are relevant to the characterization of other linguistically significant classes of verbs. As discussed in Levin and Rappaport (1989) and Levin and Rappaport Hovav (1991), verbs of motion fall into a class of verbs of inherently directed motion, the *arrive* verbs, and a class of verbs of manner of motion, which further subdivides into two classes, the *run* and *roll* verbs; see the examples in (46):

(46) a. *arrive* class: arrive, come, go, depart, fall, return, descend . . .
b. *roll* class: roll, slide, move, swing, spin, rotate . . .
run class: run, walk, gallop, jump, hop, skip, swim . . .

The *arrive* verbs specify a direction of motion but no manner or means of motion, while the *run* and *roll* verbs specify a manner or means of motion but no direction. The notion of direction is in some sense analogous to the notion of resultant state; both can be viewed as providing an event with a type of goal. Furthermore, Gentner (1978) suggests that verbs of combining can also be subdivided according to whether they describe the manner or means of combining (e.g., *stir*, *shake*, or *beat*) or the result of this process (e.g., *mix* or *blend*). The importance of the notions of result/direction and manner/means in the organization of verb meaning has also received considerable support from research in child language acquisition. Gentner (1978), Gropen (1989), Gropen, Pinker, Hollander, and Goldberg (1991), and Pinker (1989) have suggested that children are sensitive to this distinction in their acquisition of new words.

We conclude by pointing out an interesting generalization about possible verb meanings that emerges from these studies: there do not seem to be verbs in English that lexicalize both manner/means and result/direction components. Why should these meaning components be in complementary distribution? In Levin and Rappaport Hovav (1991), we suggest that results and directions, unlike means or manners, can be used to delimit the time course of an event.

Specifically, the notions of result and direction seem to be closely tied to the notion of telicity (boundedness in time), which figures prominently in the literature on the lexical aspect of verbs – the inherent temporal structure of the event denoted by a verb (Dowty, 1979; Vendler, 1957; among others). In contrast, the notions of means and manner appear to be connected to the notion of durativeness. The complementary distribution of these meaning components may reflect the impossibility of having a verb that denotes an event that is both bounded and not bounded in time. Further research will perhaps give more insight into this aspect of the "syntax of lexical semantics".

Appendix: How many *clear* verbs are there?

In this appendix, we briefly discuss why the set of *clear* verbs has sometimes been taken to be larger than we have suggested in this paper; see, for example, Fraser (1971), Hook (1983).[20] A variety of other verbs have been cited as showing the same possible pattern of expression of arguments as *clear*, and particularly the ability to be found in the "NP V NP *of* NP" syntactic frame. However, many of these verbs are more accurately grouped with the *wipe* verbs in their basic sense; these include the verb *prune*, cited by Fraser, and the verbs *shear*, *skim*, *shave*, and *wring*, cited by Hook, and the verb *trim* cited by both Fraser and Hook. These verbs lexicalize a means component, and, like other *wipe* verbs, are not found in the causative/inchoative alternation. Despite being grouped with the *clear* verbs in some work, they are only occasionally found with *of* phrases, again under the same circumstances as the other *wipe* verbs. The presence of these phrases can receive the explanation we proposed in section 6 for *of* phrases found with *wipe* verbs.

The verb *strip* is one of two verbs frequently found with *of* phrases that require slightly different treatment. We believe that, despite this property, this verb is not a *clear* verb. It does not participate in the causative/inchoative alternation that is a hallmark of change of state verbs (*Monica stripped the dresser*/ **The dresser stripped*). Furthermore, only when used to describe the stripping of furniture or walls does it lexicalize a manner component. Although this verb is found more often in the "NP V NP *of* NP" frame than other *wipe* verbs, it is significant that in this frame the manner component – removing strips – is completely lost. The verb *strip* in this frame become a *deprive* verb and simply means "cause to come to be in a state of being without", as in (47); such uses cannot be paraphrased by the "NP V NP FROM NP" frame:

[20]Hook's list of alternating verbs is much more extensive than Fraser's. We find that a number of verbs he lists do not easily enter into the same range of syntactic frames as *clear*; among them are *abstract*, *loot*, *plunder*, and *sap*. None of these verbs alternates easily for us. We do not consider them further.

(47) Rastropovich was stripped of his Soviet citizenship in 1978 . . . (Example from the AP news wire)

We suggest that this shift in the meaning of *strip* is an idiosyncratic property of this verb, an idiosyncrasy of the kind we expect to find in the lexicon.

Finally, we turn briefly to the verb *drain*, which again shows the expression of arguments typical ot *clear* verbs. We chose not to include it among the *clear* verbs in our earlier discussion for expository purposes, although we believe, that, like the *clear* verbs, it is a verb of change of state. Like other change-of-state verbs, *drain* participates in the causative/inchoative alternation (*The lifeguard drained the pool/The pool drained slowly*); however, unlike the *clear* verbs listed in (10), it does not take its name from a resultant state, as reflected in the fact that it is not deadjectival. This verb is not unique in this respect; there are other change of state verbs that are not related to adjectives (e.g., *thaw*, *freeze*, *melt*, *break*, *shrink*), suggesting that the verb *drain* has been correctly included with the *clear* verbs in other work.

References

Anderson, S.R. (1971). On the role of deep structure in semantic interpretation. *Foundations of Language*, *7*, 387–396.

Apresjan, Ju.D. (1973). Regular polysemy. *Linguistics*, *142*, 5–32.

Atkins, B.T. (1991). Building a lexicon: The contribution of lexicography. *International Journal of Lexicography*, *4:4*. To be co-published in M. Bates & R. Weischedel (Eds.), *Challenges in natural language processing*. Cambridge, UK: Cambridge University Press.

Atkins, B.T., Kegl, J., & Levin, B. (1988). Anatomy of a verb entry: From linguistic theory to lexicographic practice. *International Journal of Lexicography*, *1*, 84–126.

Boguraev, B. (1991). Building a lexicon: The contribution of computers. *International Journal of Lexicography*, *4:4*. To be co-published in M. Bates & R. Weischedel (Eds.), *Challenges in natural language processing*. Cambridge, UK: Cambridge University Press.

Boguraev, B., Byrd, R.J., Klavans, J.L., & Neff, M. (1989). From structural analysis of lexical resources to semantics in a lexical knowledge base. Position paper prepared for the Workshop on Lexicon Acquisition, IJCAI, Detroit.

Brousseau, A.-M. & Ritter, E. (1991). A non-unified analysis of agentive verbs. *Proceedings of the Tenth West Coast Conference on Formal Linguistics*.

Brugman, C., & Lakoff, G. (1988). Cognitive topology and lexical networks. In S. Small, G. Cottrell & M. Tanenhaus (Eds.), *Lexical ambiguity resolution* (pp. 477–508). Los Altos, CA: Morgan Kaufmann.

Burzio, L. (1986). *Italian syntax: A government-binding approach*. Dordrecht: Reidel.

Carter, R.J. (1976). Some constraints on possible words. *Semantikos*, *1*, 27–66.

Carter, R.J. (1988). *On linking: Papers by Richard Carter* (Lexicon Project Working Papers 25), B. Levin & C. Tenny (Eds.). Cambridge, MA: Center for Cognitive Science, MIT.

Chomsky, N.A. (1986). *Knowledge of language*. New York: Praeger.

Clark, E.V., & Clark, H.H. (1979). When nouns surface as verbs. *Language*, *55*, 767–811.

Cruse, D. (1986). *Lexical semantics*. Cambridge, UK: Cambridge University Press.

Dowty, D.R. (1979). *Word meaning and Montague grammar*. Dordrecht: Reidel.

Fillmore, C.J. (1967). The grammar of *hitting* and *breaking*. In R. Jacobs & P. Rosenbaum (Eds.), *Readings in English transformational grammar* (pp. 120–133). Waltham, MA: Ginn.

Fraser, B. (1971). A note on the *spray paint* cases. *Linguistic Inquiry*, *2*, 603–607.

Gentner, D. (1978). On relational meaning: The acquisition of verb meaning. *Child Development*, *49*, 988–998.

Green, G. (1974). *Semantics and syntactic regularity*. Bloomington, IN: Indiana University Press.

Gropen, J. (1989). *Learning locative verbs: How universal linking rules constrain productivity*. Unpublished doctoral dissertation, MIT, Cambridge, MA.

Gropen, J., Pinker, S., Hollander, M., & Goldberg, R. (1991). Affectedness and direct objects: The role of lexical semantics in the acquisition of verb argument structure. *Cognition*, this volume.

Guerssel, M., Hale, K., Laughren, M., Levin, B., & White Eagle, J. (1985). A cross-linguistic study of transitivity alternations. In W.H. Eilfort, P.D. Kroeber, & K.L. Peterson (Eds.), *Papers from the parasession on causatives and agentivity* (pp. 48–63). Chicago, IL: Chicago Linguistic Society.

Hale, K.L., & Keyser, S.J. (1986). *Some transitivity alternations in English* (Lexicon Project Working Papers 7). Cambridge, MA: Center for Cognitive Science, MIT.

Hale, K.L., & Keyser, S.J. (1987). *A view from the middle* (Lexicon Project Working Papers 10). Cambridge, MA: Center for Cognitive Science, MIT.

Hook, P.E. (1983). The English abstrument and rocking case relations. *Papers from the Nineteenth Regional Meeting of the Chicago Linguistic Society*, 183–194.

Jackendoff, R.S. (1990). *Semantic structures*. Cambridge, MA: MIT Press.

Jeffries, L. & Willis, P. (1984). A return to the spray paint issue. *Journal of Pragmatics*, *8*, 715–729.

Keyser, S.J., & Roeper, T. (1984). On the middle and ergative constructions in English. *Linguistic Inquiry*, *15*, 381–416.

Laughren, M. (1988). Towards a lexical representation of Warlpiri verbs. In W. Wilkins (Ed.), *Thematic relations* (pp. 215–242). New York: Academic Press.

Leech, J. (1981). *Semantics*. Cambridge, UK: Cambridge University Press.

Levin, B. (1991). Building a lexicon: The Contribution of Linguistic Theory. *International Journal of Lexicography 4:4*. To be co-published in M. Bates & R. Weischedel (Eds.), *Challenges in natural language processing*. Cambridge, UK: Cambridge University Press.

Levin, B., & Rappaport, M. (1989). Approaches to unaccusative mismatches. *Proceedings of the 19th Annual Meeting of the North-Eastern Linguistics Society*, 314–328.

Levin, B., & Rappaport Hovav, M. (1991). The lexical semantics of verbs of motion: The perspective from unaccusativity. In I. Roca (Ed.), *Thematic structure*: *Its role in grammar*. Berlin: Walter de Gruyter.

Levin, B., & Rapoport, T.R. (1988). Lexical subordination. *Papers from the 24th Regional Meeting of the Chicago Linguistic Society*, 275–289.

McClure, W. (1990). A lexical semantic explanation for unaccusative mismatches. In K. Dziwirik, P. Farrell, & E. Mejias-Bíkandi (Eds.), *Grammatical relations: A cross-theoretical perspective* (pp. 305–318). Stanford, CA: CSLI.

Norvig, P. (1989). Building a large lexicon with lexical network theory. In U. Zernik (Ed.), *Proceedings of the First International Lexical Acquisition Workshop*.

Oehrle, R.T. (1976). *The grammatical status of the English dative alternation*. Unpublished doctoral dissertation, MIT, Cambridge, MA.

Ostler, N.D.M. (1979). *Case-linking: A theory of case and verb diathesis applied to classical Sanskrit*. Unpublished doctoral dissertation, MIT, Cambridge, MA. Revised as N.D.M. Ostler (1980). *A theory of case linking and agreement*. Bloomington, IN: Indiana University Linguistics Club.

Ostler, N.D.M. (1980). Origins, orientations and endpoints: Evidence for a finer analysis of thematic relations. *Studies in English Linguistics*, *8*, 10–23.

Perlmutter, D.M. (1978). Impersonal passives and the unaccusative hypothesis. *Proceedings of the Fourth Annual Meeting of the Berkeley Linguistics Society*, 157–189.

Pinker, S. (1989). *Learnability and cognition: The acquisition of argument structure*. Cambridge, MA: MIT Press.

Pustejovsky, J. (1989). *The generative lexicon*. Unpublished manuscript, Brandeis University, Waltham, MA.

Rappaport, M., & Levin, B. (1988). What to do with theta-roles. In W. Wilkins (Ed.), *Thematic relations* (pp. 7–36). New York: Academic Press.

Rosen, C. (1984). The interface between semantic roles and initial grammatical relations. In D.M. Perlmutter & C. Rosen (Eds.), *Studies in relational grammar 2* (pp. 38–77). Chicago, IL: University of Chicago Press.

Schwartz-Norman, L. (1976). The grammar of "content" and "container". *Journal of Linguistics*, *12*, 279–287.

Smith, C.S. (1970). Jespersen's "move and change" class and causative verbs in English. In M.A. Jazayery, E.C. Palome, & W. Winter (Eds.), *Linguistic and literary studies in honor of Archibald A. Hill: Vol 2. Descriptive linguistics* (pp. 101–109). The Hague: Mouton.

Talmy, L. (1975). Semantics and syntax of motion. In J.P. Kimball (Ed.), *Syntax and semantics 4* (pp. 181–238). New York: Academic Press.

Talmy, L. (1985). Lexicalization patterns: Semantic structure in lexical forms. In T. Shopen (Ed.), *Language typology and syntactic description 3. Grammatical categories and the lexicon* (pp. 57–149). Cambridge, UK: Cambridge University Press.

Tenny, C. (1987). *Grammaticalizing aspect and affectedness*. Unpublished doctoral dissertation, MIT, Cambridge, MA.

Van Valin, R.D., Jr. (1990). Semantic parameters of split intransitivity. *Language*, *66*, 221–260.

Vendler, Z. (1957). Verbs and times. *Philosophical Review*, *56*, 143–160. Reprinted in Z. Vendler (1967). *Linguistics in philosophy*. Ithaca, NY: Cornell University Press.

Zaenen, A. (in preparation). Unaccusativity in Dutch: An integrated approach. In J. Pustejovsky (Ed.), *Semantics and the lexicon*. Dordrecht: Kluwer.

6

Affectedness and direct objects: The role of lexical semantics in the acquisition of verb argument structure*

Jess Gropen

Department of Psychology, McGill University.

Steven Pinker & Michelle Hollander

Department of Brain and Cognitive Sciences, Massachusetts Institute of Technology.

Richard Goldberg

Department of Psychology, University of Maryland.

How do speakers predict the syntax of a verb from its meaning? Traditional theories posit that syntactically relevant information about semantic arguments consists of a list of thematic roles like "agent", "theme", and "goal", which are linked onto a hierarchy of grammatical positions like subject, object and oblique

*We thank Kay Bock, Melissa Bowerman, Susan Carey, Eve Clark, Adele Goldberg, Jane Grimshaw, Beth Levin, Ken Wexler, and an anonymous reviewer for their helpful comments on an earlier draft. We are also grateful to the directors, parents, and especially children of the following centers: Angier After School Program, Bowen After School Care Program, Children's Village, Creative Development Center, MIT Summer Day Camp, Needham Children's Community Center, Newton Community Service Center, Newton-Wellesley Children's Corner, Plowshares Child Care Program, Recreation Place, Red Barn Nursery School, Rosary Academy Learning Center, Second Church Nursery School, Leventhal-Sidman Jewish Community Center, Temple Beth Shalom, Underwood After School Program, and the Zervas Program. This research is part of the first author's MIT doctoral dissertation. It was supported by NIH grant HD 18381 to the second author, a grant from the Alfred P. Sloan Foundation to the MIT Center for Cognitive Science, and by an NIH NRSA Postdoctoral Fellowship to the first author, which he held at the Department of Linguistics, Stanford University. Michelle Hollander is now at the Department of Psychology, University of Michigan.

object. For verbs involving motion, the entity caused to move is defined as the "theme" or "patient" and linked to the object. However, this fails for many common verbs, as in *fill water into the glass *and* *cover a sheet onto the bed. *In more recent theories verbs' meanings are multidimensional structures in which the motions, changes, and other events can be represented in separate but connected substructures; linking rules are sensitive to the position of an argument in a particular configuration. The verb's object would be linked not to the moving entity but to the argument specified as "affected" or caused to change as the main event in the verb's meaning. The change can either be one of location, resulting from motion in a particular manner, or of state, resulting from accommodating or reacting to a substance. For example,* pour *specifies how a substance moves (downward in a stream), so its substance argument is the object* (pour the water/*glass); fill *specifies how a container changes (from not full to full), so its stationary container argument is the object* (fill the glass/*water). *The newer theory was tested in three experiments. Children aged 3;4–9;4 and adults were taught made-up verbs, presented in a neutral syntactic context* (this is mooping), *referring to a transfer of items to a surface or container. Subjects were tested on their willingness to encode the moving items or the surface as the verb's object. For verbs where the items moved in a particular manner (e.g., zig-zagging), people were more likely to express the moving items as the object; for verbs where the surface changed state (e.g., shape, color, or fullness), people were more likely to express the surface as the object. This confirms that speakers are not confined to labeling moving entities as "themes" or "patients" and linking them to the grammatical object; when a stationary entity undergoes a state change as the result of a motion, it can be represented as the main affected argument and thereby linked to the grammatical object instead.*

Introduction

There is a strong correlation in English between a verb's semantic properties and its syntactic properties, and it seems obvious that speakers can sometimes exploit this pattern to predict form from meaning. Knowing that a verb *to glip* means "to shove with one's elbow", an English speaker can confidently guess that it is a transitive verb whose agent argument is mapped onto the subject role and whose patient ("acted upon") argument is mapped onto the object role. Thus the speaker would use the verb in *John glipped the dog* but not *The dog glipped John* or *John glipped to the dog*. There is evidence that children can do this as well (see Gropen, Pinker, Hollander, Goldberg, & Wilson, 1989; Pinker, 1984). Furthermore this procedure of *linking* (or *canonical mapping*; see Pinker, 1984) would work not only in English but in most other languages; agents of actions are generally subjects (Keenan, 1976), and patients are generally objects (Hopper & Thompson, 1980). What is not so obvious, however, is exactly what these linking regularities are or how they are used.

Early theories: Lists of primitive thematic roles

The first theories of linking, developed by Fillmore (1968), Gruber (1965), and Jackendoff (1972), shared certain assumptions. Each posited a list of primitive "thematic roles" – such as agent, patient, theme (moving entity in a motion event), goal, source, and location – that specified the role played by the argument with respect to the event or state denoted by the predicate. These thematic roles were linked to "grammatical relations" (subject, direct object, and oblique object) according to some canonical scheme. Usually grammatical relations are arranged in a hierarchy like "subject–object–oblique" and thematic relations are arranged in a hierarchy like "agent–patient/theme–source/location/goal". Then the thematic relations specified by the verb are linked to the highest available grammatical relation (see Bowerman, 1990; Grimshaw, 1990; Pinker, 1984; for reviews). Thus a verb with an agent and a theme would have a subject and an object; a verb with an agent and a goal, or a theme and a goal, would have either a subject and an object (e.g., *enter*) or a subject and an oblique object (e.g., *go*); and a verb with an agent, a theme, and a goal (e.g., *put*) would have a subject, an object, and an oblique object.

Theories of linking based on lists of primitive thematic roles were influential in both linguistic theory (e.g., Bresnan, 1982; Chomsky, 1981) and language acquisition research (e.g., Bowerman, 1982a; Marantz, 1982; Pinker, 1984) through the first half of the 1980s, until a number of problems became apparent.

First, the early theories predict that all verbs denoting a kind of event with a given set of participant types should display the same linking pattern, and that is not true. This is especially notable among "locative" verbs that refer to an agent causing an entity (the "content" or "figure" argument, usually analyzed as a patient and theme) to move to a place (the "container" or "ground" argument, usually analyzed as a location or goal). There are some locative verbs, which we will call "figure-object" verbs, that display the standard linking pattern, where the moving entity gets mapped onto the direct object (e.g., *pour*, as in *pour water into the glass/*pour the glass with water*). Others, which we will call "ground-object" verbs, violate it (e.g., *fill*, as in **fill water into the glass/fill the glass with water*). Some others, which we will call "alternators", permit both patterns (e.g., *brush*, as in *brush butter onto the pan/brush the pan with butter*).

In some versions of the list-of-primitives theory, verbs that violate the standard linking pattern would be noncanonical or "marked" and presumably would be rarer in the language and harder to learn. Not only does this reduce the predictive power of the theory, but its predictions do not seem to be true. Supposedly noncanonical ground-object forms may in fact be more numerous than those with the supposedly canonical figure-object syntax (Gropen, Pinker, Hollander, & Goldberg, 1991; Rappaport & Levin, 1985), and both kinds are acquired at the same time (Bowerman, 1990; Pinker, 1989). Similarly, many analyses of the dative alternation take the prepositional form (e.g., *give the book to him*) as unmarked because the theme is the object and goal is an oblique object, and the double-object form (e.g., *give him the book*) as marked because the goal is the surface object and the theme assumes a "lower" grammatical relation of second object. However, verbs taking the double-object construction are extremely common, and children do not learn the construction any later than they learn the prepositional construction (Bowerman, 1990; Gropen et al., 1989; Pinker, 1984, 1989).

A third problem with the list-of-primitives assumption is that it does not naturally explain systematic semantic differences between two forms of an alternating verb that involve the same kinds of thematic roles but different linking patterns. For example, *John loaded the cart with apples* implies that the cart is completely filled with apples, but *John loaded apples into the cart* does not. This *holistic interpretation* (Anderson, 1971) is puzzling under the list-of-primitives assumption because the arguments are labeled with the same thematic roles in both forms. This phenomenon is widely seen across constructions and languages. Across constructions we see similar semantic shifts in the difference between *Kurt climbed the mountain* and *Kurt climbed up the mountain*, only the first implying that the entire mountain has been scaled, and *Sam taught Spanish to the students* versus *Sam taught the students Spanish*, the latter suggesting that the students successfully learned Spanish (see Green, 1974; Gropen et al., 1989; Hopper & Thompson, 1980; Levin, 1985; Moravscik, 1978; Pinker, 1989; for reviews). Comparing languages we frequently find homologues to the locative alternation that involve the same kinds of verbs that alternate in English, and the holistic interpretation accompanying the ground-object form, many in languages that are genetically and areally distinct from English (Foley & Van Valin, 1985; Gropen, 1989; Moravscik, 1978; Pinker, 1989; Rappaport & Levin, 1988).

A fourth problem involves the productivity of patterns of alternation. Children and adults notice that some verbs alternate between linking patterns and extend the alternation to novel verbs. This can be seen in children's errors (e.g., *Can I fill some salt into the bear?*; Bowerman, 1982a, 1988), adults' neologisms (e.g., *fax me those data*), and children's and adults' behavior in experiments, where they are presented with sentences like *pilk the book to her* and are willing to extend it to *pilk her the book* (Gropen et al., 1989, 1991; Pinker, 1984, 1989). In standard theories this productivity is thought to be accomplished by *lexical rules*, which take a verb with its canonical linking pattern and substitute new grammatical relations (or syntactic positions) for old ones; for example, $\text{NP-V-NP}_{\text{theme}}$-*into*-$\text{NP}_{\text{goal}} \rightarrow \text{NP-V-NP}_{\text{goal}}$-*with*-$\text{NP}_{\text{theme}}$ (e.g. Bresnan, 1982; Pinker, 1984).

The problem is that the verb's semantic information relevant to linking should be exhaustively captured in its list of thematic roles. But the patterns of alternation (i.e., alternative linking patterns for one verb) vary among verbs with identical lists of thematic roles. While novel *fax me the message* sounds natural, equally novel *shout me the message*, with the same list of thematic roles according to the early theories, does not. Presumably some property of the individual verbs allows speakers to distinguish the alternating verbs, which can be input to a lexical rule relating it to a second linking pattern, from the nonalternating verbs, which cannot. But whatever this property is, the straighforward list-of-primitives approach is failing to capture it. It is important to know what these properties are and why they influence linking patterns. Since children are not reliably corrected for making errors like *fill salt into the bear* or *she said me nothing*, it would be mysterious how they unlearn the errors they do make and avoid the countless tempting ones they never make, unless they can detect the diagnostic properties and use them to constrain lexical rules (Baker, 1979; Gropen et al., 1989; Pinker, 1984, 1989).

Recent theories: Semantic structure

Recent theories aimed at solving these and other problems have abandoned the assumption that a verb's syntactically relevant semantic properties can be captured in a list of thematic role labels. Instead a verb is said to have a structured semantic representation that makes explicit the agentive, causal, and temporal properties of the event that the verb refers to. Thematic roles are not primitive types but are argument positions in these multidimensional structures; though certain traditional thematic labels like "agent" and "theme" can serve as mnemonics for some of these positions, the actual roles are more finely differentiated and the verb's interaction with syntax can be sensitive to such distinctions. For example, as we shall see there may be several kinds of "themes", and there may be roles that do not have traditional thematic labels. Examples of the newer theories may be found in Grimshaw (1990), Jackendoff (1987, 1991), Levin (1985), Levin and Rappaport Hovav (1991), Pustejovsky (1991), Tenny (1988), Dowty (1991), and Pinker (1989). See Levin (1985) for a review of how these theories are related to earlier theories of semantic decomposition such as generative semantics and the work of Miller and Johnson-Laird (1976).

Moreover, whereas the content of the thematic role labels in the early theories was dictated by the physical properties of the event, usually motion (so that the "theme" was always defined as the moving entity if there was one), semantic structure theories cross-classify thematic roles in terms of more elementary and abstract relations. Since the early analyses of Gruber (1965) and Jackendoff (1972) it has been apparent that events involving physical motion and events involving more abstract changes are expressed using parallel syntactic structures.

For example, *John went from sickness to health* parallels *John went from Boston to Chicago*, presumably reflecting a common level of mental representation underlying physical motion and more abstract "motion" in state space, that is, change of state. Although early theories could capture these parallels by assigning the same thematic labels to concrete and abstract motion events (e.g., *John* would be a "theme" in both of the preceding examples), they were not equipped to capture the parallels when a *single* argument of a single verb simultaneously played several kinds of roles. This is because the semantic content of each argument was exhaustively summarized in its role label, which corresponded to its role in physical motion if it participated in a motion event. The ability of an argument to play two roles simultaneously – one motional, one nonmotional – is the key to understanding constructions such as the locative, which present such severe problems for the list-of-primitives theory.

Semantic structure and the locative alternation

In their analyses of the locative alternation, Rappaport and Levin (1985, 1988) and Pinker (1989) show how the problematic noncanonicity of verbs like *fill* disappears under a more subtle analysis of their semantic structure and a more abstract theory of linking.

Say the semantic structure of *fill the glass with water* can be rendered as something like (1), which contrasts with the semantic structure of *pour water into the glass*, rendered in (2) (see Pinker, 1989, for a more formal representation):

(1) Cause the glass to become full of water by means of causing water to be in the glass.
(2) Cause water to go downward in a stream into the glass.

In (1), the semantic roles of *glass* and *water* cannot be exhaustively captured by any single thematic label. *Glass* is both an abstract "theme" or affected entity in a change-of-state event (changing from not full to full) and the "goal" in a change of location event. *Water* is both the "theme" or affected entity in a change-of-location event and helps define the state in the change-of-state event (it is what the glass becomes full of).

Furthermore the two events are related in a specific way. The state change is the "main event" and the location change is a subsidiary "means" of achieving it. This asymmetry between main and subsidiary events is motivated by dimensions of meaning that are closely related to thematic structure. In the realm of pragmatics, the choice of *fill* over *pour* serves to make the change of fullness of the glass, rather than the motion of the water, the highlighted feature of the event. (This effect is reinforced by the fact that within the rigid word order of English, the choice of *fill* focuses the content as the "new" entity by putting it at the end of the sentence, backgrounding the "given" container by putting it immediately after the verb, and vice versa, if *pour* is used.[1]) In the realm of aspect, the event of *filling* is understood as temporally delimited at the moment that the main event is over with, namely, when the container becomes full (see Dowty, 1991; Gropen, 1989; Tenny, 1988).

Now say that there is a linking rule such as the one in (3):

(3) Link the argument that is specified as "caused to change" in the main event of a verb's semantic representation to the grammatical object.

The change or "affectedness" that is caused can either be a change of location (i.e., a motion) *or* a change of state.[2] This would correctly map the container argument of *fill* onto the object position; it is caused to change state from not full to full. The fact that it also in some sense bears the thematic role "goal" does not disrupt this mapping; since the semantic representation is a multidimensional structure rather than a single list, the "goal" relation is specified within the "means" substructure where it does not trigger the object linking rule, which distinguishes main events from means. (Instead, the goal relation triggers a linking rule for the object of the preposition *with*; the fact that it does not have a traditional thematic role label is irrelevant.)[3]

Psychologically speaking, the "semantic structure" theory renders both *pour* (traditionally canonical) and *fill* (traditionally noncanonical) as canonical, thanks to the lexicalization of a "gestalt shift" that is possible when conceptualizing

[1]Note, however, that differences between the versions of an alternating verb cannot be *reduced* to properties of pragmatic focus. The speaker can use alternative verb structures to express differences in focus *only* to the extent that the particular verbs in the language permit it; he cannot push verbs around at will to satisfy pragmatic intentions. For example, even if the listener already knows all about a bucket becoming full and only needs to know how and with what it became full, an English speaker still may not use the semantically interpretable and pragmatically appropriate **I dripped it with maple syrup*. Conversely if the listener has background knowledge that paint has been used up but does not know how or onto what, grammar prevents the speaker from using the pragmatically natural **I coated it onto the chair*. Only for alternating verbs like *sprayed paint/sprayed the wall* can the speaker avail himself or herself of either form, depending on the discourse context. Details of the semantic representation of the phrase will necessarily differ between the forms, but will generally be consistent with the discourse difference, because differences in which entity is being asserted to be "affected" are compatible with differences in which entity is focused as "new" information.

[2]There are several other "semantic fields" such as possession, existence, or knowledge, in which a theme can be caused to change; see Jackendoff (1983, 1987, 1990) and Pinker (1989), both of which use the mnemonic "GO" to correspond to all such changes.

[3]In addition, there is a linking rule mapping the agent onto the subject; a linking rule that, in combination with other rules, maps the main event theme onto the subject if the subject has not already been linked or onto the direct object otherwise; a linking rule mapping the main event patient (i.e., an acted-upon entity, whether or not it changes) onto the direct object; and linking rules that map places, paths, and certain subordinated arguments onto oblique (prepositional) objects (see Pinker, 1989). Linking rules do not specify individual prepositions; the preposition's own semantic representation selects the appropriate kind of oblique object that it can be inserted into (Jackendoff, 1987, 1990; Pinker, 1989).

locative events. An event of filling a glass by pouring water into it can be conceptualized either as "causing water to go into a glass" (water affected) or "causing a glass to become full" (glass affected). English provides the speaker with a different verb for each perspective, and the objects of both verbs are linked to arguments with the same linking rule. The rule always picks out the affected entity in the main event, whether the affectedness involves a change of location (water for *pour*) or a change of state (glass for *fill*).

The semantic structure theory in its strongest form holds that the linking pattern of a verb is fully predictable from its meaning. At first glance this may seem circular. Since every act of moving an object to a goal is also an act of affecting the goal by forcing it to accommodate an object in some way, one might worry that the "predictability" is attained post hoc by looking at the verb's linking pattern and asserting that it means "cause to change location" just in case the moving entity is seen to be the object and "cause to change state" just in case the goal is seen to be the object. The circle is broken by a key semantic property that classifies verbs a priori as referring to change of location or change of state. Most verbs do not simply mean "move" or "change"; if they did we would have hundreds of synonyms. Rather, particular verbs mean "move in such-and-such a way" or "change in such-and-such a way". If a verb specifies *how* something moves in a main event, it must specify *that* it moves; hence we predict that for verbs that are choosy about manners of motion (but not change of state), the moving entity should be linked to the direct object role. In contrast, if a verb specifies *how* something changes state in a main event, it must specify *that* it changes state; this predicts that for verbs that are choosy about the resultant state of a changing entity (but not manner of motion), the changing entity should be linked to the direct object role. By assessing speakers' judgments about the kinds of situations that a verb can naturally refer to, we can identify which feature of the verb's meaning is specified as its main event, and predict which of its arguments is the direct object.

For example, the meaning of the verb *pour* specifies the particular manner in which a substance changes location – roughly, in a downward stream. For now it does not matter exactly how we characterize the manner in which a *poured* substance moves; what is crucial is that *some* particular manner of motion is specified in the meaning of the verb. This specificity becomes clear when we compare *pour* to closely related verbs such as *drip* and *dribble*, where equally specific, yet distinct, manners of location change are specified: an event counts as *dripping* or *dribbling*, but not *pouring*, if one drop at a time changes location. Although *pour* is choosy about how a substance moves, it is *not* choosy about the resultant state of the container or goal: one may *pour* water down the drain, out the window, into a glass, and so on. This tells us that the semantic representation of *pour* (and *drip* and *dribble*) specifies a change of location as its main event, and the affectedness linking rule, operating on the semantic representation, therefore licenses only the figure-object form of the verb. In contrast, the meaning of the verb *fill* specifies the particular way in which the ground is affected: a container must undergo a change of state from being not full to being full. Yet *fill* does *not* specify anything about the manner in which a substance is transferred: one may *fill* a container by pumping liquid into it, by pouring liquid into it, by dripping liquid into it, by dipping it into a bathtub, and so on. Hence, the affectedness linking rule maps the semantic representation for *fill* onto the ground-object form, but not the figure-object form. Verbs like *cover*, *saturate*, and *adorn* also specify only a change of state of a ground, and they, too, can only encode the ground as direct object.

Advantages of the semantic structure theory of locative verbs

Aside from accounting for the equal naturalness and acquirability of verbs like *pour* and verbs like *fill*, the semantic structure theory has several additional advantages over the list-of-primitives theory.

For one, it jointly predicts which syntactic forms are related in an alternation, and how the verb's interpretation changes when it is linked to one form or another. In the semantic structure theory, a lexical rule is an operation on a verb's semantic structure.[4] A rule for the locative alternation converts a verb's main effect representation from "cause X to go to Y" to "cause Y to change by means of causing X to be in Y". For example, when applied to the semantic representation of *splash* in which the liquid argument is specified as affected (moving in a particular manner), the rule would generate a new semantic representation in which the target of the motion is specified as affected (covered in a particular way). The syntactic effects need not be specified directly; the linking rules automatically specify *splash water onto the wall* for the first meaning, and *splash the wall with water* for the second. The main advantage of dividing the labor of argument structure alternations between meaning-altering lexical rules and general linking rules is that the *form* of each alternative is explained. It is no longer an arbitrary stipulation that *splash water onto the wall* alternates with *splash the wall with water* rather than *splash the wall the water*, *splash onto the wall against water*, or countless other possibilities (and indeed, such forms are not to be found among children's errors; Pinker, 1989). Rather, the construability of surfaces as affected or "caused to change" entities renders the ground-object form predictable.

Moreover, because the two forms related in the alternation have similar, but not identical, semantic representations, subtle meaning differences between them – such as the holism effect – are to be expected. An alternating verb like *splash* has a slightly different meaning in the ground-object form, asserting a state

[4]An essentially similar formulation can be found in Pesetsky (1990), who suggests that lexical alternations are morphological operations that affix a null morpheme onto a verb. The morpheme, though phonologically empty, has a semantic representation, which thereby alters the meaning of the whole affixed form.

change of the ground. Since the most natural interpretation of a state change is that it is the entire object that undergoes the change, rather than one part, the ground is interpreted holistically in this form. (The effect may in turn be related to the fact that themes in general are treated as dimensionless points in semantic structures, without any representation of their internal geometry; see Gropen, 1989; Jackendoff, 1983, 1990; Pinker, 1989; Talmy, 1983; for discussion.) This predicts that the holism requirement, because it is just a consequence of the most natural conceptualization of state changes, can be abrogated when the addition of the figure to one part of the ground can be construed as changing its state. Indeed *a vandal sprayed the sculpture with paint* is compatible with only a splotch of paint having been sprayed, presumably because here even one splotch is construed as ruining the sculpture (Dowty, 1991; Foley & Van Valin, 1984; Rappaport & Levin, 1985).

Another advantage is that the new linking theory can be applied to a variety of constructions in a variety of languages. Besides the ubiquity of the holism effect, noted above, there is a strong cross-linguistic tendency for affected entities to be encoded as direct objects. Verbs expressing events that are naturally construed as involving an agent that brings about a direct effect on a patient, such as verbs of causation of change of position (e.g., *slide*) or state (e.g., *melt*), or verbs of ingestion (e.g., *eat*), are almost invariably transitive across languages, with patients/themes as direct objects. In contrast, verbs that fall outside this broad semantic class, and allow different arguments to be construed as affected, show more variation within and across languages. For example, either argument can appear as the direct object of verbs of emotion (e.g., *fear* vs. *frighten*), and particular arguments waffle between direct and prepositional objects across verbs of perception (e.g., *see* vs. *look at*) and verbs of physical contact without a change in the contacted surface (*hit* vs. *hit at*); see Levin (1985), Hopper and Thompson (1980), and Talmy (1985). Even in these more ambiguous verbs, the new theory predicts that there should be a correlation between the linking pattern and the construal underlying the verb meaning, and this too seems to be true. For example, Grimshaw (1990) reviews evidence that *fear* and *frighten* are not synonymous but that the latter involves causation of a change in the object argument and hence its linking pattern is predictable. In sum, although languages differ as to which verb meanings they have, the linking rule for objects and affected entities may be universal. (See Pinker, 1989, for reviews of cross-linguistic surveys that suggest that abstract linking rules for subject and second object, as well as object, and the meaning changes that accompany alternations involving them, have very wide cross-linguistic applicability.)

Finally, the semantic structure theory helps explain which verbs undergo alternations. Consider the verb *stuff*, which can alternate between *Mary stuffed mail into the sack* and *Mary stuffed the sack with mail*. In order for an action to be an instance of *stuffing*, it cannot be the case (e.g.) that Mary simply dropped letters into the sack until it was full. In fact, it wouldn't count as *stuffing* even if Mary had wadded up a few letters before dropping them in. Instead, the mail must be forced into the sack *because* the sack is being filled to a point where its remaining capacity is too small, or just barely big enough, relative to the amount of mail that is being forced in. The semantic representation of *stuff* jointly constrains the change of location that the figure undergoes and the change of state the ground undergoes. That is why the object of *stuff* can be linked either to the figure or to the ground. (We shall return to the issue of precisely how linking applies to alternating verbs.) Other alternators also denote changes or effects simultaneously specified in terms of figure and ground. For verbs like *brush* and *dab*, force is applied pushing the figure against the ground; for *load*, the insertion of a kind of contents specific to the container enables the container to act in a designated way (e.g., a camera, or a gun). See Pinker (1989) for formal semantic representations for these and other kinds of locative verbs, for evidence motivating the form of such representations, and for a discussion of precisely how they interact with linking rules.

Developmental evidence from children's errors with existing verbs

As mentioned, one of the prime challenges of the list-of-primitives theory is that children acquire the supposedly noncanonical verbs with no more difficulty than the supposedly canonical ones. The semantic structure theory is consistent with the developmental facts noted earlier because all the verbs in question are canonical. However, these data do not rule out the possibility that children create verb argument structures solely in response to examples of use of the verbs in the parental input, without deploying general mapping patterns between meaning and form. (In that case the regularities found in the adult lexicon would have to be attributed to the accumulation of individual words coined by one-time analogies during the history of the language, possibly coupled with adults noticing redundancies in their lexicons.) Better evidence concerning children's linking mechanisms comes from the study of children's errors in using verbs in syntactic structures, because errors by definition could not have been recorded directly from the input and must be the output of some productive mechanism.

Bowerman (1982a) found that children between the ages of 4 and 7 often overuse the figure-object form, as in **Can I fill some salt into the bear?* [referring to a bear-shaped salt shaker]. Errors involving incorrect ground-object forms (e.g., **I poured you with water*) also occur, but far less frequently. Both kinds of errors, and the difference in their likelihood, were also found in experiments by Gropen et al. (1991), in which 3–8-year-old children were asked to describe pictures of locative events using verbs like *pour*, *fill*, and *dump*.

Bowerman (1982a, 1988, 1990) has drawn parallels between such errors and inflectional overregularizations of irregular verbs such as *breaked*. The child is thought to acquire many irregular verb forms from parental speech before abstracting the regular "add *-ed*" rule from pairs like *walk/walked*, and then overapplying it to the previously correct irregulars (see Marcus, Ullman, Pinker, Hollander, Rosen, & Xu, 1990). Similarly in acquiring locative verbs the child would acquire individual verbs of both the figure-object and ground-object types with the correct parental syntax, before noticing that most of them had the figure-object linking pattern. This pattern would be distilled into linking rules (of the list-of-primitives variety, though restricted to locative events) and overapplied to the ground-object verbs, resulting in errors like *fill salt*. Errors in which the opposite pattern is overapplied are presumably rarer for the same reason that inflectional errors like *brang* are less common than overregularization errors.

According to the semantic structure theory the observed asymmetry in syntactic errors could have a different source. If children are prone to making systematic mistakes about verb meaning, such as the misspecification of which entity is affected, the affectedness linking rule, even when applied correctly, would yield syntactic errors. Moreover, consistent patterns in mislearning verb meanings should lead to consistent patterns in misusing verb syntax.

Gentner (1975, 1978, 1982) has gathered evidence that children do make errors in acquiring verbs' meanings (see also Pinker, 1989, for a literature review). Furthermore some of the errors fall into a systematic pattern: children have more difficulty acquiring meaning components relevant to changes of state than components relevant to changes of location. In one experiment, Gentner (1978) tested the ability of children aged 5–9 and adults to understand common cooking terms, such as *mix*, which specifies a particular change of state ("an increase in homogeneity"), and *stir*, *shake*, and *beat*, which specify particular manners of motion. Subjects were asked to verify whether each of these verbs applied to events in which a mixable substance (a combination of salt and water) or a nonmixable substance (cream, already homogeneous) was shaken or stirred. Gentner found that the youngest children, but not the older children or adults, had difficulty in distinguishing appropriate from inappropriate instances of *mixing*: the 5–7-year-olds applied the verb on 48% of the trials involving mixable substances (where it is appropriate) and on 46% of the trials involving nonmixable substances (where it is not appropriate). In contrast, the same children applied the three manner-of-motion verbs on 97% of the trials in which it is appropriate, but only on 6% of the trials in which it is inappropriate.

This asymmetry in the acquisition of verb meaning components, together with the affected-entity linking rule in (3), could explain the asymmetry in syntactic error types with locative verbs noted by Bowerman (1982a) and Gropen et al. (1991): if children frequently misinterpret a state change verb as a location change verb, they will map the wrong changing entity onto the object position, resulting in figure-object errors. For example, *fill the water* might be due to the child erroneously thinking that verbs like *fill* specify a particular manner of motion of the content argument (e.g., pouring). The prediction was tested in two experiments in Gropen et al. (1991). We showed that children between the ages of 2;6 and 8;9 not only have a tendency to make more *fill the water* (figure-object) than *pour the glass* (ground-object) errors in their speech, but they are also more likely to misrepresent the meaning of *fill* than the meaning of *pour* in comprehension. Unlike adults, they often interpreted *fill* as implying that something must be poured, even if the container ended up not full. Furthermore, there was a small tendency for the individual children who misinterpreted verbs like *fill* to be more likely to make syntactic errors with such verbs – errors in which the figure was used as the direct object.

Of course, if children are misled by the salience (to them) of the moving entity in certain locative events and mistakenly encode its manner of motion as part of the verb's meaning, they must possess a learning mechanism that at some point in development replaces the incorrect feature with the correct one. This mechanism could operate by monitoring the application of the verb *across* situations in parental speech. Sooner or later *fill* will be used by an adult to refer to an event in which there is no pouring (e.g., when a cup is filled by dripping or bailing or leaving it out during a rainstorm), so the incorrect "pouring manner" component can be expunged. But *fill* will always be used to refer to becoming full, so the state change meaning component, once hypothesized, will remain with the verb (see Pinker, 1989, for a theory outlining mechanisms of verb learning in children). If these two influences on verb learning – salience and cross-situation consistency – can be manipulated experimentally to affect speakers' construals of new verb meanings, the predictions of the semantic structure theory can be tested directly. That is the goal of the present investigation.

Developmental predictions about children's acquisition of novel verbs

We present three experiments assessing whether speakers use a verb's meaning, specifically, which argument is specified as caused to change (affected), to predict the verb's syntax. Children and adults are taught novel verbs for actions involving the transfer of objects to a surface or container. The participants are then tested on their willingness to express the figure (content) or the ground (container) argument as the direct object of the verb. The verbs are taught in a neutral syntactic context (e.g., *this is mooping*), but the meanings of the verbs are varied according to whether the figure or the ground is saliently and consistently affected in a particular way (e.g., whether the figure moves in a zig-zagging fashion, or whether the ground changes color).

According to the list-of-primitives theory, the child should assign a single thematic role to each participant in the event, drawing from the list of available primitives. This would be "theme" for the moving entity or figure, and "goal" or "location" for the destination or ground, and they would be invariably linked to object and oblique object, respectively.

In contrast, in the semantic structure theory the child would notice the thematic roles related to motion for each of the arguments, but these roles would not exhaust the syntactically relevant semantic representation of the verb. Arguments' semantic roles could be specified on several levels of semantic representation, only one of which would correspond to the motion relations, and the linking mechanism could be sensitive to the full structure of the verb. For the events with a specific manner of motion, the figure (moving entity) and ground (destination) would be encoded as theme and goal and linked to object and *to*-object respectively, as in the primitives theory. But for events with a specific state change but without a specific manner of motion, the causation of a change of the ground would be specified in the main event, and the ground would be linked to object position by the affectedness linking rule in (3). The motion of the figure would still be specified, but in a subsidiary "means" structure, as in (1), where it would not trigger the object linking rule.[5]

The predictions of Bowerman's overregularization analogy are similar, but not identical, to those of the list-of-primitives theory. Irregular forms by definition are *unpredictable*, and can only be learned by direct exposure. For example when one comes across the archaic verb *to shend*, one cannot know that its correct past tense form is *shent* unless one actually hears it in the past tense; the regular form *shended* would be offered as the default. According to the overregularization analogy, this would be true for ground-object verbs as well, and it predicts that a child should generally assign figure-object syntax to a novel locative verb if it is heard without syntactic cues, regardless of the kind of locative event it refers to. In addition, the analogy predicts some smaller proportion of uses of ground-object syntax, matching the asymmetry of errors observed in spontaneous speech, which in turn would be related to the smaller fraction of existing verbs in the language that display the ground-object pattern.

Experiment 1

In the first experiment we teach children one novel verb with the intended construal "cause X to move to Y in a zig-zagging manner", and another with the intended construal "cause Y to sag by means of placing X on it". We did not invent verbs with both a manner and a state change. On the one hand, if such a

[5]The subordinated figure argument can either be left unexpressed, as an "understood" argument, or expressed as the object of the preposition *with*. The distinction, not studied in this investigation, is discussed in Jackendoff (1987), Rappaport and Levin (1988), and Pinker (1989).

verb involved an unrelated manner and state change (e.g., "to cause X to zig-zag over to Y, causing Y to sag") it would not be linguistically possible and psychologically natural, because real verbs cannot specify multiple events unless they also specify some causal relation between them (Carter, 1976; Pinker, 1989, Ch. 5). On the other hand, if the verb involved an interpredictable manner of motion and resulting state change, the theory predicts it should alternate, and thus any mixture of figure-object and ground-object responses would be compatible with the theory and its prediction would be unclear.

The verbs are presented in a context like "this [acting out] is keating". Note that this construction involves a gerund form rather than an intransitive use of the verb, and that gerunds do not require arguments to be expressed. For example, English verbs that are obligatorily transitive can easily appear in the gerund form, as in "This [acting out or pointing] is devouring". Thus the grammatical context does not leak any grammatically relevant information to the subjects.

Method

Subjects

Sixty-four native English speakers participated: 16 children between 3;4 and 4;5 (mean 3;11); 16 between 4;7 and 5;11 (mean 5;1); 16 between 6;5 and 8;6 (mean 7;5); and 16 paid undergraduate and graduate students at MIT. The children were drawn from middle-class day-care and after-school programs in the Boston area. Eight children who failed to understand the taught verbs or were confused, distracted, or shy, were replaced in the design.

Materials

In a pretest, we used a cup and some marbles. In the experiment, to discourage subjects from making rote responses we used two separate pairs of materials: a clear packet of pennies was moved to a 20-cm felt square, or a packet of marbles was moved to a plastic square. During the teaching and testing phases, the cloth or plastic was placed on a stand consisting of either a solid square, which supported its entire surface, or a hollow frame, supporting only its perimeter.

Two verb meanings were created. In the *manner* condition, a packet was moved to a fully supported piece of material in a zig-zagging manner. In the *endstate* condition, the packet was moved in a direct path to an unsupported piece of material, which sagged under the weight of the packet. By using the same pairs of materials for both actions (within subject), we ensured that any differences in performance were not due to the salience of the materials. Corresponding to these two novel actions were two verb roots, *pilk* and *keat*. The pairing of one of the meanings with one of the roots that defined each verb was counterbalanced across subjects within each age group.

Procedure

Children were tested in a quiet area by two experimenters, one eliciting responses, the other recording data. Each novel verb was introduced to children by a puppet as a "puppet word".

Pretest. After being introduced to the materials, subjects were pretested on sentences with the verbs *pour* and *fill*. They were shown examples of pouring and filling, and descriptions were elicited; the experimenter recorded whether they used the figure (marbles) or ground (cup) as the direct object. For example, the experimenter would say: "do you know the word *fill*? . . . when I do this (moving marbles, a few at a time, into a cup) . . . and it ends up like that (the cup filled) . . . it's called *filling*." After doing this three times, the experimenter asked, "using the word *fill*, can you tell me what I'm doing?" If a subject failed to produce a sentence with an unambiguous direct object, we followed up with a prompt: "filling what?" or "filling ____?"[6] Regardless of the subject's final response, the experimenter modeled a correct sentence with *fill* (i.e., *I'm filling the cup with marbles*), and had the subject repeat it. The analogous protocol was followed for *pour*. The order of pretesting the two verbs was counterbalanced across subjects within an age group.

Teaching the novel verbs. Each subject was then taught two novel verbs: one specifying a manner (zig-zagging) and the other specifying an endstate (sagging). The verbs were taught and elicited one at a time, order counterbalanced across subjects in an age group. The experimenter first asked, "Can you say *keat*? . . . say *keat*," and then said, "let me show you what *keating* is . . . when I do this [moving a packet directly towards an unsupported square] . . . and it ends up like that [placing the packet onto the square, causing it to sag] . . . it's called *keating*." After repeating the demonstration, the experimenter said, "now let me show you something that's *not keating* . . . when I do this [moving a packet towards a *supported* square] . . . and it ends up like that [placing the packet onto the square, without changing its shape] . . . it's *not* called *keating*." The experimenter then asked, "Can you show me what keating is?" and then "Can you show me something that's not keating?" If children failed, the experimenter again showed examples and non-examples of the verb's meaning, and had the child act out the verb again, using the same materials. The teaching protocol was repeated with the second pair of materials.

The same teaching procedure was used when teaching the manner-of-motion verb. The experimenter moved a packet onto a supported square in a zig-zagging

[6]If subjects still failed to respond, the procedure called for a forced-choice question (e.g.), "Am I filling the cup or filling the marbles?", order counterbalanced. However, we had to resort to a forced-choice question on only four occasions in this investigation (0.2%), so we have grouped these data with those given in response to the fill-in-the-blank prompt.

manner, saying, "when I do this . . . and it ends up over there . . . it's called *pilking*". To illustrate what the verb was not, the experimenter then moved the packet in a bouncing manner.[7]

Testing the novel verbs. After each verb was taught, sentences containing it were elicited. The experimenter reverted to the original set of materials, asked the child to act out the verb again, asked him or her for the name of the figure (marbles or pennies), supplying it if the child did not, and asked him or her to say the verb. Then the experimenter asked, "Can you tell me, with the word *keating*, what I'm doing with the *marbles*?" while performing the action. The experimenter then verified that the child knew the names of the second set of materials, and elicited a sentence with it with a slightly different question: "Can you tell me, using the verb *keating*, what I'm doing with the *cloth*?" We posed the question these two ways to guard against the possibility that the subjects had a constant preference for either the figure-object or ground-object form, masking any potential effect of verb meaning. The figure question is a discourse context that makes the figure-object sentence pragmatically natural as a reply, and similarly the ground question makes a ground-object sentence natural (this technique was also used in Gropen et al., 1989, 1991, and in Pinker, Lebeaux, & Frost, 1987). Since both questions were asked with both verbs, order counterbalanced, this did not introduce any confound. In those trials where a subject failed to provide an unambiguous direct object, we followed up with a prompt: "keating what?" or "keating ____?"

The second verb was then taught and tested with the same protocol. Both pairs of materials were used in the teaching and syntactic testing of each verb, with the sequence of materials switched for the second verb (within subject) and balanced across subjects within an age group. In addition, we also switched the order of question types so that the sequence of items mentioned in the questions was either figure–ground–ground–figure or ground–figure–figure–ground. Together, these switches guaranteed that the same two items (i.e., marbles and felt or pennies and plastic) were mentioned in questions for both verbs within subject, so that the focusing of different materials in the questions could not account for any

[7]Note that the difference in instructions between manner and state-change verbs does not provide syntactic information that the child can use to predict the syntactic differences between the verbs. In most grammatical theories, *over there* and *like that* are both prepositional phrases. In particular, *like* in this context is not an adjective: adjectives do not take direct objects, only prepositional phrases and clauses; prepositions do take direct objects, but do not take the comparative *-er* suffix; cf. **A is liker B than C*. The fact that *over there* refers to a location (semantics typical of a PP) and *like that* refers to a state (semantics typical of an AP) is syntactically irrelevant: PPs can refer to states (e.g., *in this state; with red paint all over it; in a mess*) and APs can refer to locations (e.g., *very close to the edge*; *closer to the edge*). Of course, children could be attending to the semantics of the phrases in the instructions, instead of or in addition to their real-world referents, but this is fully compatible with the intention that the independent variable be one of verb semantics. Crucially, the syntactic difference between the instructions provides no information of use to the child.

differences in a subject's performance with the two meanings. Furthermore, the combination of verb meaning, question order, and material order was counterbalanced across subjects in each age group.

Scoring

Responses containing the appropriate verb and an unambiguous direct object were scored according to whether the object consisted of the figure or the ground in the action. Responses that were made only in response to the follow-up prompt (e.g., "keating what?") were also tallied separately. When subjects used a pronoun (e.g., "you're keating it"), utterances were counted only if the referent was disambiguated by the presence of an oblique object or particle (e.g., "you keated it onto the felt" or "You keated it on"), or if the referent could be pinned down via the subsequent prompt. In addition, we noted spontaneous intrusions of English verbs and unsolicited descriptions of the actions.

Results and discussion

Table 1 presents the proportions of figure-object and ground-object responses for the manner and endstate verbs, broken down by the type of eliciting question. Responses to the original question and to the subsequent prompt are combined in the proportions reported in this and other tables presented in this paper. The actual frequencies of unprompted and prompted responses (collapsed across question types) are also reported in the tables.

Table 1. *Experiment 1: likelihood of choosing figure or ground arguments as the direct object of manner and endstate verbs*

	Age									
	3;4–4;5		4;7–5;11		6;5–8;6		Adult		Mean	
Object argument:	Figure	Ground	Figure	Ground	Figure	Ground	Figure	Ground	Figure	Ground
Manner verbs										
Figure question	1.00	0.00	1.00	0.00	1.00	0.00	0.88	0.06	0.97	0.02
Ground question	0.88	0.12	0.94	0.06	0.69	0.31	0.62	0.31	0.78	0.20
Mean	0.94	0.06	0.97	0.03	0.84	0.16	0.75	0.19	0.88	0.11
No prompt/prompt	6/24	2/0	8/23	0/1	17/10	5/0	20/4	6/0		
Endstate verbs										
Figure question	0.94	0.06	0.88	0.12	0.75	0.19	0.69	0.31	0.81	0.17
Ground question	0.56	0.38	0.69	0.31	0.38	0.62	0.44	0.56	0.52	0.47
Mean	0.75	0.22	0.78	0.22	0.56	0.41	0.56	0.44	0.66	0.32
No prompt/prompt	7/17	4/3	12/13	3/4	11/7	10/3	16/2	14/0		

A small number of unscorable responses caused some sets of proportions not to add up to 1.00 and some sets of frequencies not to add up to 32.

As predicted, children in all age groups, and adults, produced more figure-object responses when using manner verbs than when using endstate verbs, and produced more ground-object responses when using endstate verbs than when using manner verbs.

In principle, the frequencies of figure-object and ground-object responses are independent because children could fail to provide an unambiguous sentence of either type; this calls for separate analyses of the proportions of figure-object and of ground-object responses. In practice, however, ambiguous responses were rare (less than 0.5% across the three experiments), so a single number for each condition suffices to summarize the subjects' behavior. The number we chose to enter into the analyses of variance is the proportion of trials in which a figure-object form was produced. Subjects produced significantly more figure-object responses in the manner condition (mean proportion = 0.88) than in the endstate condition (0.66), $F(1, 60) = 20.59$, $p < .001$. The difference was also significant for the mid-aged children, $F(1, 15) = 5.87$, $p < .03$, and the oldest children, $F(1, 15) = 6.36$, $p < .03$, and marginally so for the youngest children, $F(1, 15) = 4.36$, $p < .06$, and the adults, $F(1, 15) = 4.36$, $p < .06$. Finally, because of a set carried over from the first verb taught to the second, the verb type effect was stronger (between subjects within each age group) for the first verb taught ($F(1, 56) = 22.40$, $p < .001$) than for the second ($F(1, 56) < 1$).

The analysis of variance also revealed a significant main effect of question type, showing that subjects were sensitive to discourse influences on object choice. They produced more figure-object sentences (and thus fewer ground-object sentences) when the figure was mentioned in the question than when the ground was mentioned, $F(1, 60) = 31.68$, $p < .001$. No other effect or interaction was statistically significant.

Although we have shown that the choice of direct object is influenced by the aspect of the situation that the verb meaning specifies, with more figure-object responses and fewer ground-object responses for manner-of-motion verbs than change-of-state verbs, figure-object responses were in the majority for both types of verbs. We found a similar overall preference in the pretest using existing verbs: 11 of the youngest children, 3 of the middle group, and 4 of the oldest group (but no adults) produced ungrammatical sentences in which the direct object of *fill* was the content argument, and none made the converse error with *pour* (see also Bowerman, 1982a; Gropen et al., 1991). Part of this preference may be attributed to an overall bias for young children to attend to manners over endstates, as documented by Gentner (1978) and Gropen et al. (1991): the linking rule would translate a bias towards the manner components of verb meaning into a preference for figure-object sentences. Indeed our choice of endstate verb may, inadvertently, have fostered such a bias. The experimenter often had to nudge the packet into the unsupported material in order to initiate the sagging, and subjects may have noticed this, thereby interpreting the action that we have been calling "change of state" as involving a particular manner as well. That is, the verb may inadvertently have been given the interconnected motion-and-state-change semantics of an alternator like *stuff* or *brush*. In fact, of the 16 children who provided overt descriptions of the meaning of the endstate verb by focusing on one of the arguments, 10 mentioned what happened to the figure (most often, that it moved downward), contrary to our intentions.

Experiment 2

In this experiment we teach children and adults a purer endstate verb. The problem with the endstate verb in Experiment 1 was that the state change was a change of shape, and by definition whenever an object changes shape its local parts must change position. To cause a change in the position of the local parts of the ground object, the figure object had to impinge on it in a particular way, and that particular way (nudging) may have been interpreted by the subjects as part of the verb meaning, rendering it an alternator and diluting the predicted effect. Here we will teach a verb in which the ground changes color, not configuration, and furthermore the proximal cause of the change is chemical, not the motion of an impinging figure. If the linking hypothesis is correct, ground-object constructions should be the response of choice in using these endstate verbs.

Method

Subjects

Sixty-four native English speakers, drawn from the same sources as in Experiment 1, participated: 16 between 3;5 and 4;5 (mean 3;10); 16 between 4;7 and 5;8 (mean 5;1); 16 between 6;7 and 8;5 (mean 7;3); and 16 adults. We replaced one child in the design for being unresponsive in the syntactic task, three children because of experimenter error, and one adult who was color-blind.

Materials

As in Experiment 1, two separate pairs of materials were used with each subject, though in this experiment the pairing of objects (figures) and surfaces (grounds) was balanced across subjects in an age group. The surface was either a 6 × 10-cm piece of absorbent paper or a piece of white felt; the object was either a 2-cm square piece of sponge or a cotton ball. All materials were kept damp: the surface was saturated with cabbage juice; the object was saturated with either water, lemon juice, or a baking soda solution. As in Experiment 1, a cup and some marbles were used in a pretest.

Two verb meanings were created, both involving taking a damp object and patting it against a damp surface. For the endstate verb, the surface changed color in an acid-base reaction from purple (the color of unadulterated cabbage juice) to either pink (when the object contained lemon juice) or green (when the object contained baking soda solution). In the manner condition, an object was moved to a surface in a particular manner, either zig-zagging or bouncing; the object was saturated with water so no color change resulted. The color of the change and the particular manner were consistent for each subject and counterbalanced across subjects. As in the previous experiment, we used the same pairs of materials for both actions (within subjects). Corresponding to these two novel actions were two verb roots, *moop* and *keat*. The pairing of verb meanings and verb roots was counterbalanced across subjects in an age group.

Procedure

The procedure and scoring were the same as in Experiment 1, except that when providing a demonstration of what the endstate verb did not refer to, the experimenter used the solution that produced the other color. In addition, in order to reduce the carry-over effects in Experiment 1 caused by questioning the same materials for both verbs, we made the following changes: the sequence of materials for the first verb was counterbalanced with the sequence for the second verb, the order of question types for the first verb was counterbalanced with the order for the second verb, and the total sequence of materials and the total sequence of question types were combined so that each material (object or surface) was mentioned in only one question per session, and each material (in a given pairing) was mentioned an equal number of times in a question within meaning condition (all counterbalancings are over subjects within each age group).

Results and discussion

Results are shown in Table 2. As predicted, subjects responded with more figure-object sentences for manner verbs than for endstate verbs. An analysis of variance on the proportion of figure-object responses reveals a significant difference for the two verb types, $F(1, 60) = 115.52$, $p < .001$. (The effect is even larger when examined between subjects using only the first verb taught, eliminating carry-over effects.) The difference between the two verb types does not just arise from responses to the follow-up prompts, but is observed for full sentence responses to the original question; $F(1, 60) = 17.55$, $p < .001$. The effect of verb type is significant within each age group: youngest children, $F(1, 15) = 9.00$, $p < .01$; middle children, $F(1, 15) = 90.00$, $p < .001$; oldest children, $F(1, 15) = 27.21$, $p < .001$; adults, $F(1, 15) = 30.77$, $p < .001$. We also replicated the effect of discourse focus seen in Experiment 1, in which subjects produced relatively more figure-object forms when the figure was mentioned in the question than when the ground was mentioned, $F(1, 60) = 10.00$, $p < .005$.

Table 2. *Experiment 2: likelihood of choosing figure or ground arguments as the direct object of manner and endstate verbs*

	Age									
	3;4–4;5		4;7–5;8		6;7–8;5		Adult		Mean	
Object argument:	Figure	Ground	Figure	Ground	Figure	Ground	Figure	Ground	Figure	Ground
Manner verbs										
Figure question	0.62	0.38	0.88	0.12	0.81	0.19	0.69	0.31	0.75	0.25
Ground question	0.44	0.56	0.62	0.38	0.69	0.31	0.62	0.38	0.59	0.41
Mean	0.53	0.47	0.75	0.25	0.75	0.25	0.66	0.34	0.67	0.33
No prompt/prompt	1/16	5/10	1/23	1/7	9/15	4/4	15/6	11/0		
Endstate verbs										
Figure question	0.19	0.75	0.00	1.00	0.25	0.75	0.00	1.00	0.11	0.88
Ground question	0.12	0.81	0.00	1.00	0.06	0.94	0.00	1.00	0.05	0.94
Mean	0.16	0.78	0.00	1.00	0.16	0.84	0.00	1.00	0.08	0.91
No prompt/prompt	3/2	5/20	0/0	5/27	2/3	14/13	0/0	29/3		

A small number of unscorable responses caused some sets of proportions not to add up to 1.00 and some sets of frequencies not to add up to 32.

What is noteworthy in these data is that in each age group figure-object sentences were in the majority for the manner verb whereas ground-object sentences were in the majority for the endstate verb. (Indeed the 4–5-year-old children and the adults expressed the stationary entity as the direct object 100% of the time when it was observed to change state.) The results show that when a change of state is salient enough, children will usually express this affected entity as a direct object, even though it would traditionally be analyzed as a "goal" to which some other "theme" in the scene is moving. (Indeed, it is possible that when children correctly grasp that the meaning of a verb involves a change of state, they *always* choose the ground-object form: the 33 children (69%) who spontaneously used a color name to explain the meaning of the endstate verb produced nothing but ground-object sentences, though we cannot rule out the possibility that both phenomena are due to general precociousness.) Interestingly, the pretest revealed the same kind of error patterns with existing verbs that have been found in previous studies: 17 children out of 48 (10, 4, and 3 from the respective age groups) incorrectly used *fill* with the ground as direct object, and only one child made the complementary error with *pour*. Thus the tendency to make errors like *fill water* does not reflect the operation of a general requirement that figures be linked to the direct object position.

Experiment 3

In this experiment we attempt to explain the holistic interpretation that accompanies alternating locative verbs such as *load* and *spray*, whereby in ground-object sentences like *John loaded the cart with apples* the ground is interpreted as being affected over its entire surface or capacity, whereas in figure-object sentences like *John loaded apples into the cart* no such interpretation is forced (Anderson, 1971; Schwartz-Norman, 1976). If the holism effect is a consequence of the fact that a state change is naturally conceptualized as applying to an entire entity, and of a rule that links entities changing state to the grammatical object, then surfaces or containers that are completely covered or filled should be more likely to be construed as affected, and thus more likely to be expressed as direct objects, than those that are only partly covered or filled.

We contrast a "partitive" condition, in which (e.g.) a peg is inserted into a hole on a board, with a "holistic" condition, in which the same action is repeated until all of the holes on the board are plugged with pegs. We predict that children and adults should produce more ground-object sentences with the verb in the holistic condition than with the verb in the partitive condition.

Method

Subject

Sixty-four native English speakers, drawn from the same sources as in the previous two experiments, participated: 16 between 3;5 and 4;10 (mean 4;0); 16 between 5;0 and 6;11 (mean 5;7); 16 between 7;0 and 9;4 (mean 7;10); and 16 adults. We replaced five children in the design for being uncooperative, inattentive, or shy, one child because of experimenter error, one child for having received contaminating intervention, and one adult for misinterpreting the task as a request to imitate a child.

Materials

Two sets of materials were used with each subject, each consisting of two types of objects and two containers. One set consisted of beads, 0.6-cm plastic eggs, a flatbed cart with six holes in its 8 × 20-cm surface, and a 10-cm square cube with four holes on one of its sides. The second set consisted of marbles, small plastic balls, an 8 × 20-cm bench with six holes, and an 8 × 60-cm board with four holes. Both kinds of objects in a set could be inserted part way into the holes of either container in that set. Each subject saw the same pairings of objects and containers, counterbalanced across subjects in an age group. In addition, two (non-interchangeable) pairs of materials were used in the teaching phase: 5-cm styrofoam disks and a muffin tray with eight cavities; and 3 × 3-cm Duplo pieces and a candy mold with 12 indentations.

Because the comparison in this experiment involves a single kind of action, performed either once or enough times to fill all the holes in a container, a between-subjects design was necessary: each subject was taught and tested on one verb meaning. Across subjects in an age group, the partitive meaning was taught and tested as often as the holistic meaning, and the mean ages of the children in different meaning conditions were matched to ±2 months for each age group. In addition, we counterbalanced the four possible combinations of objects and containers with verb meaning so that each combination of object–container pairs occurred as often in the partitive condition as it did in the holistic condition, across the subjects in an age group. The verb root *keat* was used throughout.

Procedure

After introducing the subject to the materials and verb form, the experimenter taught the verb by performing the holistic or partitive action once, using either the styrofoam and muffin tray or the Duploes and candy mold. In the partitive condition, the experimenter inserted (e.g.) a piece of styrofoam into a hole in the tray while saying "I am keating." In the holistic condition, the experimenter inserted (e.g.) styrofoam pieces into the tray, one at a time, until all of the holes in the tray were plugged. The description "I am keating" was uttered only once, but the utterance was stretched out while the experimenter inserted several pieces. The experimenter then asked the subject to "show me what keating is." The teaching sequence was repeated on the rare occasions when it was neccessary.

In eliciting sentences, we sought to increase the number of prepositional phrases uttered by making it pragmatically informative to include them (see Crain, Thornton, & Murasugi, 1987; Gropen et al., 1991). Subjects saw two types of objects or two types of containers, only one of which actually participated in the event, and had to describe the action to a blindfolded puppet. For example, when asking a ground question in the holistic condition, the experimenter would say "Here is a board . . . I can have either some marbles (pointing) . . . or some balls (pointing). Now watch this: I am keating (filling the board with the marbles) . . . Tell Marty the puppet, using the word *keat*, what I did to the *board*." The most natural response in this context is a full ground-object form, (e.g.) "You keated the board with the *marbles*," where the old information (topic) is encoded as the direct object and the new information is encoded as the prepositional object. Similarly, when asking a figure question in the holistic condition, the experimenter would say (e.g.) "Here are some marbles . . . I can have either a board (pointing) . . . or a bench (pointing). Now watch this: I am keating (filling the bench with the marbles) . . . Tell Marty, using the word *keat*, what I did to the *marbles*." The order of presentation of the two materials was balanced within subject so that the chosen material was first as often as it was second. The same procedure was used for the partitive action except that single objects were moved and named. As before, the question was followed, if necessary, with the prompt "keating ____?" or "keating what?"

Four of these questions were asked in each of two blocks of elicitation trials, in the order figure–ground–figure–ground or ground–figure–ground–figure. Each presentation of the novel action was performed with a new pair of materials, so that after four trials each of the four objects and containers had been used once. The procedure for the second block was the same as for the first, except that the experimenter reinforced the temporal endpoint of the events by saying, "I am done keating. I keated" after each presentation of an action. We counterbalanced the sequence of question types for the first and second blocks, and coordinated the total sequence of question types with the total sequence of material pairs so that each of the eight materials was mentioned in a question exactly once per session, and each material (in a given pairing) was mentioned as often in the partitive condition as it was in the holistic condition (all counterbalancings are over subjects within each age group). After each block of trials, the experimenters administered several procedures designed to assess and train children's understanding of the temporal unfolding of the event. Since the results of these procedures had no measurable effect on the second block of elicitation trials, we will not discuss them; details are reported in Gropen (1989).

The responses were scored as in Experiments 1 and 2. Acceptable ground-object forms included one passive (*the block was keated*) and two sentences in which the figure was encoded as an instrumental subject (e.g., *the bead keated the block*).

Results and discussion

Table 3 shows the proportions of figure-object and ground-object responses (collapsing across both blocks of elicitation trials) for the partitive and holistic

Table 3. *Experiment 3: likelihood of choosing figure or ground arguments as the direct object of partitive and holistic verbs*

	Age									
	3;5–4;10		5;0–6;11		7;0–9;4		Adult		Mean	
Object argument:	Figure	Ground	Figure	Ground	Figure	Ground	Figure	Ground	Figure	Ground
Partitive verbs										
Figure question	0.88	0.12	0.88	0.12	0.78	0.22	0.84	0.16	0.84	0.16
Ground question	0.84	0.16	0.88	0.12	0.69	0.31	0.72	0.28	0.78	0.22
Mean	0.86	0.14	0.88	0.12	0.73	0.27	0.78	0.22	0.81	0.19
No prompt/prompt	5/50	4/5	40/16	7/1	45/2	13/4	45/5	11/3		
Holistic verbs										
Figure question	0.81	0.19	0.59	0.41	0.69	0.31	0.84	0.16	0.73	0.27
Ground question	0.47	0.53	0.31	0.69	0.69	0.31	0.56	0.44	0.51	0.49
Mean	0.64	0.36	0.45	0.55	0.69	0.31	0.70	0.30	0.62	0.38
No prompt/prompt	25/16	18/5	16/13	30/5	42/2	18/2	45/0	18/1		

verbs. As predicted, subjects used more ground-object forms when the verb referred to a holistic action (ground completely filled) than when referring to a partitive action (ground partly filled). The comparison is significant in an analysis of variance whose dependent variable is the proportion of figure-object responses; $F(1, 56) = 4.36$, $p < .05$. The actual effect consists of subjects strongly preferring the figure-object sentence with partitive verbs, but being indifferent between figure-object and ground-object sentences with holistic verbs. This can be seen in a set of two-tailed *t*-tests: for partitive verbs, the difference between proportions of figure-object and ground-object responses is significantly different from zero in every age group except the oldest children: young children, $t(7) = 3.29$, $p < .02$; middle children, $t(7) = 3.00$, $p < .025$; oldest children, $t(7) = 1.69$, $p = .14$; adults, $t(7) = 2.61$, $p < .05$. In contrast, the difference between proportions of figure-object and ground-object responses in the holistic condition is not significantly different from zero for any of the age groups.

As in previous experiments, subjects produced relatively more figure-object forms when the figure was mentioned in the question than when the ground was mentioned, $F(1, 56) = 16.55$, $p < .001$. A significant interaction of verb meaning and question type indicates that the effect of question type is greater in the holistic condition than in the partitive condition, $F(1, 56) = 5.33$, $p < .05$. This reflects a tendency for subjects to avoid the ground-object form of the partitive verb, even in response to a ground question, but to respond to the ground question with a ground response for holistic verbs.

We have shown that children interpret completely filled or covered surfaces as more worthy of being expressed as the direct object of a novel verb. This manifests itself most strongly as an outright avoidance of ground-object sentences when the surface is only partly filled. This is exactly what we would expect if speakers respected the holism constraint, according to which ground-object sentences imply holistic effects, and hence partitive effects imply the avoidance of ground-object sentences. In other words, subjects should avoid saying (e.g.) *you keated the board with the ball* in the partitive condition for the same reason that English speakers avoid saying *Mary loaded the cart with the apple(s)* in the situation where most of the cart remains empty. In contrast, it is not unnatural to say *Mary loaded apples into the cart* or *Mary put apples into the cart* even when she fills it. This is consistent with our finding that subjects did not avoid uttering figure-object sentences in either condition.

General discussion

The three experiments clearly show that children (from 3 to 9) and adults, when faced with a locative verb and no syntactic information about how to use it, show no across-the-board tendency to express the caused-to-move or figure entity as the direct object. Rather, when the goal of the motion changes state, whether it be shape (Experiment 1), color (Experiment 2), or fullness (Experiment 3), speakers are more likely to select that goal as the direct object.

These findings add developmental evidence to the list of problems recently recognized as plaguing earlier theories of linking such as those of Gruber (1965), Fillmore (1968), and Jackendoff (1972), where a verb's syntactically relevant semantic argument structure consists of a single set of thematic roles drawn from a fixed list and determined on the basis of motion if the verb refers to motion. It supports the more recent theories (e.g., Dowty, 1991; Grimshaw, 1990; Jackendoff, 1987, 1990; Pinker, 1989; Rappaport & Levin, 1985, 1988; see Levin, 1985, for a review) that posit a multilayered semantic structure in which information about motion, other changes, and their causal relations are specified, and in which linking rules are triggered by arguments in specific semantic sub-structures. Specifically, we have demonstrated the operation of a linking rule that interprets "themes" as entities that are "caused to change" or "affected" as part of the verb's main event representation, and maps them onto the direct object position, whether the change be location, state, or something else. Thus even when a learner registers that a verb can refer to a salient motion along a path to a goal, this motion event does not exhaust his or her syntactically relevant semantic representation of the verb; if there is a consistent state change serving as the end to which the motion is merely a means, the motion can be represented in this subordinate role, and the state change, as superordinate main event, can trigger the linking to direct object.

The results reinforce a theory that helps to explain many properties of English and other languages: why different verbs (e.g., *pour* and *fill*) have seemingly different linking patterns, the prevalence and lack of markedness of verbs whose moving entities are not objects, and the nonsynonymity (holism effect) of constructions with alternating verbs. Indeed the psycholinguistic foundation of the holism effect – that a state is most naturally predicated of the object considered in its entirety – was directly demonstrated in Experiment 3, where subjects, knowing only that a surface was holistically affected, were likely to describe the event with novel verbs using ground-object syntax.

In its strongest form the semantic structure theory predicts that verbs' syntactic argument structures are completely predictable from their semantic representations, for all verbs, speakers, ages, and languages. For many years this proposition has seemed clearly false, given the seemingly arbitrary differences between verbs within and across languages, and the existence of children's errors. The semantic structure theory, however, posits a richness and fine grain to verbs' semantic representations that might render the extreme claim defensible. All differences in syntactic argument structures should be accompanied by subtle, though measurable differences in semantic structure. In the next section we discuss how the theory would characterize such an interplay between syntax and semantics.

How are linking rules used in language?

According to the version of semantic structure theory discussed here, linking rules are not isolable bits of knowledge particular to a language, like a vocabulary item or rule of morphology, but are an inherent part of the interface between lexical semantics and syntactic argument structure. Thus they should have pervasive (though indirect) effects coordinating the semantics and syntax of predicates. In this section we examine these effects as they might operate in the experiments reported here and in the language acquisition process.

1. In the experiments

In all three experiments we influenced the syntactic privileges that subjects assigned to a novel verb presented with no syntactic information: children (in each age group) and adults were more likely to express the stationary goal entity as direct object (and less likely to express the moving entity as direct object) when the goal entity underwent a change of shape, color, or fullness than when it stayed the same and an entity moved to it in a characteristic fashion.

However, one might wonder (as did one of the reviewers of an earlier version of this paper) whether the semantic structure theory should predict that *all* of the uses of state-change verbs should have the ground as the direct object, and all of the uses of the manner verbs should have the figure as the direct object. This would be true only if we could have controlled subjects' construal of the verb *completely* in the few demonstrations of its meaning we were able to present (and, of course, if we could have prevented all lapses of attention, forgetting, idiosyncratic interest in the nonspecifically changing entity, response bias, and carry-over effects), which is not practical. In a person's real-life experience, any inappropriate construal of a verb's meaning as including some irrelevant semantic dimension (e.g., manner for an endstate verb or vice versa) can be expunged as the person witnesses the verb being used in circumstances that lack that feature, as noted. But even with our brief teaching situations, we were able to find a consistent significant effect in the predicted direction superimposed on the various uncontrollable factors. Moreover, the partial dilution of the effect, especially in Experiment 1, is understandable from independent sources of evidence, such as the manner bias demonstrated by Gentner (1978) and Gropen et al. (1991) and the partially faulty, alternator-like semantics of the verb we designed. In Experiment 2, where the endstate verb was better designed, children of all ages and adults preferred to express the stationary ground surface as the direct object, a preference that was absolute for two of the groups. (Of course, since subjects are literally free to construe a wetted surface as "affected" even if it does not change color or any other feature, we could not prevent them from ever using the ground-object form in the manner condition.) In Experiment 3, previous examination of the range of meanings allowed by existing alternating verbs helped make sense of the magnitudes of effects obtained: both figure-object and ground-object forms are compatible with a holistic event, but a partitive event lacking any obvious state change should strongly bias a choice of the figure-object form.

Furthermore, an experiment reported in Gropen (1989) is consistent with our conjecture that some nonpredicted sentences in these studies were lawful consequences of subjects' construing events in ways we could not completely control. The experiment was similar to the holistic condition of Experiment 3 except that subjects were also asked whether the event was best described as *putting* or *covering*. This was thought to assess in part their uncontrolled personal construals of the event as kinds of motions (for which *put* would be the most appropriate existing verb) or kinds of changes (for which *cover* would be most appropriate). Subjects (3;7 to adult) who chose *cover* preferred the ground-object form 91% of the time when using the novel verb; subjects who chose *put* preferred it only 61% of the time.

2. Novel coinages

The real-life case closest to our experiments is one where a speaker coins a novel verb (or interprets such a novel coinage by another speaker for the first time). Such coinages can occur when stems are invented out of the blue, perhaps influenced by phonetic symbolism (such as the recent verbs *snarf* (retrieve a computer file), *scarf* (devour), *frob* (randomly try out adjustments), *mung* (render inoperable), and *ding* (reject)). They can also occur when a stem is borrowed from another lexical category (e.g., *He tried to Rosemary-Woods the tape*; *He nroffed and scribed the text file*; see Clark & Clark, 1979). In all such cases the argument structure of the novel verb is not predictable from existing forms in the language and must be created from the verb's meaning by linking rules.

3. Recording a verb used in a sentence

Whenever a verb is heard in a grammatical syntactic construction, there is, strictly speaking, no need to use a linking rule to predict that the verb can appear in that construction; that fact can be recorded directly from the input. However, the fact that verbs obey linking regularities so uniformly suggests that linking rules do play a role in their acquisition, unlike genuinely input-driven memorization such as irregular morphology or the association between a word's sound and its meaning.

The prediction of the semantic structure theory discussed in this paper is that the child must make a verb's syntax (observed from syntactic analyses of parental sentences) compatible with its semantics (observed from the sets of situations in which the verb is used) according to the linking rules. Thus children should have trouble learning verbs whose hypothesized semantic representations are incompatible with their syntax, such as an English verb meaning something like "pour" but with the syntax of *fill* or vice versa.

Furthermore when a child hears a verb used in a full sentence, he or she could use the linking rule in the reverse direction, to guide the acquisition of the verb's meaning by directing attention to features of meaning that reliably accompany the verb but that may otherwise have gone unnoticed. For example, if an argument is heard in direct object position, the child may try out the hypothesis that the verb specifies that it is affected. The child would verify whether the referent reliably changes when used with the verb, and if it does, he or she could look for some characteristic manner if it moves, or state change if it does not, and would add it to the semantic representation of the verb. See Gleitman (1990) and Pinker (1989) for discussion and evidence.[8]

Finally, note that even when a child witnesses the syntactic privileges of a verb, he or she may forget them, but if the meaning is remembered the linking rules can reconstruct them. See Pinker (1989, pp. 330–341) for a discussion of verb errors in children's spontaneous speech that suggests that this process does occur.

4. Generalizing a verb from one construction to another

The most common setting where a speaker may be expected to apply linking rules productively is in generalizing from one construction that a verb is heard in to a new, related construction. For example, a learner might be faced with generalizing from a figure-object form of an alternating verb like *daub paint on the board* to a ground-object verb form like *daub the board with paint*, or vice versa, in the absence of having heard one of the two forms. See Gropen et al. (1989), Bowerman (1988), and Pinker (1984, 1989) for reviews of experimental and naturalistic evidence that adults and children frequently make such generalizations.

Within the semantic structure theory, these generalizations are enabled not by a single lexical rule specifying the syntactic linking of the new form (as in the list-of-primitives theory), but by a combination of a specific lexical rule and general linking rules (Pinker, 1989; Rappaport & Levin, 1988). The lexical rule is reduced to a simple manipulation of a verb's semantic structure, effecting a gestalt shift: the rule takes a semantic representation like "cause X to go into/onto Y" and generates a new, related representation like "cause Y to change by means of causing X to be in/on Y" (or vice versa). The linking rules would create the corresponding syntactic structures automatically. As mentioned in the Introduction, this division of labor helps explain the forms of the syntactic structures that are related by an alternation, the change of interpretation (e.g., holism) that

[8]Note that this is distinct from the proposal of Landau and Gleitman (1985) and Gleitman (1990) that the child must use a *set* of argument structures to deduce the idiosyncratic semantic content of the verb (e.g., whether the verb refers to *opening*, *closing*, *breaking*, or *melting*) from those argument structures, without having to note the contexts in which the verb is used. Pinker (1989) and Grimshaw and Pinker (1990, in preparation) examine this particular proposal in detail, and discuss evidence suggesting that it is unlikely to be an important factor in learning lexical semantics.

accompanies it, and its verbwise selectivity. If this characterization of a lexical rule as a simple semantic operation is correct, it would mean that linking rules are used whenever a verb is extended to a new construction for the first time.

Note, though, that the lexical rule cannot be applied freely to just any locative verb. If it could, a nonalternating motion verb like *pour* could be the basis for the creation of a similar verb predicating a state change resulting from pouring (something like "be poured upon"), and the linking rule would generate the ungrammatical **pour the glass with water*. True, we pointed out in the Introduction that alternating verbs like *stuff* and *spray* are generally different from nonalternators in simultaneously constraining properties of the figure and ground arguments in their definitions, but this raises the question of why non-alternators like *pour* and *fill* cannot have secondary meanings, involving simultaneous figure and ground constraints, that would make them eligible for the construction that they do not, in fact, appear in.

Pinker (1989) and Gropen et al. (1989), drawing on Levin (1985) and Green (1974), suggest that lexical rules apply freely only within narrowly circumscribed subclasses of verbs within the broad class that is generally associated with an alternation. For example, the English locative rule applies freely not to all verbs involving motion of contents to a container or surface, but only to verbs of simultaneous contact and motion (e.g., *smear*, *brush*, *dab*), vertical arrangement (*heap*, *pile*, *stack*), ballistic motion of a mass (e.g., *splash*, *spray*, *inject*), scattering (e.g., *scatter*, *strew*, *sow*), overfilling (e.g., *stuff*, *cram*, *pack*, *wad*), and insertion of a designated kind of object (*load*, *pack*, *stock*). Virtually all other locative verbs, those that fall outside of these subclasses, are confined to one syntactic form or the other. For example verbs of enabling the force of gravity (e.g., *pour*, *dump*, *drip*, *spill*) are confined to the figure-object construction, and verbs of exact covering, filling, or saturating (e.g., *fill*, *cover*, *line*, *coat*, *soak*, *drench*) are confined to the ground-object form.[9]

[9]Goldberg (in press) suggests that once one specifies narrow subclasses of verbs belonging to a construction, one can eliminate lexical rules. The speaker could note that a verb has an intrinsic meaning that is compatible with more than one possible subclass and could use it in both accompanying constructions; constraints on alternations would reduce to constraints on possible verb meanings. See Pinker (1989, Ch. 4) for three reasons why lexical rules seem to be necessary. (1) They specify morphological changes accompanying certain alternations (e.g., English passive). (2) They dictate the semantic composition of verb meaning and construction meaning (e.g., distinguishing whether the semantic representation of a verb in one construction is a "means" or an "effect" in the representation in another construction). (3) They specify pairs of compatible semantic subclasses that are allowed to share verb roots, distinguishing them from pairs of compatible semantic subclasses that are confined to disjoint sets of verb roots. For example, verbs of "removing stuff from a surface" and "making a surface free of stuff" can share roots, as in *clean (clear, strip) the table of crumbs/crumbs from the table*, presumably because of a lexical rule. But verbs of "removing possessions from a person" and "making a person bereft of possessions," though both possible in English, must be expressed by different roots, as in *seize (steal, recover, grab) money from John/*John of his money; bilk (rob, relieve, unburden) John of his money/*money from John* (see Talmy, 1985), presumably because of the absence of a lexical rule.

Presumably the child learns the subclasses by focusing on a verb that he or she hears alternate in parental speech, and generalizing its meaning to a minimal extent. This has the effect that a subsequently encountered verb that is highly similar in meaning will be allowed to alternate as well. See Pinker (1989) for a precise definition of "highly semantically similar" and for formal details of the generalization mechanism and how it interacts with verbs' semantic representations.

5. Development of alternating subclasses in acquisition and history

There is one effect of linking rules on the language whose mode of psychological operation is not clear, and this is in motivating the *kinds* of semantic subclasses that are freely subjectable to lexical rules in a given language, that is, the kind of constraints discussed in the immediately preceding passage. It seems that which subclasses of verbs actually alternate in the language correlates with the cognitive content of the notion "affectedness": the easier it is to construe both the figure and the ground as directly "affected" by a given action, the more likely English is to allow verbs of that type to alternate. For example in verbs like *brush* and *dab*, force is applied simultaneously to the figure and the ground, an action easily construable as affecting them both. Similarly, what makes an event an instance of *stuffing*, *cramming*, or other verbs in the overfilling subclass is that force is applied to the contents in opposition to resistance put up by the container. The difference between the gravity-enabled motion subclass (*pour*, *spill*, *drip*, etc., which cannot be used in the ground-object form) and the imparted-force subclass (*splash*, *spray*, *inject*, *splatter*, etc., which alternate) may be related to the fact that when force is imparted to a substance the location and shape of the goal object is taken into account by the agent in how the force is imparted (e.g., in aiming it), and the particular pattern of caused motion defining the verb also predicts the effect on the goal (e.g., the kind of motion that makes an act *splattering* or *injecting* also dictates how a sprayed surface or injected object has changed. See Pinker, 1989, and Gropen, 1989, for explicit semantic representations of all these verbs.)

Why do English constraints on alternation show signs of having hints of cognitive motivation? It is certainly not true that the ease of construing an event as simultaneously affecting figure and ground is the *direct* cause of a speaker's willingness to allow a verb to alternate. That is because there are stable constraints within a dialect, and differences between dialects, in the specifications of the exact subclasses of verbs that can alternate. (For example, we cannot say *drip the cake with icing* even if we construe the cake as directly affected, though some English speakers can; see Pinker, 1989; Rappaport & Levin, 1985.) Instead, presumably the psychology of affectedness interacts with psycholinguistic rules of the locative alternation in more indirect ways. Over historical timespans innovative speakers may be more likely to extend a verb subclass to a new construction for the first time if the intrinsic semantics of the verbs in the subclass is cognitively compatible with the semantics of the construction (e.g., if the object argument in the new construction is easily conceptualized as being affected). And perhaps these innovations are more likely to spread through a linguistic community if many members of the community find it tempting to construe the event in the multiple ways originally entertained by the innovator. Finally, once the subclass becomes entrenched as a possible domain of a rule, it might be more easily learned by each generation if the construals it forces on the speakers are cognitively natural (see Pinker, 1989, for discussion).

6. Bootstrapping the first rules involving grammatical relations

A final implication of the semantic structure theory of linking concerns the semantic bootstrapping hypothesis (see Grimshaw, 1981; Macnamara, 1982; Pinker, 1982, 1984, 1987, 1989; Wexler & Culicover, 1980). According to this hypothesis, young children at the outset of language acquisition (younger than those studied here) might use linking regularities and word meanings to identify examples of formal syntactic structures and relations in parental speech and hence to trigger syntactic rule learning for their particular language. (This is logically independent of the claim that linking rules are used to predict *individual* verbs' syntactic privileges from their meanings after the rules of syntax for their language have been acquired.) For example, if the patient argument of a verb comes after the verb in an input sentence, the child can deduce that it is a VO language, even if the child had no way of knowing prior to that point what counted as an object in that language.

A major sticking point for the hypothesis has been the existence of seeming counterexamples to any proposed set of linking rules: for example, passives, in which the agent is not expressed as a subject, and double-object datives and ground-object locatives, where the argument traditionally analyzed as the "theme" or "patient" is not expressed as the verb's first object. The hypothesis required that parents avoid using the supposedly exceptional constructions in their speech, that the child recognizes them as exceptional by various cues, or that the child weighs and combines multiple sources of evidence to settle on the most concordant overall analysis of the construction (see Pinker, 1982, 1984, 1987, for discussion).

But if linking rules, when properly formulated, are exceptionless, the burden of filtering "marked" or "noncanonical" or "exceptional" constructions out of the input to rule-learning mechanisms is shifted. If objects are linked from "affected" or "caused to change" entities, not necessarily "moved" ones (and if subjects can be linked not only from agents but from themes in agentless semantic structures; see Pinker, 1989), then neither the child nor the parent would have to pay special attention to using or analyzing the supposedly "marked" constructions. The restriction instead is that the parent would have to use predicates whose semantic structures meshed with the young child's construal of the situation; the universal linking rules, shared by parent and child, would yield the correct syntactic analysis for the child as long as the child could identify (e.g.) which entities counted as "affected". Obviously, it is not realistic to expect that the lexical semantics of a parent's verb matches the child's cognitive representation of the described event for all situations and languages. But the fact that the new linking theory allowed us to predict the syntactic frames that children assigned to novel verbs in specific kinds of situations, including frames often treated as "marked", suggests that some sharing of construals between child and adult is plausible.

Appendix: A comparison of the semantic structure theory of linking with Melissa Bowerman's overregularization analogy

Bowerman (1990) presents an interesting discussion of the possible operation of linking rules in children's first word combinations (the 2–5-word strings produced before the age of 2). She first points out that though word order errors are not infrequent in the speech of her two daughters (about 11% of the utterances she reproduces in her tables) the errors do not seem to occur more often for verb argument structures that would be harder according to the list-of-primitives theory (e.g., double-object datives or ground-object locatives). Nor do the first correct uses of these marked constructions appear later than their supposedly unmarked counterparts. These data were among those we mentioned in the Introduction as posing a challenge to the list-of-primitives theory.

Bowerman notes that the semantic structure theory defended in this paper does not predict the same asymmetry. But she presents additional tests that, she claims, refute the newer theory as well – in particular, the hypothesis that the child's language system is innately organized to link verbs' syntactic and semantic representations in particular ways. Instead, she argues that children are not predisposed to follow any particular pattern of linking. At first they acquire verbs' syntactic properties individually from the input, and they are capable of acquiring any linking pattern between arguments and syntactic positions with equal ease. When the child notices statistically predominant linking patterns in the verbs thus acquired, the patterns are extracted as rules and possibly overextended, like inflectional overregularizations (e.g., *breaked*). As support for this proposal she cites evidence that children's use of linking rules appears only late in development (presumably after the child has had enough time to tabulate the linking patterns) and that their errors mirror the relative frequencies of the linking patterns among verbs in the language.

In this Appendix we will first outline the logic of testing for the existence of linking rules, then turn to Bowerman's two empirical tests (one claimed to refute the existence of innate linking rules, the other claimed to support the overregularization analogy); finally, we examine the overregularization analogy itself.

The logic of testing for linking rules in early speech

Linking rules, under the conception outlined here and in Pinker (1989) and Gropen (1989), are internal pointers between lexical semantic structures and grammatical relations, and hence cannot be tested directly against children's behavior, but only together with independently motivated hypotheses about each of the structures that the linking rules would link. In the experiments reported in this paper and in Gropen et al. (1991), such motivation was readily available. It seems safe to assume that in experimental subjects 3;4 and older, basic grammatical relations like object and oblique object are well developed. In the experiments reported here, we attempted to control lexical semantic structures directly, as part of our experimental manipulations; in Gropen et al. (1991), we exploited the bias previously demonstrated by Gentner (1978) and others (see Pinker, 1989, for a review) whereby children acquire manner-of-motion components of meaning more easily than change-of-state components.

Bowerman's data are far more problematic as tests for the existence of linking rules, because neither of the two entities that the linking rules would link is reliably present in the children's speech. First, there is some evidence from Bowerman herself that the girls' first meanings for several common verbs were not true semantic representations but could be quite context-bound. In Bowerman (1978, p. 982) she argues that their first uses of *put*, *take*, *bring*, *drop*, and *make go* "were restricted to relatively specific, and different, contexts" with the result that each child "may be at a loss when she wants to refer to a new act that does not fit clearly into any of these categories." This raises the possibility that many early verbs (including "nonprototypical" verbs) could be used correctly simply because they were memorized as referring to stereotyped situations and kinds of arguments. Linking rules, which apply to more schematic verb semantic structures that can refer to a particular range of situations, may not be applicable until such semantic structures are acquired, which Bowerman (1978) suggests often comes later. Second, the errors in this early state do not appear to involve linking per se, where the wrong arguments would be linked to particular grammatical positions like subject, object, or the object of particular prepositions. Rather, the errors include every possible distortion of the grammatical positions themselves: SOV, VOS, VSO, OSV, and OVS orders all occur. The ordering of subject, verb, and object is not a linking phenomenon (specific verbs do not call for SVO order; it is general across the English language), and so these errors probably reflect noisy processing or incomplete acquisition in components of the child's language system involving phrase structure and grammatical relations.[10]

But for now, let us assume that the correct utterances in Bowerman's sample

[10]Bowerman notes that the errors occur more often for prototypical agent–patient verbs than for "other" verbs, but this pattern, if general, would be difficult to explain in any theory.

involve properly represented grammatical relations and semantic structures, so that we can focus on the logic of her tests comparing different kinds of verbs.

Bowerman does not outline any specific proposals about young children's semantic representations, but points to a discussion in Pinker (1989) on the mechanisms by which verb meanings are acquired. Pinker (1989) describes three plausible (and not mutually exclusive) mechanisms. One is called event-category labeling: the child would take a pre-existing concept of a particular kind of event or state (e.g., seeing, or breaking) and use it as a hypothesis about the meaning of a verb inferred to express an instance of such an event. In general this mechanism can serve as no more than a source of first or default hypotheses; however, because many verbs corresponding to a general cognitive category like "moving an object" or "fright" vary in their precise semantic representations across languages (Gentner, 1982; Pinker, 1989; Talmy, 1985). The second learning mechanism is called semantic structure hypothesis testing: the child would add or delete substructures to his or her current representation of a verb meaning to make it conform with instances of its use. (For example, if a child incorrectly represented *fill* as requiring a pouring manner, that meaning component would be dropped when the verb was heard in connection with bailing.) The third learning mechanism is called syntactic cueing, in which the child would create semantic substructures with a set of inferences including the use of linking rules in reverse. That is, when the child hears a verb used in a sentence at a point at which enough syntax has been acquired to parse the sentence, the child would adjust the semantic representation of the verb to make it compatible with the grammatical relations of the verb's arguments, in conformity with the linking rules. For example a child who thought that *fill* meant "to pour" would change its semantics upon hearing *fill* used with a direct object referring to a full container, which implies that the verb expresses the change undergone by the container argument. Note that the subsequent use of linking rules does not care about which (if any) of these procedures was used to acquire a verb's semantic representation, as long as the verb has one.

Bowerman extracts a prediction from the operation of these mechanisms. She first lists verbs for which event-category labeling would be a sufficient learning mechanism; in particular, "prototypical agent–patient verbs" such as *open*, *fix*, *throw away*, *wash*, and *eat* should be prominent examples of such "cognitively-given" verbs. These verbs are then contrasted with stative transitive verbs such as *like*, *scare* (with an inanimate subject), *see*, *hear*, *need*, and *want*, where general cognitive concepts are associated with verbs that show variation in linking within and across languages (e.g., fright can be expressed with either *fear* or *scare*). She notes, "Regardless of which technique the child uses to determine the mapping of 'non-cognitively-given' verbs, it is clear that these verbs will require more effort than verbs whose meanings are cognitively transparent. Cognitively transparent verbs can in principle be mapped immediately (because there is only one candidate Agent, Patient, etc.); in contrast, 'something more' is needed for ambiguous verbs, and this will take extra time." But her two daughters did not use prototypical agent–patient verbs any sooner, or with fewer errors, than the "non-cognitively-given" verbs.[11]

Note, however, that Bowerman's prediction relies on an extra and gratuitous assumption. While it is true that "something more" is needed to acquire ambiguous verbs compared to unambiguous ones, that something more is not, as she suggests, "effort", or even time, but *information*. The semantic representation of an unambiguous verb could be acquired as a default by category labeling even if the child did no more than witness the verb itself expressing a single instance of the relevant event or state; for ambiguous verbs, a syntactic context or a disambiguating situation or situations would be required. But the difference is simply one of availability of information, not of inherent difficulty or time consumption other than that entailed by the difference between no information and some information. And crucially, because these are naturalistic data, the child surely *has* had access to relevant information. If a child is uttering *scare* or *like* at all she has necessarily heard those verbs used previously. If she has heard them used previously she has almost certainly heard them in contexts providing information that resolves their thematic ambiguity. One kind of context is situational: while the general event/state category pertaining to fright may be ambiguous, *to scare* involves an event and *to fear* a state (Dowty, 1991; Grimshaw, 1990; Pesetsky, 1990), and a situation in which *scare* is used to refer to an event can disambiguate them. The other kind of context is sentential: the child surely has not learned the verb from sentences like "this is scaring" but from sentences where the verb appears with a subject and an object, identifiable on many occasions as referring to either the experiencer or the stimulus. Here the syntax could cue the child, via reverse linking, to select a semantic representation of *scare* involving a causal stimulus argument. Similarly , there is no reason why it should be hard to acquire consistent semantic and syntactic representations for other "non-cognitively-given" verbs in Bowerman's list, like *ride*, *hold*, *spill*, *drop*, *wear*, *see*, *hear*, and *like*, as long as the child does not hear them in isolation but in correct sentences with their usual referents.

Thus Bowerman has not tested linking rules by themselves (which is generally impossible) but in conjunction with the extra asumption that *even with information sufficient to resolve thematic ambiguities* verbs whose meanings require the use of hypothesis testing or syntactic cueing have a lasting disadvantage compared

[11]In some cases, Bowerman's assignment of verbs to her "prototypical agent–patient" class may not exactly fit the criterion of verbs that show little variation in linking: *hit* and *cover* are classified as prototypical agent–patient verbs, though they do vary across languages (see her Note 7); for some excluded verbs, such as *hold* and *draw*, it is not clear that they do vary. Still, the patterns shown by the two children would not change much if a few verbs were recategorized.

to verbs that could have been acquired by category labeling. Note that Bowerman needed this extra assumption so that she could use her naturalistic data to test a hypothesis that is inherently better suited to being tested experimentally. According to the semantic structure theory of linking, together with the assumption that category labeling exists as one of the mechanisms for acquiring semantic structure, the ambiguous and unambiguous verbs should differ only when no disambiguating information is available. This situation is impossible to achieve in everyday life, but easy to achieve (at least in principle) in an experiment: an experimenter can present novel verbs without any syntactic context, controlling the events and states it refers to, and test whether children use the verbs with predictable syntax. Of course, that is exactly what we did in this paper with older children. A related experiment can be done by presenting novel verbs in syntactic contexts that linking rules render flatly incompatible with any reasonable semantic representation (verbs with "anticanonical" linking, where, for example, the direct object is an agent and hence not construable as "affected"), and seeing if children have more trouble learning them. This has been done with older children by Marantz (1982) and Pinker et al. (1987).

If verbs without a pre-existing concept corresponding precisely to their meanings can develop through experience without measurable disadvantage, one might wonder whether the role of linking, especially in semantic bootstrapping, has been minimized, or worse, defines a vicious circle (verbs' syntactic properties are deduced by linking rules applied to their semantic representations, verbs' semantic representations are acquired by reverse linking from syntax). The issues are discussed in detail in Pinker (1987, 1989, Ch. 6). The circle is easily broken by the fact that the verbs that inspire the hypothesization of grammatical rules are not the *same* verbs that need to be acquired with the help of their grammatical contexts; even a few unambiguous verbs would be sufficient in principle to get grammar acquisition started.[12] Moreover, no matter what the relative contributions are of nonlinguistic concepts, patterns of use across situations, and syntactic cues in how a verb was originally acquired, linking rules will govern its syntactic expression and semantic interpretation thereafter in a variety of spheres, such as refinement of its semantic representation, participation in lexical alternations, innovative uses including those leading to historical change, and holistic interpretation, as outlined in the General discussion.

[12]Note that Bowerman's data also do not test the semantic bootstrapping hypothesis, which asserts the prototypical semantic relations are cues used to hypothesize rules involving grammatical relations (which can then be used for all verbs, regardless of semantics), not that the rules themselves are specific to particular kinds of semantic relations. Semantic bootstrapping, like linking, is best tested experimentally: children hearing a language containing only situationally ambiguous or anticanonical verbs would have trouble learning its grammar; see Pinker (1984, Ch. 2).

Are children's linking errors strongly input driven?

Bowerman presents independent evidence in support of her claim that linking regularities must be acquired completely from parental speech. She suggests that errors attributable solely to linking rules (i.e., where the language does not contain lexical alternations, like the locative, that allow the appearance of a verb in one construction to predict its appearance in a related one via a lexical rule) occur only late in development, presumably after the child has tabulated enough data. Specifically, errors where experiencer-subject psychological verbs are used with stimulus subjects (e.g., *It didn't mind me very much*), reflecting the majority pattern in English, do not occur until the 6–11-year age range in Bowerman's two daughters.

Upon wider examination the data pattern provides little if any support for the hypothesis, however. Because lexical alternations are ubiquitous in English, Bowerman was able to rule out many possible examples of linking on the grounds that an existing English alternation might have been the source. But this does not mean that the alternation in fact was the source. In Hebrew, there are no verbs that can be used in identical form in causative and intransitive constructions, but Berman (1982) notes that 2-year-old children acquiring Hebrew use intransitive verb forms as causative transitives with agent subjects and theme objects, just as English-speaking children do. Moreover, even in English young children use verbs with nonadult but appropriate linking patterns that could not have been analogized from existing alternations. For example, Bowerman herself (1982b) presents 14 examples where children, as young as 2, causativized transitive verbs to form double-object structures (e.g., *I want to watch you this book*). This pattern of alternation is for all practical purposes nonexistent in English (Pinker, 1989). Most strikingly, the particular transitive verbs that children incorrectly link to the double-object construction are just the kinds of verbs that legitimately appear in that construction in a great variety of languages (Pinker, 1989), suggesting a common underlying psychological bias in linking. (See Pinker, 1984, Ch. 8, and Pinker, 1989, Chs. 1 and 7, for other examples of linking errors that are not based on existing English lexical alternations.)

Finally, let us examine Bowerman's data on psychological verbs, consisting of nine errors from her two daughters. One has an experiencer subject, the minority pattern in English. Of the eight with stimulus subjects, one consists of a sequence of two incorrect forms and a correct form: *I am very fond. Everyone's fond of me. I am very fonded.* Note that the second incorrect form in this sequence is a passive whose active verb source would *not* differ in linking from the correct English form (experiencer subject); the error is in converting an adjective to a passive. The other incorrect form in the sequence may also have been intended as a passive, given that the child followed it with nonpassive and clearly passive recastings of the predicate with the linking pattern it would have if it were indeed a passive, and given children's tendency to leave forms ending in *t* or *d* unmarked in past and participle forms (see Pinker & Prince, 1988). Even if it was intended as a nonpassive adjective, its experiencer subject follows no common English linking pattern for such predicates. A third example is a double-object form (*You know what pictures me uncle?*), which does not occur at all in English with stimulus subjects verbs. Three others are intransitive with prepositionally marked stimulus arguments (*approved to you; reacted on me; picture to me like*), of which the great majority in English actually have experiencer subjects; there are only a tiny number with stimulus subjects (*appeal*, *matter*; Talmy, 1985; Beth Levin, personal communication). This leaves only three errors containing transitive usages with stimulus subjects, reportedly the majority pattern in English, out of the nine linking errors with psych verbs listed. Thus when the grammatical properties of the errors and of English verbs are examined with more precision, one finds no clear evidence for Bowerman's assertion that most children's errors follow the statistically dominant linking pattern for English psychological verbs.

Do alternative linking patterns act like irregular inflection?

Bowerman gives no explicit account of how her alternative learning mechanism works or how its operation predicts developmental patterns or linguistic regularities. But the guiding analogy, inflectional overregularization, seems more misleading than helpful when examined in detail (see Marcus et al., 1990; Pinker & Prince, 1988). First, whereas irregularly inflected verbs are fewer in number and higher in average token frequency than regular ones, the exact opposite may be true of ground-object and figure-object locative verbs (Rappaport & Levin, 1985; Gropen et al., 1991). Second, verbs fall into inflectional paradigms specifying a past tense form for every verb, in which the presence of an irregular is sufficient to block the regular rule. This allows the child to recover from inflectional overregularization when he or she hears the irregular a sufficient number of times. But no such paradigm organization is apparent for locative argument structures and the overregularization analogy leaves the unlearning of such errors unexplained (Gropen et al., 1991; Pinker, 1989). Third, whereas any particular irregular pattern occurs with an unpredictable set of verbs (by definition), the ground-object linking pattern occurs *predictably* with verbs having a particular kind of meaning (in children as well as adults). Fourth, whereas any particular irregular pattern is an arbitrary memorization and supports no further grammatical inferences, the ground-object form is lawfully associated with a particular shift in interpretation (in children as well as adults), the one we have referred to as "holistic". Fifth, whereas the child's course of acquiring irregular verbs is mainly governed by frequency of exposure (since the verbs' unpredictability requires them to be memorized by rote; see Marcus et al., 1990), the developmental course of ground-object forms is influenced by specific, independently measurable aspects of their semantic development (Gropen et al., 1991). Sixth, while particular irregular patterns and the verbs they take vary radically from language to language, the ground-object form and the verbs that use it show highly similar patterns across unrelated languages. A learning mechanism that recorded any statistically predominant linkage between figure versus ground and direct versus oblique object predicts that these widespread and mutually consistent patterns should not occur. In contrast, it would be shocking to find an *i–a* alternation in the past tense inflection of the translations of *sing* in language after language, other than those historically close to English. The fact that these linking patterns do occur counts as evidence against Bowerman's claim that children learn the syntactic argument structure of verbs like *fill* in the same way that they learn the past tense forms of verbs like *sing*.

In sum, we find Bowerman's data interesting in suggesting that, in the presence of linguistic and nonlinguistic contextual information, young children can acquire verb representations even if the verbs do not unambiguously label preformed concepts for kinds of events, states, and arguments. But we see two problems in her claim that children learn all aspects of linking from the statistics of parental speech, with all possible linking patterns being equally easy to acquire. Methodologically, she tries to exploit her naturalistic data to test a hypothesis that can only be tested clearly with experimental materials in which a verb's semantic and syntactic contexts can be manipulated. Theoretically she appeals to the metaphor of irregular morphology; we have shown that when one examines the linguistic and psychological facts in detail, the metaphor falls apart. The ground-object form is just not an example of linguistic irregularity.

Note that we are not suggesting that learning plays a small role in the acquisition of argument structure. The child must learn details of the semantic structures of individual verbs, the kinds of verb structures permitted in the language, and which kinds of verbs lexical rules apply to. But the evidence suggests that linking rules, which show little or no cross-linguistic variation and which enforce pervasive systematicities among these learned structures, are more plausibly seen as one of the causes of such learning rather than as one of its products.

References

Anderson, S.R. (1971). On the role of deep structure in semantic interpretation. *Foundations of Language*, *6*, 197–219.

Baker, C.L. (1979). Syntactic theory and the projection problem. *Linguistic Inquiry*, *10*, 533–581.

Berman, R.A. (1982). Verb-pattern alternation: The interface of morphology, syntax, and semantics in Hebrew child language. *Journal of Child Language*, *9* 169–191.

Bowerman, M. (1978). Systematizing semantic knowledge: Changes over time in the child's organization of word meaning. *Child Development, 49,* 977–987.
Bowerman, M. (1982a). Reorganizational processes in lexical and syntactic development. In E. Wanner & L.R. Gleitman (Eds.), *Language acquisition: The state of the art* (pp. 319–346). New York: Cambridge University Press.
Bowerman, M. (1982b). Evaluating competing linguistic models with language acquisition data: Implications of developmental errors with causative verbs. *Quaderni di Semantica, 3,* 5–66.
Bowerman, M. (1988). The 'no negative evidence' problem: How do children avoid constructing an overly general grammar? In J.A. Hawkins (Ed.), *Explaining language universals* (pp. 73–101). Oxford: Blackwell.
Bowerman, M. (1990). Mapping thematic roles onto syntactic functions: Are children helped by innate "linking rules"? *Journal of Linguistics, 28,* 1253–1289.
Bresnan, J. (1982). The passive in lexical theory. In J. Bresnan (Ed.), *The mental representation of grammatical relations* (pp. 3–86). Cambridge, MA: MIT Press.
Carter, R.J. (1976). Some constraints on possible words. *Semantikos, 1,* 27–66.
Chomsky, N. (1981). *Lectures on government and binding*. Dordrecht: Foris Publications.
Clark, E.V., & Clark, H.H. (1979). When nouns surface as verbs. *Language, 55,* 767–811.
Crain, S., Thornton, R., & Murasugi, K. (1987). Capturing the evasive passive. Paper presented at the Twelfth Annual Boston University Conference on Language Development (pp. 23–25). October.
Dowty, D.R. (1991). Thematic proto roles and argument selection. *Language, 67.*
Fillmore, C.J. (1968). The case for case. In E. Bach & R.J. Harms (Eds.), *Universals in linguistic theory* (pp. 1–90). New York: Holt, Rinehart, and Winston.
Foley, W.A., & Van Valin, R.D. (1984). *Functional syntax and universal grammar*. New York: Cambridge University Press.
Foley, W.A., & Van Valin, R.D. (1985). Information packaging in the clause. In T. Shopen (Ed.), *Language typology and syntactic description. Vol. 1: Clause structure* (pp. 282–364). New York: Cambridge University Press.
Gentner, D. (1975). Evidence for the psychological reality of semantic components: The verbs of possession. In D.A. Norman & D.E. Rumelhart (Eds.), *Explorations in cognition* (pp. 211–246). San Francisco: W.H. Freeman.
Gentner, D. (1978). On relational meaning: The acquisition of verb meaning. *Child Development, 49,* 988–998.
Gentner, D. (1982). Why nouns are learned before verbs: Linguistic relativity vs. natural partitioning. In S.A. Kuczaj II (Ed.), *Language development. Vol. 2: Language, thought, and culture* (pp. 301–334). Hillsdale, NJ: Erlbaum.
Gleitman, L.R. (1990). Structural sources of verb meaning. *Language Acquisition, 1,* 3–55.
Goldberg, A. (in press). The inherent semantics of argument structure: The case of the English ditransitive construction. *Cognitive Linguistics.*
Green, G.M. (1974). *Semantics and syntactic regularity*. Bloomington: Indiana University Press.
Grimshaw, J. (1981). Form, function, and the language acquisition device. In C.L. Baker & J.J. McCarthy (Eds.), *The logical problem of language acquisition* (pp. 165–182). Cambridge, MA: MIT Press.
Grimshaw, J. (1990). *Argument Structure*. Cambridge, MA: MIT Press.
Grimshaw, J., & Pinker, S. (1990). Using syntax to deduce verb meaning. Paper presented to the Fifteenth Annual Boston University Conference on Language Development, 19–21 October.
Grimshaw, J., & Pinker S. (in preparation). How could children use verb syntax to learn verb meaning?
Gropen, J. (1989). Learning locative verbs: How universal linking rules constrain productivity. PhD dissertation, MIT.
Gropen, J., Pinker, S., Hollander, M., & Goldberg, R. (1991). Syntax and semantics in the acquisition of locative verbs. *Journal of Child Language, 18,* 115–151.
Gropen, J., Pinker, S., Hollander, M., Goldberg, R., & Wilson, R. (1989). The learnability and acquisition of the dative alternation in English. *Language, 65,* 203–257.
Gruber, J. (1965). Studies in lexical relations. PhD dissertation, MIT.

Hopper, P.J., & Thompson, S.A. (1980). Transitivity in grammar and discourse. *Language, 56,* 251–299.
Jackendoff, R.S. (1972). *Semantic interpretation in generative grammar.* Cambridge, MA: MIT Press.
Jackendoff, R.S. (1978). Grammar as evidence for conceptual structure. In M. Halle, J. Bresnan, & G. Miller (Eds.), *Linguistic theory and psychological reality* (pp. 201–228). Cambridge, MA: MIT Press.
Jackendoff, R.S. (1983). *Semantics and cognition.* Cambridge, MA: MIT Press.
Jackendoff, R.S. (1987). The status of thematic relations in linguistic theory. *Linguistic Inquiry. 18,* 369–411.
Jackendoff, R.S. (1990). *Semantic structures.* Cambridge, MA: MIT Press.
Jackendoff, R.S. (1991). Parts and boundaries. *Cognition, 41,* 9–45.
Keenan, E.O. (1976). Towards a universal definition of "subject". In C. Li (Ed.), *Subject and topic* (pp. 303–333). New York: Academic Press.
Landau, B., & Gleitman, L.R. (1985). *Language and experience.* Cambridge, MA: Harvard University Press.
Levin, B. (1985). Lexical semantics in review: An introduction. In B. Levin (Ed.), *Lexical semantics in review* (pp. 1–62). Lexicon Project Working Papers No. 1, MIT Center for Cognitive Science.
Levin & Rappaport Hovav (1991). Wiping the slate clean: A lexical semantic exploration. Cognition, *41,* 123–151.
Macnamara, J. (1982). *Names for things: A study of human learning.* Cambridge, MA: MIT Press.
Marantz, A.P. (1982). On the acquisition of grammatical relations. *Linguistische Berichte: Linguistik als Kognitive Wissenschaft, 80/82,* 32–69.
Marcus, G., Ullman, M., Pinker, S., Hollander, M., Rosen, T.J., & Xu, F. (1990). *Overregularization.* MIT Center for Cognitive Science Occasional Paper No. 41.
Miller, G.A., & Johnson-Laird, P.N. (1976). *Language and perception.* Cambridge, MA: Harvard University Press.
Moravscik, E.A. (1978). On the case marking of objects. In J.H. Greenberg *et al.* (Eds.), *Universals of Human Language, Vol. 4: Syntax* (pp. 249–289). Stanford, CA: Stanford University Press.
Pesetsky, D. (1990). Psych predicates, universal alignment and lexical decomposition. Unpublished manuscript, Department of Linguistics and Philosophy, MIT.
Pinker, S. (1982). A theory of the acquisition of lexical interpretive grammars. In J. Bresnan (Ed.), *The mental representation of grammatical relations* (pp. 655–726). Cambridge, MA: MIT Press.
Pinker, S. (1984). *Language learnability and language development.* Cambridge, MA: MIT Press.
Pinker, S. (1987). The bootstrapping problem in language acquisition. In B. MacWhinney (Ed.), *Mechanisms of language acquisition* (pp. 399–441). Hillsdale, NJ: Erlbaum.
Pinker, S. (1989). *Learnability and cognition: The acquisition of argument structure.* Cambridge, MA: MIT Press.
Pinker, S., Lebeaux, D.S., & Frost, L.A. (1987). Productivity and constraints in the acquisition of the passive. *Cognition, 26,* 195–267.
Pinker, S., & Prince, A. (1988). On language and connectionism: Analysis of a parallel distributed processing model of language acquisition. *Cognition, 28,* 73–193.
Pustejovsky, J. (1991). The syntax of event structure. *Cognition, 41,* 47–81.
Rappaport, M., & Levin, B. (1985). A case study in lexical analysis: The locative alternation. Unpublished manuscript, MIT Center for Cognitive Science.
Rappaport, M., & Levin, B. (1988). What to do with theta-roles. In W. Wilkins (Ed.), *Thematic relations.* New York: Academic Press.
Schwartz-Norman, L. (1976). The grammar of 'content' and 'container'. *Journal of Linguistics, 12,* 279–287.
Talmy, L. (1983). How language structures space. In H. Pick & L. Acredolo (Eds.), *Spatial orientation: Theory, research, and application.* New York: Plenum.
Talmy, L. (1985). Lexicalization patterns: Semantic structure in lexical forms. In T. Shopen (Ed.), *Language typology and syntactic description. Vol. 3: Grammatical categories and the lexicon* (pp. 57–149). New York: Cambridge University Press.
Tenny, C. (1988). The aspectual interface hypothesis. *Proceedings of the North East Linguistics Society,* 18.
Wexler, K., & Culicover, P. (1980). *Formal principles of language acquisition.* Cambridge, MA: MIT Press.

7

Semantic networks of English*

George A. Miller and Christiane Fellbaum
Cognitive Science Laboratory, Princeton University.

Principles of lexical semantics developed in the course of building an on-line lexical database are discussed. The approach is relational rather than componential. The fundamental semantic relation is synonymy, which is required in order to define the lexicalized concepts that words can be used to express. Other semantic relations between these concepts are then described. No single set of semantic relations or organizational structure is adequate for the entire lexicon: nouns, adjectives, and verbs each have their own semantic relations and their own organization determined by the role they must play in the construction of linguistic messages.

Introduction

Communicative competence in English presupposes a remarkable lexical database. Not only is long-term semantic memory vast in size, but it is so organized that retrieval for production or comprehension can proceed at conversational rates. Many psychologists have been fascinated by the complexity and importance of this memory and have devised ingenious methods to explore and analyze the cognitive processes it must entail. In the century since Francis Galton first

* Preparation of this paper was supported in part by contract N00014-86-K-0492 with the Office of Naval Research, in part by contract MDA903-86-K-0242 with the Army Research Institute, and in part by a grant from the James S. McDonnell Foundation. The work on WordNet that provides the background for the paper was done in collaboration with Amalia Bachman, Richard Beckwith, Marie Bienkowski, Patrick Byrnes, Roger Chaffin, George Collier, Michael Colon, Melanie Cook, Fiona Cowie, Derek Gross, Brain Gustafson, P.N. Johnson-Laird, Judy Kegl, Benjamin Martin, Elana Messer, Katherine Miller, Antonio Romero, Daniel Treibel, Randee Tengi, Anton Vishio, and Pamela Wakefield. The views and conclusions contained herein are those of the authors and should not be represented as official policies of ONR, ARI, the McDonnell Foundation, or Princeton University.

introduced word associations, these various methods of investigation have led to many important psychological insights. Indeed, the accumulated observations relevant to the nature and organization of semantic memory now seem adequate to support serious theoretical attempts to characterize this aspect of human cognition.

In at least one respect, however, the current state of our information about lexical memory does not yet seem adequate. The problem is that the English lexicon is too large and varied to be incorporated properly into an experimental format. Consequently, most of the psycholinguistic research of central interest has been conducted on relatively small samples of words, often concentrating on nouns that denote concrete objects and neglecting other syntactic categories. This strategy is experimentally convenient, but leaves open may questions about the generality of the experimental conclusions. All too frequently, an interesting lexical hypothesis is advanced, fifty or a hundred words testing or illustrating it are considered, and extensions to the rest of the lexicon are left as an exercise for the reader.

One motive for undertaking the work described in this paper was to expose some of the more important psycholinguistic generalizations about lexical memory to the full range of the common English vocabulary. The decision to strive for breadth of lexical coverage means, of course, that experimentation must be abandoned as the principal method of research. The work has more the character of a field trip – a mapping expedition through neglected regions of the lexicon. When our explorations suggest unexpected psycholexical hypotheses, as they sometimes do, an experiment may be devised as a more objective test. But the principal method has been lexicographic, rather than experimental.

Lexicographic methods are constructive – they are intended to result in dictionaries. One way to adapt such methods to the psychological hypotheses of interest here is to use them to construct a model of lexical memory. That is to say, one way to test your understanding of something is to try to build one for yourself. With this thought in mind and taking inspiration from the widespread use of computers to simulate cognitive processes, in 1985 a group of psycholinguists at Princeton University began to build a lexical database along the lines of various hypotheses about semantic memory that were then current in psychological journals. It has now grown into an on-line representation of a major part of the English lexicon that aims to be psychologically realistic. As this is written, the system, named WordNet, contains over 54,000 different lexical entries organized into some 48,000 sets of synonyms (Miller, 1990). Only the most robust psycholexical hypotheses have survived.

The purpose of his report is not to describe WordNet or the applications of it that have been undertaken. In the course of building the database certain preconceptions had to be modified, a number of novel problems arose that had not been anticipated, and some familiar problems came to be seen in a new light.

No claim is made that what we have learned could not have been learned in other ways, or was not anticipated by other scientists, but the experience of testing psycholinguistic principles against the full scope of the English lexicon did give us our own perspective on lexical semantics – on what is important and what has been neglected, and what still lies beyond the reach of principles currently known to us. It is that perspective we hope to share in this report.

The lexical matrix

Lexical semantics begins with a recognition that a word is a conventional association between a lexicalized concept and an utterance that plays a syntactic role. This definition of "word" raises at least three classes of problems for research. First, what kinds of utterances enter into lexical associations? Second, what is the nature and organization of the lexicalized concepts that words can express? And third, what syntactic roles do different words play? Although it is impossible to ignore any of these questions while considering only one, the emphasis here will be on the second class of problems, those dealing with the semantic structure of the English lexicon.

Since the word "word" is used to refer both to the utterance and to its associated concept, discussions of this lexical association are vulnerable to terminological confusion. In order to reduce ambiguity, therefore, we will use "word form" to refer to the physical utterance or inscription and "word meaning" to refer to the lexicalized concept that a word form can express. Then the starting point for lexical semantics can be said to be the mapping between word forms and word meanings (Miller, 1986). A conservative initial assumption is that different syntactic categories of words may have different kinds of mappings.

It must be emphasized that a person who knows a word does not experience its form and its meaning as two separate things, but as two aspects of a unitary phenomenological entity. If you are a normal person and you know some common word – *table*, say – you cannot see or hear *table* without thinking of its meaning, and you will rarely entertain that concept without at least a subvocal use of *table*. Since form and meaning can vary independently, however, it is not unreasonable to distinguish them for theoretical purposes. A simple way to represent that distinction – one often found in discussions of the functional dissociations that are observed as a consequence of cortical injuries (Shallice, 1988) – is by a flow chart: one box for forms, another box for meanings, with arrows going back and forth between them. That representation has the advantage that two different kinds of relations are clearly distinguished: one box contains a system of formal relations between forms, the other contains a system of semantic relations between meanings. However, a box-and-arrow representation is too abstract to serve as a guide for the construction of a model like WordNet.

A box-and-arrow representation provides no easy way to incorporate the fact that the associations between forms and meanings are many : many – some forms have several different meanings, and some meanings can be expressed by several different forms. The arrows between boxes must be replaced by a lexical matrix that maps between forms and meanings. Without this many : many mapping, it is impossible to discuss the relation between two important and related problems of lexical storage – polysemy and synonymy. Polysemy and synonymy are problems that arise in the course of gaining access to information in the mental lexicon: a listener or reader who recognizes a word form must cope with its polysemy; a speaker or writer who hopes to express a meaning must decide between synonyms. Polysemy is a source of ambiguities that can lead to the retrieval of irrelevant information; synonymy is a source of alternative terminologies that can result in failures to retrieve relevant information.

In order to simulate this many : many lexical mapping it is necessary to have some way to represent both word forms and word meanings. Written words provide a reasonably satisfactory solution for the forms, but how meanings should be represented poses a critical question for any theory of lexical semantics. Lacking an adequate psychological theory, methods developed by lexicographers provide an interim solution: definitions can play the same role in a simulation that meanings play in the mind of a language user.

How meanings are to be represented by definitions in a theory of lexical semantics depends on whether the theory is intended to be constructive or merely differential. In a constructive theory, the representation should contain sufficient information to support an accurate construction of the concept (by either a person or a machine). The requirements of a fully constructive theory are not easily met, and there is some reason to believe that the definitions found in most standard dictionaries do not meet them (Miller & Gildea, 1987). Someone whose concept of tables was limited to the information that can be found in a dictionary definition of *table* would not be able to use or understand the word in everyday discourse. The gloss found in one leading dictionary, *a piece of furniture consisting of a flat slab fixed on legs*, is intelligible only to a reader who already knows what a table is. Lexicographers may aspire to constructive definitions (Landau, 1984), but you are at risk if your understanding is limited to what you have found in a dictionary.

In a differential theory, on the other hand, it is assumed that the user already has the concept, and that meanings can be represented by any symbols that make it possible to distinguish among them. The requirements for a differential theory are more modest, yet sufficient for the construction of the desired mappings. If the person who reads the definition needs merely to identify a familiar concept, then a synonym (or near synonym) is often sufficient. For example, someone who knows that *board* can mean either a piece of lumber or a group of people assembled for some purpose will be able to pick out the intended meaning with no more help than *plank* or *committee*. The synonym sets, {*board*, *plank*} and {*board*, *committee*} can serve as unambiguous designators of these two meanings of *board*. These synonym sets (synsets) do not explain what the concepts are; they merely signify that the concepts exist. People who know English are assumed to have already mastered the concepts, and are expected to recognize them from the words listed in the synsets.

A lexical matrix, therefore, can be represented for theoretical purposes by a mapping between written words and the synsets to which they belong. Since English is particularly rich in synonyms, synsets are often sufficient for differential purposes. Sometimes, however, a single word is not available, in which case the polysemy must be resolved by a short gloss; for example, {*board*, (a person's meals, provided regularly for money)} can serve to differentiate this sense of *board* from the others; it can be regarded as a synset with a single member. The gloss is not intended for use in constructing a new lexical concept by someone not already familiar with it, and it differs from a synonym in that it is not used to gain access to information stored in the mental lexicon. It fulfills its purpose if it enables a person who knows English to differentiate this meaning from others with which it could be confused.

Once a method of representation for lexical meanings is established, a central problem for lexical semantics is to characterize relations between meanings.

Semantic relations

The mental lexicon is organized by semantic relations. Since a semantic relation is a relation between meanings, and since meanings can be represented by synsets, it is natural to think of semantic relations as pointers between synsets. It is characteristic of semantic relations that they are reciprocated: if there is a semantic relation R between meaning $\{x, x', \ldots\}$ and meaning $\{y, y', \ldots\}$, then there is also a relation R′ between $\{y, y', \ldots\}$ and $\{x, x', \ldots\}$. For the purposes of the present discussion, the names of the semantic relations will serve a dual role: if the relation between the meanings $\{x, x', \ldots\}$ and $\{y, y', \ldots\}$ is called R, then R will also be used to designate the relation between word forms belonging to those synsets. It would be logically tidier to introduce separate terms for the relation between meanings and for the relation between forms, but even greater confusion might result from the introduction of so many new technical terms.

The following examples illustrate (but do not exhaust) the kinds of semantic relations we have worked with.

Synonymy

From what has already been said, it should be obvious that the most important semantic relation is similarity of meaning, since the ability to judge that relation is a prerequisite for the representation of meanings in a lexical matrix. According to one definition (usually attributed to Leibniz) two expressions are synonymous if the substitution of one for the other never changes the truth value of a sentence in which the substitution is made. By that definition, true synonyms are rare, if they exist at all. A weakened version of this definition would make synonymy relative to a context: two expressions are synonymous in a context C if the substitution of one for the other in C does not change the truth value. For example, the substitution of *plank* for *board* in carpentry contexts does not alter truth values, although there are other contexts of *board* where that substitution would be totally inappropriate. But even local synonymy – synonymous in a context – is insufficient for the needs of a lexical semanticist: some words (particularly verbs) express very similar concepts, yet cannot be interchanged without making the sentence ungrammatical. Synonymy is simply one end of a continuum on which similarity of meaning can be graded; it may be the case that semantically similar words can be interchanged in more contexts than can semantically dissimilar words (Miller & Charles, 1991). But the important point is that theories of lexical semantics do not depend on truth-functional conceptions of synonymy; semantic similarity is sufficient. It is convenient to assume that the relation is symmetrical, however: if x is similar to y, then y is equally similar to x.

Hyponymy

Another semantic relation that has received much attention is hyponymy/hypernymy (variously called subordination/superordination, subset/superset, or the ISA relation): *maple* is a hyponym of *tree*, and *tree* is a hyponym of *plant*. A meaning $\{x, x', \ldots\}$ is said to be a hyponym of the meaning $\{y, y', \ldots\}$ if native speakers of English accept sentences constructed from such frames as *An x is a (kind of) y*. The relation can be represented by including in $\{x, x', \ldots\}$ a pointer to its superordinate, and including in $\{y, y', \ldots\}$ pointers to its hyponyms.

Hyponymy is transitive and asymmetrical (Lyons, 1977, vol. 1), and, since there is normally a single superordinate, this semantic relation generates a hierarchical semantic structure where a hyponym is said to be below its superordinate. Such hierarchical representations are widely used by computer scientists to construct information retrieval systems, and are called inheritance systems (Fahlman, 1979): the hyponym inherits all the features of the more generic concept and adds at least one feature that distinguishes it from its superordinate and from any other hyponyms of that superordinate. For example, *maple* inherits the features of its superordinate, *tree*, but is distinguished from other trees by the hardness of its wood, the shape of its leaves, the use of its sap for syrup, etc. (Exceptions, skipping levels, and conflicts can be incorporated in nonmonotonic inheritance systems – Touretzky, 1986 – but will not be discussed here; see Flickinger, 1989, and Evans and Gazdar, 1990, for applications of nonmonotonic inheritance theory in the lexicon and other areas of descriptive linguistics.)

A seminal paper by Collins and Quillian (1969) attempted to show that the time needed to respond Yes or No to such statements as *A canary is a canary*, *A canary is a bird*, and *A canary is an animal* increased as the number of hyponymic levels increased. When further experiments demonstrated that reaction times are not always reliable predictors of the number of links in such taxonomic hierarchies, many psycholinguists assumed that the principles underlying inheritance systems are not applicable to the organization of semantic memory. Without reviewing the extensive debate on this question we will simply state that there are many other reasons to assume that the inheritance arguments are correct, and that reaction times do not measure what Collins and Quillian initially assumed.

Antonymy

Another familiar semantic relation is antonymy, which turns out to be surprisingly difficult to define. The antonym of a word *x* is sometimes *not-x*, but not always. For example, *rich* and *poor* are antonyms, but to say that someone is not rich does not mean that they must be poor; many people consider themselves neither rich nor poor. Antonymy, which seems such a simple symmetrical relation, is at least as complex as the other semantic relations, yet speakers of English have no trouble recognizing antonyms when they see them. One complication (discussed below) arises from the need to distinguish clearly between antonymy as a relation between word forms and antonymy as a relation between word meanings.

Meronymy

Synonymy, hyponymy, and antonymy are familiar semantic relations. They apply widely throughout the lexicon and people do not need special training in linguistics in order to appreciate them. Another relation sharing these advantages is the part-whole (or HASA) relation, known to lexical semanticists as meronymy/holonymy. A meaning $\{x, x', \ldots\}$ is a meronym of a meaning $\{y, y', \ldots\}$ if native speakers of English accept sentences constructed from such frames as *A y has an x* (*as a part*) or *an x is a part of y*. The meronymic relation is transitive (with qualifications) and asymmetrical (Cruse, 1986), and can be used to construct a part hierarchy (with some reservations, since a meronym can have many holonyms). We assume that the concept of a part of a whole can be a part of a concept of the whole, although we recognize that the implications of this assumption deserve more discussion than they will receive here.

These and other similar relations serve to organize the mental lexicon. They can all be thought of, or represented by, pointers or labeled arcs from one synset to another. Thus, semantic relations represent associations that form a complex semantic network; knowing where a word is located in that network is an important part of knowing the word's meaning. It is a rigid network, yet open enough to admit new meanings and new associations as vocabulary growth proceeds. It is not profitable to discuss these relations in the abstract, however, because they play different roles in organizing the lexical knowledge associated with different syntactic categories.

Nouns

When psychologists think about the organization of lexical memory it is nearly always the organization of nouns that they have in mind. Consequently, there has been considerable speculation about the semantic organization of nominal concepts. It is generally agreed that they are organized hierarchically into levels, from specific to generic, although the associations required to realize that structure are still moot (Smith, 1978).

The topmost, or most generic level of the hierarchy is almost vacuous semantically. It is possible to put some empty abstraction designated, say, {*entity*}, at the top; to make {*object*} and {*idea*} its immediate hyponyms, and so to continue down to more specific meanings, thus pulling all nouns together into a single hierarchical structure. In practice, however, these abstract concepts carry little semantic information; it is doubtful that people could even agree on the appropriate words to express them. The alternative is to select a relatively small number of generic concepts and to treat each one as the unique beginner of a separate hierarchy. Different workers make different choices, of course, but we have found that the following set of 26 unique beginners provides a place for every English noun:

{*act, action, activity*}	{*natural object*}
{*animal, fauna*}	{*natural phenomenon*}
{*artifact*}	{*person, human being*}
{*attribute, property*}	{*plant, flora*}
{*body, corpus*}	{*possession, property*}
{*cognition, ideation*}	{*process*}

{*communication*}	{*quantity, amount*}
{*event, happening*}	{*relation*}
{*feeling, emotion*}	{*shape*}
{*food*}	{*society*}
{*group, collection*}	{*state, condition*}
{*location, place*}	{*substance*}
{*motive*}	{*time*}

These hierarchies vary widely in size and are not mutually exclusive – some cross-referencing is required – but on the whole they cover distinct conceptual domains.

If these hierarchies were inheritance systems, there would be no reason to limit the number of levels they might contain. In fact, however, they seldom go more than ten levels deep, and those cases usually contain technical levels that are not part of the everyday vocabulary. For example, a Shetland pony is a pony, a horse, an equid, a perissodactyl, a herbivore, a mammal, a vertebrate, and an animal: nine levels, of which five are technical. Some are deeper than others: the hierarchy of man-made artifacts sometimes goes six or seven levels deep (*roadster*→ *car*→ *motor vehicle*→ *wheeled vehicle*→ *vehicle*→ *conveyance*→ *artifact*), whereas the hierarchy of persons runs about three or four (one of the deepest is *televangelist*→ *evangelist*→ *clergyman*→ *spiritual leader*→ *person*). If information associated with these concepts was stored redundantly, rather than inherited, the more generic information would be repeated over and over, so each additional level would put an increasing burden on lexical memory – a possible reason for limiting the number of levels.

These hierarchies of nominal concepts have been said to have a level, somewhere in the middle, where most of the distinguishing features are attached. It is referred to as the base level of the noun lexicon, and concepts at this level are basic concepts (Rosch, Mervis, Gray, Johnson & Boyes-Braem, 1976). For lexical concepts at the base level, people can list many distinguishing features. Above the base level, descriptions are brief and general. Below the base level, little is added to the features that distinguish basic concepts. The best examples are to be found in the hierarchical lexicon for concrete objects.

Although the overall structure of noun hierarchies is generated by the hyponymy relation, details are given by the features that distinguish one concept from another. For example, a canary is a bird that is small, yellow, sings, and flies, so not only must *canary* be entered as a hyponym of *bird*, but the attributes of small size and yellow color must also be included, as well as the activities of singing and flying. Moreover, *canary* must inherit from *bird* the fact that it has a beak and wings with feathers. In order to make all of this information available when *canary* is activated, it must be possible to associate *canary* appropriately with at least three different kinds of information:

(1) Parts: *beak*, *wings*
(2) Attributes: *small*, *yellow*
(3) Functions: *sing*, *fly*

Each type of distinguishing feature must be treated differently.

Parts

Since *beak* and *wing* are meronyms of *bird*, this semantic relation provides an obvious way to attach parts to a hierarchy: meronyms can serve as features that hyponyms can inherit. Consequently, meronymy and hyponymy become intertwined in complex ways. For example, if *beak* is a meronym of *bird*, and if *canary* is a hyponym of *bird*, then *beak* must be an inherited meronym of *canary*. Although these connections may appear complex when dissected in this manner, they are rapidly deployed in language comprehension: for example, most people overlook the inferences involved in establishing a connection between the sentences: *It was a canary. The beak was injured*. Of course, after *canary* has inherited *beak* often enough, the fact that canaries have beaks may come to be stored redundantly with the other features of *canary*, but that possibility does not mean that the general structure of people's lexical knowledge is not organized hierarchically.

The connections between meronymy and hyponymy are further complicated by the fact that parts are hyponyms as well as meronyms. For example, {*beak*, *bill*, *neb*} is a hyponym of {*mouth*, *muzzle*}, which in turn is a meronym of {*face*, *countenance*} and a hyponym of {*orifice*, *opening*}. A frequent problem in establishing the proper relation between hyponymy and meronymy arises from a general tendency to attach features too high in the hierarchy. For example, if *wheel* is said to be a meronym of *vehicle*, then sleds and spacecraft will inherit wheels they should not have.

Meronymy has been said to be particularly important in defining the basic objects in a hyponymic hierarchy (Tversky & Hemenway, 1984), but we have found it to occur primarily in the {*body*, *corpus*}, {*natural object*}, and {*artifact*} hierarchies;[1] we have not explored whether a basic level can be defined for more abstract concepts.

[1] Meronyms are also common in the {*quantity*, *amount*} hierarchy, where small units of measurement are parts of larger units. We assume that these meronyms are not what Tversky and Hemenway had in mind.

Attributes

The fact that canaries are small should be expressed by the adjective *small*. There is no semantic relation comparable to synonymy, hyponymy, or meronymy that can serve this function, however. Instead, adjectives are said to modify nouns, or nouns are said to serve as arguments for attributes: Size (*canary*) = *small*. For theoretical purposes, however, the fact that a canary is small can be represented by a pointer in much the same way as the fact that a canary is a bird. Formally, the difference is that there is no return pointer from *small* back to *canary*. That is to say, although people will list *small* when asked for the features of canaries, when asked to list small things they are unlikely to think of canaries. The pointer from *canary* to *small* is interpreted with respect to the immediate superordinate of *canary*, that is, *small for a bird*, but that anchor to a head noun is lost when *small* is accessed alone.

The use of modification to introduce attributes as distinguishing features of nominal concepts provides a semantic link from noun hierarchies to adjectives, whose semantic structure is discussed further below.

Functions

The term "function" has served many purposes, both in psychology and linguistics, so we are obliged to explain what sense we attach to it in this context. A functional feature of a nominal concept is intended to be a description of something that instances of the concept normally do, or that is normally done with or to them. This usage feels more natural in some cases than in others. For example, it seems natural to say that the function of a pencil is to write or the function of an umbrella is to protect from the elements, but to say that the function of a canary is to fly or to sing is less felicitous. What we really have in mind here are all the features of nominal concepts that are described by verbs or verb phrases. Lacking any better term, we will use "function", although the thought has not escaped us that a more precise analysis might distinguish several different kinds of functional features. These nominal concepts can play various semantic roles as arguments of the verbs with which they co-occur in a sentence: instruments (knife–cut), materials (wallpaper–attach; wool–knit), products (hole–dig; picture–paint), containers (box–hold), etc.

The need for functional features is most apparent when attempting to characterize a concept like {*ornament*, *decoration*}. An ornament can be any size or shape or composition; parts and attributes fail to capture the meaning. But the function of an ornament is clear: it is to make something else appear more attractive. At least since Dunker (1945) described functional fixedness, psychologists have been aware that the uses to which a thing is normally put are a central part of a person's conception of that thing. To call something a box, for example, suggests that it should function as a container, which blocks the thought of using it for anything else. There are also linguistic reasons to assume that a thing's function is a feature of its meaning (Katz, 1964).

In terms of the approach to lexical semantics being developed here, functional information should be included by pointers to verb concepts, just as attributes are included by pointers to adjective concepts. In many cases, however, there is no single verb that expresses the function. And in cases where there is a single verb, it can be circular. For example, if the noun *hammer* is defined by a pointer to the verb *hammer*, both concepts are left in need of definition. More appropriately, the noun *hammer* should point to the verb *hit*, because it usually plays the semantic role of instrument and is used for hitting; the verb *hammer* is a conflation of its superordinate *hit* and the instrument used to do it. The semantic role of nouns like *hammer*, *wallpaper*, or *box* tend to be the same wherever they occur in sentences, independent of their grammatical role. That is to say, in both *John hit the mugger with a hammer* and *The hammer hit him on the head*, the semantic role of *hammer* is that of an instrument. Similarly, *wool* is a semantic material in each of the following sentences: *She knitted the wool into a scarf*, *She knitted a scarf out of the wool*, and *This wool knits well*. This consistency in mapping onto the same semantic role independently of syntax is not a feature of all nominal concepts, however: what is the function of *apple* or *cat*? The details are obviously complicated and we do not feel that we have yet achieved a satisfactory understanding of these functional attributes of nominal concepts.

Kinship terminology

Because kinship provides valuable information about the organization of a society, linguistic anthropologists have devoted considerable attention to kinship terminology (Goodenough, 1956; Romney & D'Andrade, 1964; Wallace & Atkins, 1960). But kin terms are a specialized lexical subfield of nouns that do not fit easily into the system of semantic relations available in WordNet. For example, it can be shown (Greenberg, 1949; Miller & Johnson-Laird, 1976) that English kinship terminology can be specified in terms of the primitive relations PARENT OF (and its inverse, CHILD OF) and SPOUSE OF, but these primitive relations are not included among the semantic relations used to build WordNet.

When a description of the semantics of kin terms is limited to those semantic relations having broad application throughout the noun lexicon, only a part of the kinship structure can be captured. For example, *father* and *son* can be represented as hyponyms of *man*, as antonyms of *mother* and *daughter* respectively, and as meronyms of *family*. But the semantic relations that would be required for a more adequate account of English kin terms are not needed outside of this limited lexical domain. There is no reason that the missing relations – generational and affinal – could not be added in order to obtain a more complete theory of semantic relations, but they are considered too specialized for inclusion in WordNet.

Adjectives

Two kinds of modifiers are usually distinguished. Roughly, those that modify nouns are called adjectives; those that modify anything else are called adverbs. We have not explored the semantics of adverbs, but have assumed that, since the majority of them are derived from adjectives by adding an −*ly* suffix, adverbs must have the same semantic organization as adjectives.

Predicative adjectives

A predicative adjective is one that can be used in the predicate of a sentence. For example, *strong* is a predicative adjective in *the man is strong*. A few adjectives can only be used predicatively: *the man is alive* is acceptable, but not the *the alive man*. However, most adjectives can be used attributively: *the strong man*. The important point to understand is that many adjectives cannot be used predicatively. For example, *the former champion* is admissible, but *the champion is former* is not. In dictionaries, non-predicative adjectives are often defined with some phrase like "of or pertaining to" something.

The distinction between predicative and non-predicative adjectives is complicated by the fact that some adjectives can be both: *nervous* is predicative in *a nervous person*, but not in *a nervous disorder*. Linguists have provided several criteria for distinguishing between them (Levi, 1978):

(1) Predicative and non-predicative adjectives cannot be conjoined: *the tall and corporate lawyer* is odd.
(2) Non-predicative adjectives are not gradable: *the extremely natal day* is odd.
(3) Non-predicative adjectives cannot be nominalized: the predicative use of *nervous* in *the nervous person* admits such constructions as *the person's nervousness*, but its non-predicative use in *the nervous disorder* does not.

Note that numbers are a special class of non-predicative adjectives: they do not conjoin (*the young and three friends*), they are not gradable (*the highly three friends*), and they cannot be nominalized (*the friends' threeness*).

By all three criteria, non-predicative adjectives resemble nouns that are used as adjectives. For example, in *baseball game* the noun *baseball* is used as an adjective to modify *game*, but, like a non-predicative adjective, the nominal adjective does not conjoin (*the long and baseball game*), is not gradable (*the extremely baseball game*), and cannot be nominalized (*the game's baseballness*). Consequently, non-predictive adjectives can be considered stylistic variants of modifying nouns; we have assumed that they are entered in lexical memory as a special class of adjectives, and are defined by pointers to the pertinent noun concept. Thus, the meanings expressed by non-predicative adjectives are assumed to have the same hierarchical semantic organization that nominal meanings have.

Semantic structure

The semantic organization of predicative adjectives is entirely different from that of nouns – a prime example of syntactic–semantic linking. Nothing like the hyponymic relation that generates nominal hierarchies is available for adjectives: it is not clear what it would mean to say that one adjective "is a kind of" some other adjective. Some people find it natural to think of the semantic organization of adjectives, not as a hierarchical tree, but as an abstract hyperspace of *N* dimensions.

The basic semantic relation among adjectives is antonymy. The importance of antonymy first became obvious from results obtained with word association tests. When the probe word in a word association test is a familiar adjective, the response commonly given by adults is the antonym of the probe. For example, when the probe is *good*, the common response is *bad*; when the probe is *bad*, the response is *good*. This mutuality of association is a salient feature of the data for adjectives (Deese, 1964, 1965). It is acquired as a consequence of these pairs of words being used together frequently in the same phrases and sentences (Charles & Miller, 1989; Justeson & Katz, 1989).

The importance of antonymy is understandable when it is recognized that the function of predicative adjectives is to express values of attributes, and that most attributes are bipolar. Antonyms are adjectives that express values at opposite poles of an attribute. That is to say, *x is Adj* presupposes that there is an attribute A such that A(x) = *Adj*. To say *The package is heavy* presupposes that there is an attribute Weight such that Weight(*package*) = *heavy*. The antonym of *heavy* is *light*, which expresses a value at the opposite pole of the Weight attribute.

This account leaves two questions unanswered. First, if antonymy is so important, why do many adjectives seem to have no antonym? Second, and closely related, when two adjectives have similar meanings, why do they not have the same antonym? For example, continuing with Weight, what is the antonym of *ponderous*? *Ponderous* is often used where *heavy* would also be appropriate, yet *ponderous* has no obvious antonym. And why do *heavy* and *weighty*, which are closely similar in meaning, have different antonyms, *light* and *weightless*, respectively?

The problem here is that the antonymy relation between word forms is different from the antonymy relation between word meanings. Except for a handful of frequently used Anglo-Saxon adjectives, most antonyms of predicative adjectives are formed by a morphological rule that adds a negative prefix (usually *un-*) and changes the polarity of the meaning. Morphological rules apply to word forms, not to word meanings; they generally have a semantic reflex, of course, and in the case of antonymy the semantic reflex is so striking that it deflects attention away from the underlying morphological process. But the important consequence of the morphological origin of many antonym pairs is that antonymy is not a semantic relation between word meanings, but rather is a semantic relation between word forms – which precludes the simple representation of antonymy by pointers between synsets. To continue with Weight, it is not appropriate to introduce antonymy by labeled pointers between {*heavy*, *weighty*, *ponderous*, *massive*} and {*light*, *weightless*, *airy*}. People who know English will judge *heavy/light* to be antonyms, and perhaps *weighty/weightless*, but they will pause and be puzzled when asked whether *heavy/weightless* or *ponderous/airy* are antonyms. The word meanings are opposed, but the word forms are not familar antonym pairs.

For this reason, it is necessary to look for structure inside the synsets. Gross, Fischer, and Miller (1989) propose that adjective synsets be regarded as clusters of adjectives associated by semantic similarity with a focal adjective (one or more) that relates the cluster to a contrasting cluster at the opposite pole of the attribute. Thus, *ponderous* is similar to *heavy* and *heavy* is the antonym of *light*, so a conceptual opposition of *ponderous/light* is mediated by *heavy*. Gross et al. distinguish between direct antonyms like *heavy/light*, which are conceptual opposites that are also associated pairs, and indirect antonyms, like *heavy/weightless*, which are conceptual opposites that are not associatively paired. Under this formulation, all predicative adjectives have antonyms; those lacking direct antonyms have indirect antonyms, that is, are synonyms of adjectives that have direct antonyms. Direct antonyms can be represented by an antonymy pointer between synsets containing a single word form; indirect antonyms must add a synonym pointer that indicates membership in the cluster.

Gradation

Most discussions of antonymy distinguish between contradictory and contrary terms. This terminology originated in logic, where two propositions are said to be contradictory if the truth of one implies the falsity of the other, and are said to be contrary if only one proposition can be true, but both can be false. Thus, *alive* and *dead* are said to be contradictory terms because the truth of *Sam is dead* implies the falsity of *Sam is alive*, and vice versa. And *fat* and *thin* are said to be contrary terms because *Sam is fat* and *Sam is thin* cannot both be true, but both can be false if Sam is of average weight. However, Lyons (1977, vol. 1) has pointed out that this definition of contrary terms is not limited to opposites, but can be applied so broadly as to be almost meaningless. For example, *Sam is a chair* and *Sam is a dog* cannot both be true, but both can be false, so *dog* and *chair* must be contraries. Lyons argues that gradability, not truth functions, provides the better explanation of these differences. Contraries are gradable, contradictories are not.

Gradable adjectives can be identified as those whose value can be multiplied by such adverbs of degree as *very*, *decidedly*, *intensely*, *rather*, *quite*, *somewhat*, *pretty*, *extremely* (Cliff, 1959). In some cases, gradation is lexicalized. For example, gradation orders such strings of adjectives as *frigid*, *cold*, *cool*, *tepid*, *warm*, *hot*, *scalding*. Surprisingly little gradation is lexicalized in English, however. Some attributes allow it: size, age, value, brightness, warmth, for example. But most gradation is accomplished by morphological rules for the positive, comparative, and superlative degrees, which can be extended if *less* and *least* are used to complement *more* and *most*.

Gradation must be added to antonymy and synonymy as a semantic relation organizing lexical memory for adjectives (Bierwisch, 1989). Although gradation is conceptually important, however, it does not play an important role in the adjective lexicon, and so is not coded in WordNet.

Markedness

Most attributes have an orientation. It is natural to think of them as dimensions in a hyperspace, where one end of each dimension is anchored at the point of origin of the space. The point of origin is the expected or default value; deviations from it merit comment, and are called the marked value of the attribute.

The antonyms *long/short* illustrate this general linguistic phenomenon known as markedness. In an important paper on German adjectives, Bierwisch (1967) noted that only unmarked spatial adjectives can take measure phrases. For example, *The train is ten cars long* is acceptable; the measure phrase, *ten cars*, describes how long the train is. But when the antonym is used, as in *The train is ten cars short*, the result is not acceptable (unless it has already been established that the train is short). Thus, the primary member, *long*, is the unmarked term; the secondary member, *short*, is marked and does not take measure phrases without special preparation. Note that the unmarked member lends its name to the attribute, *long* → *length*.

Measure phrases are inappropriate with many attributes, yet markedness is a general phenomenon that characterizes nearly all direct antonyms. In nearly every case, one member of a pair of antonyms is primary: more customary, more frequently used, less remarkable, or morphologically related to the name of the attribute. The primary term is the default value of the attribute, the value that would be assumed in the absence of information to the contrary. In a few cases (e.g., *wet/dry*, *hot/cold*) it is arguable which term should be regarded as primary, but for the vast majority of pairs the marker is explicit in the form of a negative prefix: *un* + *pleasant*, *im* + *patient*, *il* + *legal*, for example.

Color adjectives

One large class of adjectives is organized differently, and deserves special note. English color terms can serve either as adjectives or nouns, yet they are not nominal adjectives: they can be graded, nominalized, and conjoined with other predicative adjectives. But the bipolar pattern of direct and indirect antonymy that is observed for other predicative adjectives does not hold for color adjectives. Only one attribute is clearly described by direct antonyms: lightness, whose polar values are expressed by *light/dark* or *white/black*. Students of color vision can produce evidence of oppositions between red and green, and between yellow and blue, but those are not treated as direct antonyms in lay speech. The semantic organization of color terms is given by the dimensions of color perception: lightness, hue, and saturation (or chroma), which define the color solid.

Speculation about the evolution of color terminology (Berlin & Kay, 1969) suggests that it begins with a single, conventional attribute, lightness. Exotic languages are still spoken that have only two color terms to express values of that attribute, and it has been shown that this lexical limitation is not a consequence of perceptual deficits (Heider, 1972; Heider & Olivier, 1972). As technology advances and makes possible the manipulation of color, the need for greater terminological precision grows and more color terms are added. They are added along lines determined by innate mechanisms of color perception, however, rather than by the established patterns of linguistic modification – a reversal of the Sapir–Whorf hypothesis that linguistic habits constrain thought.

Selectional preferences

Adjectives are selective about the nouns they modify. The general rule is that if the referent denoted by a noun does not have the attribute whose value is expressed by the adjective, then that adjective–noun combination requires a figurative or idiomatic interpretation. For example, a building or a person can be tall because buildings and persons have height as an attribute, but streets and yards do not have height, so *tall street* or *tall yard* do not admit a literal reading. It is really a comment on the semantics of nouns, therefore, when we say that adjectives vary widely in their breadth of application. Adjectives expressing evaluations (*good/bad*, *clean/dirty*, *desirable/undesirable*) can modify almost any noun; those expressing activity (*active/passive*, *fast/slow*) or potency (*strong/weak*, *brave/cowardly*) also have wide ranges of applicability (cf. Osgood, Suci, & Tannenbaum, 1957). From the perspective of modification, a noun is simply a bundle of attributes – including attributes that are inherited as well as those required as distinguishing features.

A nominal concept must contain more than a mere list of its attributes. It must also contain information about the expected values of those attributes: for example, although both buildings and persons have the attribute of height, the expected height of a building is much greater than the expected height of a person. It is usually assumed, therefore, that the meaning of a noun must include information about the expected values of its attributes; the adjective simply modifies those values above or below their default values. The denotation of an adjective–noun combination such as *tall building* cannot be the intersection of two independent sets, the set of tall things and the set of buildings, for then all buildings would be included.

How adjectival information modulates nominal information is not a question to be settled in terms of lexical representations. We assume that the interactions between adjectives and nouns are not prestored, but are computed as needed by some on-line interpretative process. "The nominal information must be given priority; the adjectival information is then evaluated within the range allowed by the nominal information" (Miller & Johnson-Laird, 1976, p. 358).

Verbs

Verbs are arguably the most important lexical category of a language. Every English sentence must contain at least one verb, but, as grammatical sentences like *It is raining* show, they need not contain (referential) nouns. Yet there are far fewer verbs than nouns in the language. For example, the *Collins English Dictionary* lists 43,636 different nouns and 14,190 different verbs. Verbs are more polysemous than nouns: the nouns in *Collins* have on the average 1.74 senses, whereas verbs average 2.11.[2]

Verbs are also the most complex lexical category. Representing the meanings of verbs presents difficulties for any theory of lexical semantics, but special difficulties for the present program. To begin with, we have chosen to represent word meanings in terms of semantic relations. The more popular approach has been semantic decomposition (Gruber, 1976; Jackendoff, 1972; Miller & Johnson-Laird, 1976; Schank, 1972), with perhaps the best-known example being the decomposition of *kill* into *cause to become not alive* (McCawley, 1968). But

[2] We are indebted to Richard Beckwith for these figures.

semantic decomposition of verbs yields such abstract components as CAUSE, STATE, NEG, PATH, etc., many of which cannot be expressed by verbs. Because our present concern is to understand semantic relations between verbs, we will not begin by decomposing them into irreducible semantic atoms that are not verbs. Indeed, there is no incontrovertible evidence that verbs actually are organized in lexical memory in terms of their irreducible meaning components. Although it can be shown that speakers are able to decompose verb meanings – in order to predict a verb's idiosyncratic syntactic behavior, for example (Pinker, 1989) – the fact that verbs with complex decompositions can be thought of and understood as quickly as verbs with simpler decompositions (Fodor, Fodor, & Garrett, 1975) is usually interpreted to mean that semantic components are not stored in the lexicon, but are part of an inferential system that can use the lexicon. A relational analysis, on the other hand, takes words – entries in a speaker's mental lexicon – as its primative units.

In many respects, however, the relational analysis proposed here resembles semantic decomposition. For example, the CAUSE subpredicate of generative semantics is analogous to a semantic relation linking verb pairs like *show/see* and *feed/eat*. Other semantic components do not play an overt role in the relational analysis of the verb lexicon, but are implicit in some of the relations. Thus, NEG is implicit in certain opposition relations, for example, between the contradictory verbs *have* and *lack*: *lack* can be decomposed as NEG(*have*). Or, again, Talmy's (1985) semantic element MANNER is part of the semantic relation that is here called "troponymy"; it relates such verb pairs as *stroll/walk* and *mumble/talk*. The difference between a decompositional and a relational analysis, therefore, is subtle but important; certain elements of a decompositional analysis constitute, in part, the semantics of some of the relations of our analysis.

In the course of exploring semantic relations between verbs we found that the kinds of relations used to build networks of nouns and adjectives either could not be imported straightforwardly into the verb lexicon, or that our intuitions about those relations changed when they were applied to verbs. Finally, we discovered that some semantic relations cluster in certain areas of the verb lexicon, and so determine patterns of lexicalization that we had not anticipated.

In part, the complexity of the English verb arises from its role as a predicate that takes noun phrases as arguments. It is not merely that the number of arguments can vary, but also that the nature of those arguments and the many different relations into which they can enter are lexicalized in the verb. Finding the invariant framework that supports this enormous variety is a considerable challenge.

At present, we have organized some 8,500 verb forms into about 5,000 synsets. We divided the verbs into 14 semantically distinct groups: verbs of bodily care and functions, change, cognition, communication, competition, consumption, contact, creation, emotion, motion, perception, possession, social interaction, and weather verbs. Another file contains stative verbs such as *exceed*, *differ*, and *match*. The stative verbs do not form a semantically coherent group and share no semantic properties other than that they denote states rather than actions or events.

The major division into 14 semantically coherent groups of action and event verbs and one group of semantically diverse stative verbs reflects the division between the major conceptual categories EVENT and STATE adopted by both Jackendoff (1983) and Dowty (1979).

Several of the groups are headed by a topmost verb, similar to the "unique beginner" heading a noun file. These topmost verbs resemble the "core components" of Miller and Johnson-Laird (1976). They express the basic concepts to which the semantically more elaborate verbs in the groups are linked via different relations.

Hyponymy in the verb lexicon

The sentence frame used to test hyponymy between nouns, *An x is a y*, is not suitable for verbs, because it requires that *x* and *y* be nouns: *to strut is a kind of to walk* is not a felicitous sentence. Even when this formula is used with verbs in the gerundive form, we notice a difference between nouns and verbs. Although people are quite comfortable with statements like *A robin is a bird* or *A hammer is a tool*, they are likely to question the acceptability of such statements as *Smacking is hitting* or *Mumbling is talking*, where the superordinate is not accompanied by some qualification. The semantic distinction between two verbs in a superordinate relation is different from, and somehow greater than, the features that distinguish two nouns in a hyponymic relation.

An examination of "verb hyponyms" and their superordinates shows that lexicalization involves many kinds of semantic elaborations across different semantic fields. For example, Talmy's (1985) analysis of motion verbs treats them as conflations of *move* and such semantic components as MANNER and CAUSE, exemplified by *slide* and *pull*, respectively. Other motion verbs can be said to encode SPEED (*run*) or the MEDIUM of displacement (*bus*). Similarly, English verbs denoting different kinds of *hitting* express the DEGREE OF FORCE used by the agent (*chop*, *slam*, *whack*, *swat*, *rap*, *tap*, *peck*, etc.) Since our aim is to study the relations between verbs, rather than between the building blocks that make them up, we have merged the different kinds of elaborations that distinguish a "verb hyponym" from its superordinate into a manner relation that we have dubbed troponymy (from the Greek *tropos*, manner or fashion.) The troponymy relation between two verbs can be expressed by the formula *To* V_1 *is to* V_2 *in some manner* (Fellbaum & Miller, 1990). Troponyms can be related to their superordinates along many semantic dimensions, subsets of which tend to cluster within a given semantic field. Troponyms of communication verbs often encode the speaker's intention or motivation for communicating, as in *beg*, *persuade*, or *flatter*. Among contact verbs many troponyms are conflations of the verbs *hit*, *cut*, and *fasten*, with nouns denoting instruments or materials, for example, *hammer*, *club*, *knife*, *saw*, *cable*, *tape*. Clark and Clark (1979) show that a wide variety of denominal verbs are readily created and interpreted by native speakers. Many of the verbs cited by Clark and Clark are troponyms resulting from the conflation of the base verb and a noun, which is a productive process for coining neologisms.

Troponymy is the most frequently found relation among verbs; that is, most lexicalized verb concepts refer to an action or event that constitutes a manner elaboration of another activity or event. In this respect the verb lexicon resembles the noun lexicon, where most nouns can be expressed as "kinds of" other nouns. But the organization of verb troponyms with respect to each other differs from that of noun hyponyms.

Verb taxonomies

In trying to construct verb taxonomies using the troponymy relation, it became apparent that verbs cannot easily be arranged into the kind of tree structures onto which nouns can be mapped. First of all, verbs tend to have a much more shallow, bushy structure; in most cases, the number of hierarchical levels does not exceed four. Second, within a semantic field, not all verbs can be grouped under a single top node, or unique beginner. Motion verbs, for example, have two top nodes, {*move*, *make a movement*}, and {*move*, *travel*, *displace*}. Verbs of possession can be traced up to the three verbs {*give*, *transfer*}, {*take*, *receive*}, and {*have*, *hold*}; for the most part their troponyms encode ways in which society has ritualized the transfer of possessions: *bequeath*, *donate*, *inherit*, *usurp*, *own*, *stock*, etc.

In addition to being relatively shallow, virtually every verb taxonomy shows what might be called a bulge, that is to say, a level far more richly lexicalized than the other levels in the same hierarchy. Call this layer *L0*, the layer above it *L + 1*, and the layer below *L − 1*. Most of the verbs in a hierarchy cluster at *L0*, and the troponymy relation between these verbs and their superordinate is semantically richer than between verbs on other levels. Consider the taxonomy arising from the verb *walk*: the superordinate of *walk* is {*move*, *travel*, *displace*}; troponyms of *walk* are *march*, *strut*, *traipse*, *amble*, *mosey*, *slouch*, etc. (We have coded some 65 different lexicalized manners of *walk*.) Although a statement relating *L + 1* to *L + 2* – *To walk is to move in some manner* – is perfectly fine, statements relating *L0* to *L + 1* – *To march/strut/traipse/amble . . . is to walk in some manner* – seem more felicitous; that is, more semantic features are added in the lexicalization of these *L0* troponyms than in the lexicalization of *walk*. The semantic relation between *walk* and its many troponyms appears closer than that between *move* and *walk*.

In most hierarchies, *L − 1*, the level below the most richly lexicalized one, has relatively few verbs. For the most part, they tend not to be independently lexicalized, but are compounded from their superordinate and a noun. Examples from the *walk* hierarchy would be *goose-step* and *sleepwalk*; among the consumption verbs we find verbs with incorporated nouns like *breastfeed* and *bottlefeed*.

As one descends in a verb hierarchy, the range of nouns that the verbs on a given level can take as potential arguments decreases. Thus, *walk* can take a subject referring either to a person or an animal; most troponyms of *walk*, however, are restricted to human subjects (some birds can be said to *strut*, but they cannot *shuffle* or *saunter*). On the other hand, {*move*, *travel*} can take not only person and animal subjects, but also vehicles, or objects moved by external forces.

Meronymy in the verb lexicon

Like hyponymy, meronymy is a relation well suited to nouns, but less well suited to verbs. To begin with, for sentences based on the formula *An x is a part of a y* to be acceptable, both *x* and *y* must be nouns. It might seem that using the nominalizing gerundive form of the verbs would convert them into nouns, and as nouns the HASA relation should apply. For example, Rips and Conrad (1989) asked subjects to judge questions like *Is thinking a part of planning?* and obtained consistent patterns of response. But this change in syntactic category does not overcome the fundamental meaning differences between nouns and verbs. Fellbaum and Miller (1990) argue that, first, verbs cannot be taken apart in the same way as nouns, because the parts of verbs are not analogous to the parts of nouns. Nouns and noun parts have distinct, delimited referents. The referents of verbs, on the other hand, do not have the kind of distinct parts that characterize objects, groups, or substances. Verbs cannot be broken up into referents denoted solely by verbs. And, second, the relations among parts of verbs differ from those found among noun parts. The relation between *moving* and *rising*, for example, differs from the relation between *branch* and *tree*. Any acceptable statement about part-relations among verbs always involves the temporal relation between the activities that the two verbs denote. One activity or event is part of another activity or event only when it is part of, or a stage in, its temporal realization.

Some activities can be broken down into sequentially ordered subactivities. For the most part, these fall into the class of activities termed scripts by Schank and Abelson (1977); they tend not to be lexicalized in English: *eat at a restaurant*, *clean an engine*, *get a medical check-up*, etc. However, the analysis into lexicalized subactivities that is possible for these verb phrases is not available for the majority of simple verbs in English. Consider the relation between the verbs *fatten* and *feed*. Although neither activity is a discrete part of the other, the two are connected in that when you fatten (a goose or a cow), you necessarily also feed it. The relation between the two activities denoted by these verbs is different from that holding between an activity like *get a medical check-up* and its temporally sequential subactivities, like *visit* (*the doctor*) and *undress*. *Fattening* and *feeding* are carried on simultaneously. Yet most people accept *feeding is a part of fattening* and reject *fattening is a part of feeding*, even though neither activity can be considered a subactivity of the other.

Consider also the relations among the activities denoted by the verbs *snore*, *dream*, and *sleep*. Snoring or dreaming can be a part of sleeping, in the sense that the two activities are, at least partially, temporally co-extensive: the time that you spend snoring or dreaming is a proper part of the time you spend sleeping. And it is true that when you stop sleeping you also necessarily stop snoring or dreaming.

As a final example, consider the pair *succeed* and *try*. The activities denoted by these verbs occur in a sequential order: to succeed at something, you must first have tried. But even though these two activities are sequentially ordered, and one is a precondition for the other, neither is part of the other in the same way that *visiting the doctor* is part of *getting a medical check-up* or *branch* is part of *tree*.

The differences between pairs like *fatten* and *feed*, *snore* and *sleep*, and *succeed* and *try* are due to the temporal relations between members of each pair. The activities can be simultaneous (as with *fatten* and *feed*); one can include the other (as with *snore* and *sleep*); or one can precede the other (*try* and *succeed*). All the pairs have in common that engaging in one activity necessitates either engaging, or having engaged in, the other activity. For each of the pairs, we can say that a kind of generalized entailment relation holds between the two verbs.

Entailment

Entailment, or strict implication, is defined for propositions; a proposition *P* entails a proposition *Q* if and only if there is no conceivable state of affairs that could make *P* true and *Q* false. We can say that entailment is a semantic relation because it involves reference to the states of affairs that *P* and *Q* represent. We will generalize the term here to refer to the relation between two verbs V_1 and V_2 that holds when the statement *Someone* V_1 entails *Someone* V_2; this use of entailment can be called lexical entailment. Thus we say that *snore* entails *sleep* because the statement *He is snoring* entails *He is sleeping*; the second statement necessarily holds if the first one does. We shall assume that lexical entailments include the different relations illustrated by the pairs *fatten/feed*, *snore/sleep*, and the backward presupposition holding between *succeed/try*. These kinds of lexical entailment can be distinguished on the basis of temporal relations that the members of the verb pairs bear to one another.

Given the set of verbs related by entailment, we can classify them exhaustively into three mutually exclusive categories on the basis of temporal inclusion. A verb V_1 will be said to include a verb V_2 if there is some stretch of time during which the activities denoted by the two verbs co-occur, but no time during which V_2 occurs and V_1 does not. If there is a time during which V_1 occurs, but V_2 does not, V_1 will be said to properly include V_2.

The first kind of entailment we can distinguish is the backward presupposition holding between verbs such as *succeed* and *try*, or *parole* and *arrest*, where no temporal inclusion relation holds between the two verbs. The second category is comprised of pairs like *snore* and *sleep*, or *buy* and *pay*: *snore* entails *sleep* and is properly included by it; *buy* entails *pay* and properly includes it. The third category consists of such pairs as *mumble* and *talk*, or *smack* and *hit*, where the first verb in the pair entails the second and the two are mutually inclusive, or temporally co-extensive.

This categorization yields a simple generalization: if V_1 entails V_2, and if a temporal inclusion relation holds between them, then we can cast the relation between the two verbs in terms of a part–whole treatment.

Entailment and troponymy

Some verb pairs that are related by entailment and temporal inclusion are also related by troponymy: *mumble* and *talk*, for example, satisfy the generalization just stated, as do *strut* and *walk*. Strutting entails walking, the two activities are temporally co-extensive (one must necessarily be walking while one is strutting), and walking can be said to be a part of strutting. But *strut* is also a troponym of *walk*, because *strut* is also *to walk in a certain manner*.

By contrast, a verb like *snore* entails and is included in *sleep*, but is not a troponym of *sleep*; *get a medical check-up* entails and includes *visit the doctor*, but is not a troponym of *visit the doctor*; and *buy* entails *pay*, but is not a troponym of *pay*. The verbs in these pairs are related only by entailment and proper temporal inclusion. The important generalization here is that verbs related by entailment and proper temporal inclusion cannot be related by troponymy. For two verbs to be related by troponymy, the activities they denote must be temporally co-extensive. One can sleep before or after snoring, buying includes activities other than paying, and visiting the doctor is not temporally co-extensive with getting a medical check-up, so none of these pairs are related by troponymy.

If the entailment relation in such pairs is stated as *to* V_1 *entails to* V_2, the temporal inclusion may go in either direction; that is to say, either one of the two verbs may properly include the other. In the case of *snore/sleep*, the second verb properly includes the first, while in the pair *buy/pay*, the *buy* properly includes *pay*.

The causal relation

The causal relation picks out pairs of verb concepts, such as *show/see* and *have/own*. The first verb in the pair denotes the cause of the activity, event, or state referred to by the second verb. In contrast to the other relations we have distinguished, the subject of the causative verb has a referent that is distinct from the subject of the "resultative". We have coded not only the independently lexicalized causative–resultative pairs like *feed/eat*, *raise/rise*, and *frighten/fear*, but also the large groups of motion and change verbs with identical causative and "anticausative" verb forms, such as *roll*, *bounce*, *move*, and *grow*, *break*, *rot* (see, for example, Levin, 1985, and Pinker, 1989, for a conceptual analysis of these verbs). The troponyms of the verbs in a causative–resultative pair inherit the relation of their relative superordinate. For example, all the troponyms of *give* (*bequeath*, *donate*, *pass on*, *allocate*, *grant*, *assign*, etc.) can be said to cause someone to *have*, *own*, or *possess* something.

Carter (1976) notes that causation is a kind of entailment; this can be expressed in the following formula: if V_1 necessarily causes V_2, then V_1 also entails V_2. Causative entailment is like backward presupposition and distinct from other kinds of entailment when V_2 denotes a resulting state: in these cases, there is no temporal overlap between the two verbs. For example, A must first *donate* something to B before B *owns* it.

The cause relation, like the other entailment relations, is asymmetrical: *feeding* someone causes this person to *eat*, but if someone *eats*, this does not entail that he is *fed*. However, when the subject of *eat* is not a potentially independent agent, like an infant or a confined animal, *eating* does entail *feeding*. In these cases, depending on the semantic make-up of the subject's referent, the direction of entailment may be reversed. Because the entailment here is dependent on the subject's semantic features, it is no longer a lexical relation between the two verbs.

As Gropen, Pinker, and Roeper (in preparation) have shown, the cause relation is understood by young children. When children are shown a certain action accompanied by a sentence containing a nonsense verb form used intransitively, they will use that verb form as a transitive causative when shown the same action in a causative setting. This indicates that, like troponymy, the cause relation may be used productively by speakers to create new verb senses from given verb forms.

The four categories of lexical entailment we have distinguished are displayed diagrammatically in Figure 1.

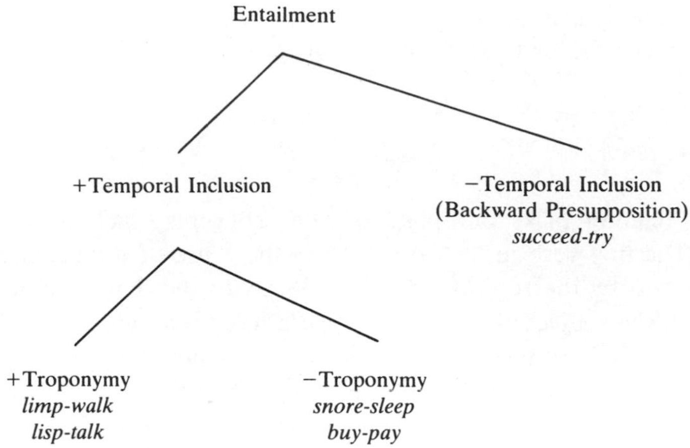

Figure 1. *A graphical representation of the relations among three kinds of lexical entailments between English verbs.*

Opposition relations in the verb lexicon

There is evidence that opposition relations are psychologically salient not only among adjectives, but also among verbs. For example, one of the authors has experienced in the course of teaching foreign languages that students, when given only one member of an antonymous or opposed verb pair, will insist on being taught the other member. Language learners are convinced that it is easier to learn semantically opposed words together. In building our database for verbs, we found that, after synonymy and troponymy, antonymy or opposition is the most frequently coded relation between verbs.

The semantics of the opposition relations among verbs are complex. As in the case of adjectives, much of the opposition among verbs is based on the morphological markedness of one member of an opposed pair. And, like the semantically similar adjective pairs *weighty/weightless* and *heavy/light*, there are pairs like *fall/rise* and *ascend/descend* that seem identical in meaning, yet are distinguished by the way their members pick out their direct antonyms: *rise/descend* and *ascend/fall* are conceptually opposed, but are not directly antonymous word forms.

Many de-adjectival verbs formed with a suffix such as *-en* or *-ify* inherit opposition relations from their root adjectives: *lengthen/shorten*, *strengthen/weaken*, *prettify/uglify*, for example. These are, for the most part, verbs of change and would decompose into BECOME-Adjective or MAKE-Adjective. As in the case of the corresponding adjectives, these are direct antonyms. Synonyms of these verbs, when they exist, are generally of Latin or Greek origin and tend to be more constrained in the range of their potential arguments; that is to say, they are usually reserved for more specialized uses. Thus, *fortify* is a synonym of *strengthen*, but its opposition to *weaken* is conceptual: *fortify/weaken* are indirect antonyms. In short, de-adjectival verbs can be represented by the same configuration that was described earlier for adjectives.

As in the case of adjectives, a variety of negative morphological markers attach to verbs to form their respective opposing members. Examples are *tie/untie*, *approve/disapprove*, and *bone/debone*. The semantics of these morphological oppositions is not simple negation. *To untie* is a kind of undoing, and the sense of this verb is one of reversing an action; it does not mean *to not tie*. A pair of verbs like *approve/disapprove* are gradables: the two lexicalized terms are points on a scale (of approval, in this case). Gradable verbs, like gradable adjectives, can be modified by degree adverbs, such as *quite*, *rather*, or *extremely*. Perhaps the most striking example illustrating that negative morphology is not always simple negation is seen in such pairs as *bone/debone* where, despite the lexical opposition induced by the presence of a negative prefix, there is no semantic opposition at all – both verbs refer to the same activity of removing the bones of an animal (Horn, 1989). In some pairs, the marked member cannot be inferred simply from the morphological marker because the opposition derives from the prefixes themselves: *emigrate/immigrate*, *exhale/inhale*, *predate/postdate*.

Other pairs whose members seem to be direct antonyms are *rise/fall* and *walk/run*. Members of these pairs are associated only with each other, and much less so with verbs that are synonyms of their respective opposites and that express the same concept as that opposite. These pairs are illustrative of an opposition relation that is found quite systematically in the verb lexicon between co-troponyms (troponyms of the same superordinate verb). For example, the motion verbs *rise* and *fall* both conflate the superordinate *move* with a semantic component denoting the direction of motion; they constitute an opposing pair because the direction of motion, upward or downward, is opposed. Similarly, the opposition between *walk* and *run*, two co-troponyms of {*move*, *travel*}, is due to the opposing manners (roughly, slow or fast, respectively) that distinguish each troponym from its superordinate. And the opposition of *whisper* and *shout*, which are co-troponyms of *speak*, derives from the opposition between a soft manner and a loud manner of speaking.

Many verb pairs are not only in an opposition relation, but also share an entailed verb. Examples are *fail/succeed* (both entail *try*), *hit/miss* (entailing *aim*), and *win/lose* (entailing *play* or *gamble*). Such verbs tend to be contradictories, and, like contradictory adjectives, they do not tolerate degree adverbs. Some opposition relations interact with the entailment relation in a systematic way. Cruse (1986) distinguishes an opposition relation that holds between verb pairs like *damage* and *repair*, and *remove* and *replace*. One member of these pairs, Cruse states, constitutes a "restitutive". This kind of opposition also always includes entailment, in that the restitutive verb always presupposes the "deconstructive" one. Many reversive *un*-verbs also presuppose their unprefixed, opposed member: in order to *untie* or *unscrew* something, you must first *tie* or *screw* it.

Still other kinds of lexical oppositions illustrate the variety and complexity of verb antonymy. Some pairs, called converses, are opposites that are associated with no common superordinate or entailed verb: *predate/postdate*, *buy/sell*, *loan/borrow*, *teach/learn*, etc. They have in common that they occur within the same semantic field: they refer to the same activity, but from the viewpoint of different participants. This fact would lead one to surmise that their strong lexical association is probably due to their frequent co-occurrence in the language.

Most of the antonymous verbs are change verbs. Change verbs denote changes of state, and most states can be expressed in terms of attributes. There are also many opposition relations among stative verbs: *exclude/include*, *differ/equal*, *wake/sleep*. Among change verbs and stative verbs we find not only that opposition relations are frequent, but that virtually no other relation (other than synonymy) holds these verbs together. Thus, the organization of this suburb of the lexicon is flat – there are no superordinates (except the generic *change* and *be*) and virtually no troponyms. Change verbs and stative verbs thus have a structure resembling that of the adjectives, with only synonymy and opposition relations.

Syntactic properties and semantic relations

In recent years the lexicon has gained increasing attention from linguists. The verb lexicon in particular has been the subject of research in pursuit of a theory of lexical knowledge. The work of Levin (1985, 1989) and others has focused on properties of verbs as lexical items that combine with noun arguments to form sentences. This research analyzes the constraints on verbs' argument-taking properties in terms on their semantic make-up, based on the assumption that the distinctive syntactic behavior of verbs and verb classes arises from their semantic components.

The WordNet project was not designed to represent everything that people know about every word, so it excludes much of a speaker's lexical knowledge about both semantic and syntactic properties of words. There is no evidence that the syntactic behavior of verbs (or of any other lexical category) serves to organize lexical memory. But one cannot disregard the substantial body of research (cited in Levin, 1989) showing undeniable correlations between a verb's semantic make-up and its syntax, and the possible implications for children's acquisition of lexical knowledge (Pinker, 1989; Gleitman, 1990).

In recognition of the syntactic regularities that accompany the semantic make-up of many verbs, WordNet includes for each verb synset one or several "sentence frames", which specify the subcategorization features of the verbs in the synset by indicating the kinds of sentences they can occur in. We limited the total number of frames by distinguishing only those variables in the frames that we hoped were significant predictors of syntactic subclasses. The frames we have coded indicate argument structure (external and internal arguments), obligatory prepositional phrases and adjuncts, sentential complements, and animacy of the noun arguments. This information permits one quickly to search a major portion of the verb lexicon for the kinds of semantic–syntactic regularities studied by Levin and others. One can either search for all the synsets that share one or more sentence frames in common and compare their semantic properties; or one can start with a number of semantically similar verb synsets and see whether they exhibit the same syntactic properties.

As a case in point consider verbs like *fabricate* and *compose*, which are part of the creation verb class. Many creation verbs participate in a syntactic alternation that Levin (1989) terms the material/product alternation, illustrated by the following examples:

She knitted a sweater from the rabbit's wool.
She knitted the rabbit's wool into a sweater.

They cast a bell from the bronze.
They cast the bronze into a bell.

Some verbs, like *fabricate* and *compose*, which also share membership in the class of creation verbs, do not participate in this syntactic alternation, despite their semantic similarity to verbs like *knit* and *cast*. In discussing these verbs, Fellbaum and Kegl (1988) point out that the data suggest a need for a fine-grained subclassification of creation verbs that distinguishes a class of verbs referring to acts of mental creation (such as *fabricate* and *compose*) from verbs denoting the creation from raw materials (such as *bake* and *cast*). Such a distinction would account for the systematic difference among the verbs in most cases. (Levin (1989) distinguishes these verbs in terms of membership in one of two classes: the BUILD class, which comprises verbs like *bake*, and the CREATE class constituted by such verbs as *compose* and *fabricate*.) However, English does not have a lexicalized generic verb denoting the concepts of *create from raw material* and *create mentally*, which would allow us to capture this generalization by means of different superordinates whose troponyms differ syntactically. But we can formulate the observation in terms of the difference in the manner relations that link verbs like *cast* on the one hand, and verbs like *compose* on the other hand, to their common superordinate *create*. This example demonstrates how syntactic differences between apparently similar verbs can be cast in terms of the particular way that we chose to represent the meanings of words in WordNet.

Viewing the verb lexicon in terms of semantic relations can also provide clues to an understanding of the syntactic behavior of verbs. Fellbaum and Kegl (1989) studied a class of English verbs that participate in the following transitive–intransitive alternation:

Mary ate a bag of pretzels.
Mary ate.

An analysis of the troponyms of the verb *eat* showed that they fall into two syntactic classes: those that must always be used transitively, and those that are always intransitive. The first class includes the verbs *gobble*, *guzzle*, *gulp*, and *devour*; the second class is comprised of verbs like *dine*, *graze*, *nosh*, and *snack*. Fellbaum and Kegl suggest that this syntactic difference is not just a transitivity alternation characteristic of a single verb, but is semantically motivated. They show the English lexicon has two verbs *eat*, and that each verb occupies a different position in the lexicon. That is to say, each verb is part of a different taxonomy. Intransitive *eat* has the sense of "eat a meal". In some troponyms of this verb, such as the denominals *dine*, *breakfast*, *picnic*, and *feast*, the intransitive *eat* has become conflated with hyponyms of the noun *meal*. These verbs are all intransitive because they are all troponyms of the intransitive verb that means "eat a meal". Other intransitive troponyms of this verb are *munch*, *nosh*, and *graze*; although these are not conflations of *eat* and a noun, they are semantically related in that they refer to informal kinds of meals or repasts. By contrast, the transitive verb *eat* has the sense of "ingest in some manner", and its troponyms all refer to a specific manner of eating: *gobble*, *gulp*, *devour*, etc.[3] Thus, the semantics of the troponyms in each case provide a classification in terms of two distinct hierarchies matching the syntactic distinction between the two verb groups. A number of other English verbs, such as verbs of drawing and writing, exhibit a similar behavior.

Summary: The structure of the verb lexicon

Different parts of the verb lexicon have distinct structures. Some parts can be cast into a taxonomic framework by means of the troponymy relation; this is generally true for verbs of creation, communication, motion, and consumption verbs. In such verb hierarchies, which tend to be much flatter than noun hierarchies, we can distinguish one level that is more richly lexicalized than the other levels. In other semantic domains, different kinds of manner relations create distinct patterns of lexicalization. Stative verbs and verbs of change exhibit an entirely

[3] Kenneth Hale (personal communication) informs us that two *eat* verbs having this semantic distinction are found cross-linguistically.

different structure: they tend to be organized in terms of opposition and synonymy relations and they can be mapped into the antonymous dumbbells that characterize the adjective lexicon. With the exception of opposition, verb relations can all be cast in terms of entailment; we distinguished four different kinds of entailment.

Lexicalization of English verbs can be said to occur mostly via the troponymy relation; the cause relation, too, holds between a great number of verb pairs. Both relations are productive; that is, speakers create verbs that are troponyms of existing verbs, and new verbs are used causatively if they meet certain semantic specifications. The two other kinds of entailment, proper inclusion and backward presupposition, are not systematically distributed throughout the English verb lexicon. These relations are also much less frequently found in the lexicon than are troponymy, cause, and entailment.

Conclusion

We believe that this attempt to treat a large and representative sample of the English lexicon in terms of semantic relations has led to a useful and coherent account of the semantic structure of lexical memory. Of major interest are the striking differences in this relational structure for words in different syntactic categories.

References

Austin, J.L. (1962). *How to do things with words*. Oxford: Clarendon Press.

Berlin, B., & Kay, P. (1969). *Basic color terms: Their universality and evolution*. Berkeley and Los Angeles: University of California Press.

Bierwisch, M. (1967). Some semantic universals of German adjectives. *Foundations of language*, *3*, 1–36.

Bierwisch, M. (1989). The semantics of gradation. In M. Bierwisch & E. Lang (Eds.), *Dimensional adjectives: Grammatical structure and conceptual interpretation*. (pp. 71–261). Berlin: Springer-Verlag.

Carter, R. (1976). Some constraints on possible words. *Semantikos*, *1*, 27–66.

Charles, W.G., & Miller, G.A. (1989). Contexts of antonymous adjectives. *Applied Psycholinguistics*, *10*, 357–375.

Clark, E.V., & Clark, H.H. (1979). When nouns surface as verbs. *Language*, *55*, 767–811.

Cliff, N. (1959). Adverbs as multipliers. *Psychological Review*, *66*, 27–44.

Collins, A.M., & Quillian, M.R. (1969). Retrieval time from semantic memory. *Journal of Verbal Behavior and Verbal Learning*, *8*, 240–247.

Cruse, D.A. (1986). *Lexical semantics*. New York: Cambridge University Press.

Deese, J. (1964). The associative structure of some English adjectives. *Journal of Verbal Learning and Verbal Behavior*, *3*, 347–357.

Deese, J. (1965). *The structure of associations in language and thought*. Baltimore: Johns Hopkins Press.

Dowty, D.R. (1979). *Word meaning and Montague grammar*. Dordrecht: Reidel.

Dunker, K. (1945). On problem solving. *Psychological monographs*, *58* (whole no. 270).

Evans, R., & Gazdar, G. (1990). *The DATR papers: February 1990*. Cognitive Science Research Paper CSRP 139, School of Cognitive and Computing Science, University of Sussex, Brighton, U.K.

Fahlman, S. (1979). *NETL: A system for representing and using real-world knowledge*. Cambridge, MA: MIT Press.

Fellbaum, C., & Kegl, J. (1988). Taxonomic hierarchies in the verb lexicon. Presented at the EURALEX Third International Congress, Budapest, Hungary.

Fellbaum, C., & Kegl, J. (1989). Taxonomic structures and cross-category linking in the lexicon. In: J. Powers & K. de Jong (Eds.), *Proceedings of the Sixth Eastern State Conference on Linguistics* (pp. 94–103). Columbus, Ohio: Ohio State University.

Fellbaum, C., & Miller, G.A. (1990). Folk psychology or semantic entailment? A reply to Rips and Conrad. *Psychological Review*, *97*, 565–570.

Flickinger, D. (1989). *Lexical rules in the hierarchical lexicon*. Ph.D. dissertation, Linguistics Department, Stanford University, California.

Fodor, J.D., Fodor, J.A., & Garrett, M.F. (1975). The psychological unreality of semantic representations. *Linguistic Inquiry*, *6*, 515–532.

Gleitman, L. (1990). The structural sources of verb meaning. *Language Acquisition*, *1*, 3–55.

Goodenough, W.H. (1956). Componential analysis and the study of meaning. *Language*, *32*, 195–216.

Greenberg, J.H. (1949). The logical analysis of kinship. *Philosophy of Science*, *16*, 58–64.

Gropen, J., Pinker, S., & Roeper, T. (in preparation). The role of directness of causation in children's productive lexical and periphrastic causatives. Cambridge, MIT.

Gross, D., Fischer, U., & Miller, G.A. (1989). The organization of adjectival meanings. *Journal of Memory and Languages*, *28*, 92–106.

Gruber, J. (1976). *Lexical structures in syntax and semantics*. New York: North-Holland.

Heider, E.R. (1972). Universals in color naming and memory. *Journal of Experimental Psychology*, *93*, 10–20.

Heider, E.R., & Olivier, D.C. (1972). The structure of color space in naming and memory for two languages. *Cognitive Psychology*, *3*, 337–354.

Horn, L. (1989). Morphology, pragmatics, and the *un*-verb. In J. Powers & K. de Jong (Eds.), *Proceedings of the Fifth Eastern State Conference on Linguistics* (pp. 210–233). Columbus, Ohio: Ohio State University.

Jackendoff, R.S. (1972). *Semantic interpretation in generative grammar*. Cambridge, MA: MIT Press.

Jackendoff, R.S. (1983). *Semantics and cognition*. Cambridge, MA: MIT Press.

Justeson, J., & Katz, S. (1989). Co-occurrences of antonymous adjectives and their contexts. Yorktown Heights, NY: IBM Research Report.

Katz, J.J. (1964) Semantic theory and the meaning of "good". *Journal of Philosophy*, *61*, 739–766.

Landau, S.I. (1984). *Dictionaries: The art and craft of lexicography* (pp. 1–62). New York: Scribners.

Levi, J.N. (1978). *The syntax and semantics of complex nominals*. New York: Academic Press.

Levin, B. (1985). Introduction. In B. Levin (Ed.), *Lexical semantics in review*. Cambridge, MA: Center for Cognitive Science, Massachusetts Institute for Technology.

Levin, B. (1989). Towards a lexical organization of English verbs. Manuscript, Evanston: Northwestern University.

Lyons, J. (1977). *Semantics* (2 vols) New York: Cambridge University Press.

McCawley, J.D. (1968). Lexical insertion in a transformational grammar without deep structure. In B.J. Darden, C.-J.N. Bailey, & A. Davison (Eds.), *Papers from the fourth regional meeting, Chicago Linguistic Society* (pp. 71–80). Chicago: Department of Linguistics, University of Chicago.

Miller, G.A. (1986). Dictionaries in the mind. *Language and Cognitive Processes*, *1*, 171–185.

Miller, G.A. (Ed.). (1990). WordNet: An on-line lexical database. *International Journal of Lexicography*, *3*, 235–312.

Miller, G.A., & Charles, W. (1991). Contextual correlates of semantic similarity. *Language and Cognitive Processes*, *6*, 1–28.

Miller, G.A., & Gildea, P.M. (1987). How children learn words. *Scientific American*, *257*, 94–99.

Miller, G.A., & Johnson-Laird, P.N. (1976). *Language and perception*. Cambridge, MA: Harvard University Press.

Osgood, C.E. , Suci, G.J., & Tannenbaum, P.H. (1957). *The measurement of meaning*. Urbana, IL: University of Illinois Press.

Pinker, S. (1989). *Learnability and cognition: The acquisition of argument structure*. Cambridge, MA: MIT Press.

Rips, L., & Conrad, F. (1989). Folk psychology of mental activities. *Psychological Review*, *96*, 187–207.

Romney, A.K., & D'Andrade, R.G. (1964). Cognitive aspects of English kin terms. *American Anthropologist*, *66*, 146–170.

Rosch, E., Mervis, C.B., Gray, W., Johnson, D., & Boyes-Braem, P. (1976). Basic objects in natural categories. *Cognitive Psychology*, *8*, 382–439.

Schank, R.C. (1972). Conceptual dependency: A theory of natural language understanding. *Cognitive Psychology*, *3*, 552–631.

Schank, R.C., & Abelson, R. (1977). *Scripts, goals, plans, and understanding*. Hillsdale, NJ: Erlbaum.

Shallice, T. (1988). *From neuropsychology to mental structure*. New York: Cambridge University Press.

Smith, E.E. (1978). Theories of semantic memory. In W.K. Estes, (Ed.), *Handbook of learning and cognitive processes* (vol. 5). Hillsdale, NJ: Erlbaum.

Talmy, L. (1985). Lexicalization patterns: Semantic structure in lexical forms. In T. Shopen, T. (Ed.), *Language typology and syntactic description*, *3*, *Grammatical categories and the lexicon* (pp. 57–149). New York: Cambridge University Press.

Touretzky, D.S. (1986). *The mathematics of inheritance systems*. Los Altos, CA: Morgan Kaufmann.

Tversky, B., & Hemenway, K. (1984). Objects, parts, and categories. *Journal of Experimental Psychology: General*, *113*, 169–193.

Wallace, A.F.C., & Atkins, J. (1960). The meaning of kinship terms. *American Anthropologist*, *62*, 58–79.

Language Index

Name Index

Subject Index